Engaging with God

Engaging with God

A biblical theology of worship

David Peterson

APOLLO8 (an imprint of Inter-Varsity Press),
38 De Montfort Street, Leicester LE1 7GP, England

© David Peterson, 1992

First published 1992
Reprinted 1992, 1994, 1998, 1999, 2000

British Library Cataloguing in Publication Data
A catalogue record for this book is available from the British Library.

ISBN 0-85111-428-8

Typeset in Great Britain by Nuprint Ltd, Haprenden,m Herts AL5 4SE.

Printed in Great Britain by Creative Print and Design (Wales), Ebbw Vale

Contents

Foreword

Christians are adept at the loose use of language. What exactly does 'bless' mean? And what is the purpose and character of the type of Christian meeting that we call a 'service'? In this book David Peterson addresses himself to the latter of these two questions and he does a notable service for his readers. He rightly recognizes that to call a Christian meeting 'worship' gives a one-sided impression of an occasion on which we do something, and that we need to realize more and more that it should be an 'engagement' with God, in which he acts towards us and we act towards him – in the context of a fellowship or mutual bond between the various people taking part.

All this is dealt with in a manner that is biblical, comprehensive, practical and simple. That is to say, the author cuts back through the undergrowth of our inherited traditions to the clarity and straightforwardness of the biblical teaching and lets it challenge us. He gives an overview of Scripture teaching as a whole, which brings out the varying accents of its different parts and which will provide a valuable aid for the more academic study of the topic: the book reflects a thorough knowledge of the scholarly literature on every page. He writes, however, with a practical bent to help Christians today to retrieve the richness of biblical worship, so that the church can be built up and become more faithful to its intended pattern. And, despite the scholarship behind it, all this is done with a beautiful simplicity and clarity that makes the book readily available to a wide circle of readers.

Here, then, is the guide to the biblical teaching on worship which has long been needed. It needs no recommendation from me, for its virtues are manifest, but I am glad to introduce the author to a wider public. David Peterson is a lecturer at Moore Theological College in Sydney, Australia, and already the author of a major work on *Hebrews and Perfection* (Cambridge: Cambridge University Press, 1982). This new book will further enhance his reputation as a fine scholar with a lively concern for the life of God's people.

I. Howard Marshall

Abbreviations

AB	Anchor Bible
AnBib	Analecta Biblica
BJRL	*Bulletin of the John Rylands Library*
BNTC	*Black's New Testament Commentary*
BTB	*Biblical Theology Bulletin*
BZAW	Beiheft zur Zeitschrift für die alttestamentliche Wissenschaft
CBQ	*Catholic Biblical Quarterly*
CGNTC	*Cambridge Greek New Testament Commentary*
EQ	*Evangelical Quarterly*
ET	English Translation
ExpT	*Expository Times*
FS	Festschrift
GNC	Good News Commentaries
HSM	Harvard Semitic Monographs
HTR	*Harvard Theological Review*
ICC	*International Critical Commentary*
ISBE	*International Standard Bible Encyclopedia*, 4 volumes. Edited by G. W. Bromiley. Grand Rapids: Eerdmans, 1979-1988
JBL	*Journal of Biblical Literature*
JEH	*Journal of Ecclesiastical History*
JSNT	*Journal for the Study of the New Testament*
JSNTS	*Journal for the Study of the New Testament Supplement*

JSOT	*Journal for the Study of the Old Testament*
JSOTS	*Journal for the Study of the Old Testament Supplement*
JSS	*Journal of Semitic Studies*
JTS	*Journal of Theological Studies*
LXX	Septuagint
NCB	New Century Bible
NEB	New English Bible
NICOT	*New International Commentary on the Old Testament*
NICNT	*New International Commentary on the New Testament*
NIDNTT	*New International Dictionary of New Testament Theology*, 4 volumes. Edited by C. Brown. Paternoster: Exeter, 1975-1986.
NIGTC	*New International Greek Testament Commentary*
NIV	New International Version
NovT	*Novum Testamentum*
NovTSup	Supplement to *Novum Testamentum*
NRSV	New Revised Standard Version
NTS	*New Testament Studies*
NRTh	*Nouvelle Revue Théologique*
RB	*Revue Biblique*
RSPT	*Revue des Sciences Philosophiques et Théologiques*
RSV	Revised Standard Version
RTR	*Reformed Theological Review*
SBT	Studies in Biblical Theology
SJLA	Studies in Judaism in Late Antiquity
SNTSMS	Society for New Testament Studies Monograph Series
SNTU	Studien zum Neuen Testament und seiner Umwelt
TDNT	*Theological Dictionary of the New Testament*, 10 volumes. Edited by G. Kittel and G. Friedrich. Translated by G. W. Bromiley. Grand Rapids: Eerdmans, 1964-1976
TDOT	*Theological Dictionary of the Old Testament*. Edited by G. J. Botterweck and H. Ringgren. Translated by J. T. Willis and D. E. Green. Grand Rapids: Eerdmans, 1974-

THAT	*Theologisches Handwörterbuch zum Alten Testament,* 2 volumes. Edited by E. Jenni and C. Westermann. München: Kaiser, 1975-1976
TNTC	*Tyndale New Testament Commentary*
TOTC	*Tyndale Old Testament Commentary*
TynB	*Tyndale Bulletin*
TWAT	*Theologisches Wörterbuch zum Alten Testament,* 6 volumes. Edited by G. J. Botterweck, H. Ringgren and H.-J. Fabry. Stuttgart: Kohlhammer, 1970-
WBC	Word Biblical Commentary
WUNT	*Wissenschaftliche Untersuchungen zum Neuen Testament*
ZNW	*Zeitschrift für die neutestamentliche Wissenschaft*

Introduction

> ✳ Worship is the supreme and only indispensable
> activity of the Christian Church. It alone will endure,
> like the love for God which it expresses, into heaven,
> when all other activities of the Church will have
> passed away. It must therefore, even more strictly
> than any of the less essential doings of the Church,
> come under the criticism and control of the revelation
> on which the Church is founded.[1] ✳

Considering the outpouring of books on worship in recent years,
it is obviously a subject of great interest and importance for
contemporary Christians. Yet, sadly, worship is an issue that
continues to divide us, both across the denominations and within
particular congregations. Even those who desire to bring their
theology and practice under the criticism and control of the
biblical revelation can find themselves in serious conflict with
one another. Most of us are more conditioned by custom and
personal preference in this matter than we would care to admit!

Despite the so-called 'experiments in worship' that are widespread today, church-goers regularly express dissatisfaction and
confess that they are still uncertain about the meaning and
purpose of what is commonly called worship. Many are defen-
sive about their traditions because they cannot see the need for
significant change. Some wander from church to church, looking

for the particular pattern of ministry that appeals to them. Above all, what seems to be so lacking in congregational life, and in books purporting to advise us about church services, is any serious attempt to grapple with a broadly based biblical theology of worship. What, after all, does the Bible mean by 'worship' and how does it relate to the other great issues of the Christian life?

What really is worship?

In everyday speech, Christian worship is usually identified with certain public religious activities, such as going to church or more particularly singing hymns, saying prayers, listening to sermons or participating in the Lord's Supper. Yet few would want to deny that private devotions are an important aspect of worship. Scripture indicates in various ways that a genuine relationship with God will be grounded in a life of personal prayer and praise. Indeed, one of the issues in the contemporary scene is a hungering for more self-expression and personal fulfilment in church services. People want to be stirred and challenged, or comforted and consoled, at an individual level. They want church services to be a source of encouragement for them in their everyday discipleship. Although this may to some extent reflect the preoccupation of our age with self-development and self-realization, it is a reminder that genuine worship will have both a private and a public dimension.

Is worship, then, essentially an experience or feeling? Is it to be identified with a special sense of the presence of God, or with some kind of religious ecstasy or with expressions of deep humiliation before God? Are there special moments in a Christian meeting when we are truly 'worshipping' God? Are church services to be measured by the extent to which they enable the participants to enter into such experiences? Such a subjective approach is often reflected in the comments people make about Christian gatherings, but it has little to do with biblical teaching on the matter. Furthermore, it creates significant problems for relationships amongst Christians, since not all will share in the same experience and some will inevitably be made to feel that their worship is inferior. Worship must involve certain identifiable attitudes, but something is seriously wrong when people equate spiritual self-gratification with worship![2]

Words, words, words

A traditional starting-point for discussions about Christian worship has been the observation that the English word 'worship' means by derivation 'to attribute worth', suggesting that to worship God is to ascribe to him supreme worth. This definition draws attention to the notion that we are to render to God the glory or praise that is due to him (*e.g.* Ps. 96:7–8; Rev. 5:12), but does it provide an adequate basis for exposing the totality of scriptural teaching on the subject? Worship defined in this way need not have anything at all to do with the particularity of biblical revelation. It leaves open the possibility of people making their own assessment of God's worth and the response which they consider to be adequate.[3]

The fact that some worship in the Old Testament was regarded as unacceptable to God (*e.g.* Gn. 4:3–7; Ex. 32; Is. 1), is a reminder that what is impressive or seems appropriate to us may be offensive to him. When New Testament writers talk about acceptable worship, they similarly imply that there are attitudes and activities that are definitely not pleasing to God (*e.g.* Rom. 12:1–2; 14:17–18; Heb. 12:28–29; 13:16).

There is a large vocabulary of words in Scripture that can contribute to our understanding of the whole theme or doctrine of worship. One of the aims of this book is to discover what can be learned from observing how certain key worship terms are used in both Old and New Testaments. If a definition of worship is to be attempted, it cannot simply be based on the derivation or common application of the English word 'worship'.

Worship as a life orientation

The theme of worship is far more central and significant in Scripture than many Christians imagine. It is intimately linked with all the major emphases of biblical theology such as creation, sin, covenant, redemption, the people of God and the future hope. Far from being a peripheral subject, it has to do with the fundamental question of how we can be in a right relationship with God and please him in all that we do. One way or another, most of the books from Genesis to Revelation are concerned with this issue.

Although there is a preoccupation with what may be termed specifically 'religious' activities in various Old Testament contexts, ritual provisions are set within the broader framework of teaching about life under the rule of God. In fact, worship theology expresses the dimensions of a life orientation or total relationship with the true and living God. This becomes even more obvious when the theme of worship in the New Testament is examined. Contemporary Christians obscure the breadth and depth of the Bible's teaching on this subject when they persist in using the word 'worship' in the usual, limited fashion, applying it mainly to what goes on in Sunday services.

Christianity emerged at a time when Jewish and pagan authors were giving new interpretations to old ideas about worship. How different is the perspective of the New Testament writers and why do they adapt the familiar terminology of worship as they do? How do they envisage that God is to be approached, honoured and adored?

Such questions cannot be answered simply by examining what the early Christians did when they met together, or by reflecting on what they said about the significance of those gatherings. The first disciples were drawn into what may be called a worshipping relationship with Jesus Christ on the basis of his words and actions, culminating in his death and resurrection and the consequent outpouring of the Holy Spirit. Following his own example, they began to use some of the language of worship to indicate the significance of his person and work and to explore the dimensions of the relationship with God which they now enjoyed in him. Jesus' teaching about the functions of the Jewish temple being fulfilled by him began one line of development. His teaching about his death as a sacrifice inaugurating a new covenant was another source of inspiration for early Christian theology.

Worship in the New Testament is a comprehensive category describing the Christian's total existence. It is coextensive with the faith-response wherever and whenever that response is elic-

18

ited. Consequently, 'our traditional understanding of worship as restricted to the cultic gathering of the congregation at a designated time and place for rite and proclamation will no longer do. This is not what the New Testament means by worship.'[4]

Divine and human action

There is no doubt that Scripture has much to say about the part we play in the adoration and service of God. So, worship is often defined quite broadly as our response to God.[5] However, there is an important theological context to be considered when worship is presented in such terms. That is, we need to ask what role God plays in the engagement or relationship which is true and acceptable worship. At one level we must discover from his own self-revelation in Scripture what pleases him. We cannot simply determine for ourselves what is honouring to him.

More fundamentally, the Bible tells us that God must draw us into relationship with himself before we can respond to him acceptably.[6] The worship provisions of the Old Testament are presented as an expression of the covenant relationship established by God between himself and Israel. Similarly, in the New Testament, worship theology is intimately connected with the establishment and outworking of the new covenant. Acceptable worship under both covenants is a matter of responding to God's initiative in salvation and revelation, and doing so in the way that he requires.

In particular, we need to take seriously the extraordinary biblical perspective that acceptable worship is something *made possible for us by God*. Of special significance in this regard is the Old Testament teaching about God drawing near to Israel so that his people might draw near to him. The New Testament points to the fulfilment of these ideas in the person and work of Jesus Christ. Again, the Old Testament teaches that the sacrificial system, which was given by God to be the means of dealing with the problem of sin and maintaining covenant relationship with his people, was only effective because of his promise and his gracious enabling. Such teaching finds important expression in the New Testament focus on Christ's death as the means by which we are sustained in an eternal relationship with God.

Engaging with God

In one sense this whole study is an attempt to define the nature of Christian worship, so that no comprehensive definition can be offered until important questions have been faced. How can God be known and approached? What must God do to enable his people to meet with him? What difference has the coming of Jesus made to biblical perspectives on this subject? What is the relationship between the activities of the Christian meeting and what we may call the worship of everyday life? Nevertheless, as I begin to answer these questions, I will test the hypothesis that the worship of the living and true God is essentially *an engagement with him on the terms that he proposes and in the way that he alone makes possible.*[7]

How does this book approach the subject?

Before any exploration of New Testament theology can take place, there is a need to understand how people in the ancient world thought that God or the gods should be honoured. This book begins with a focus on some of the beliefs and practices of Old Testament religion, as a background for expounding New Testament perspectives. The second chapter examines the use of some key words for worship in the Old Testament and non-biblical writings. Here the question of definition is faced again, as different dimensions of Israel's engagement with God are uncovered. Observing the way that various New Testament writers employ the language of worship, and looking carefully at the relevant context in each case, subsequent chapters seek to establish a particular writer's theology of worship. Word studies lead into a broader historical and theological investigation of the theme in the relevant New Testament books.

The method followed here is that of biblical theology, which attempts to study God and his scriptural revelation with a special emphasis on the historical context of each section of Scripture. 'Systematic theology builds toward a *system;* dogmatic theology enunciates and defends *dogmas;* philosophic and speculative theologies rationally *philosophize* and speculate; however, biblical theology seeks to exegete and present that which each inspired Bible writer is himself *in situ* presenting.'[8] This discipline aims to bring the contents of the Bible to a greater degree of systematization than is found immediately in the Bible itself, but to remain 'as close as possible to the method God himself has used in giving us his revelation'.[9] As well as interpreting key passages in their immediate context, this method seeks to expose the progressive and developing character of God's revelation within the pages of Scripture. This perspective can be lost or obscured by any attempt to organize and integrate the biblical evidence on purely logical or thematic grounds.

Considering the urgency of the practical issues raised in this introduction, some readers may feel frustrated at the prospect of a detailed analysis of biblical teaching when they are looking for advice about improving next Sunday's church services! I believe, however, that we have enough how-to-do-it books and not enough reflection on worship as a total biblical idea. Worship is a subject that should dominate our lives seven days a week. Vitality and meaning will not be restored to Christian gatherings until those who lead and those who participate can recover a biblical perspective on their meetings, seeing them in relation to God's total plan and purpose for his people. Nevertheless, this book offers important practical conclusions as the argument progresses and it is my hope that it will contribute significantly to the renewal of Christian life and witness, when congregations gather, and when they move out again to serve God in their everyday lives.

I want to express my gratitude to Dr Bruce Winter, Warden of Tyndale House, Cambridge, and to his Academic Sub-Committee, for the granting of a fellowship, which enabled me to write so much of this book in the stimulating and encouraging environment of that institution. I am also greatly indebted to Dr Peter Jensen, Principal of Moore Theological College, Sydney, and to the College Council, for the provision of study leave and financial assistance to pursue my research overseas. Appreciation must also be expressed to Professor Howard Marshall, who has kindly read and criticized much of my material and wrote the Foreword. Dr Peter O'Brien, Dr John Kleinig, and Dr John Woodhouse also responded to various sections of the book with

keen insight and helpful comments. This work is dedicated with
much affection to my sons, Mark, Chris and Daniel.

Notes
[1] W. Nicholls, *Jacob's Ladder: The Meaning of Worship*, Ecumenical Studies in
Worship No. 4 (London: Lutterworth, 1958), p. 9.
[2] G. Kendrick, *Worship* (Eastbourne: Kingsway, 1984 = *Learning to Worship as a
Way of Life*, Minneapolis: Bethany House, 1985, p. 32), rightly condemns a
particular expression of this: 'as if the highest achievement of our whole
pilgrimage on earth was to enter some kind of praise-induced ecstasy!'
[3] Note the helpful criticism of this common approach to the subject by P. W.
Hoon, *The Integrity of Worship* (Nashville: Abingdon, 1971), pp. 91–94.
[4] P. W. Hoon, *Worship*, p. 17 (*cf.* also pp. 31–32). Nevertheless, Hoon's own
study proceeds on the basis of the traditional understanding because he admits
that a radical new mind-set is required to deal effectively with such biblical
insights in relation to liturgical thinking.
[5] Thus, J. E. Burkhart, *Worship: A Searching Examination of the Liturgical Experience* (Philadelphia: Westminster, 1982), p. 17, defines worship as 'the celebra-
tive response to what God has done, is doing, and promises to do'. R. P.
Martin, *The Worship of God: Some Theological, Pastoral and Practical Reflections*
(Grand Rapids: Eerdmans, 1982), p. 4, similarly defines worship quite narrowly as 'the dramatic celebration of God in his supreme worth in such a
manner that his "worthiness" becomes the norm and inspiration of human
living'.
[6] Note the helpful discussion of this issue by C. E. B. Cranfield, 'Divine and
Human Action. The Biblical Concept of Worship', *Interpretation* 12, 1958,
pp. 387–398. However, I think his argument for a special presence of Christ in
baptism or the Lord's Supper is arbitrary.
[7] Put another way, worship in the Bible may be viewed as a 'reciprocal
exchange' between God and his people, expressed in word and action, according to C. Westerman, *Elements of Old Testament Theology* (ET, Atlanta: John
Knox, 1982), p. 187. However, it seems to me that Westerman has too readily
conceded that worship in the Old Testament is essentially a cultic or institutional expression of the relationship with God.
[8] F. I. Andersen, 'Biblical Theology', in G. G. Cohen (ed.), *The Encyclopedia of
Christianity* (Marshalltown, Delaware: National Foundation for Christian Education, 1968), Vol. 2, pp. 63–70 (p. 63). *cf.* C. H. H. Scobie, 'The Challenge of
Biblical Theology', *TynB* 42 (1991), pp. 31–61, 163–194.
[9] F. I. Andersen, 'Biblical Theology', pp. 65–66. Earlier, Andersen says: 'As
soon as any extra-Biblical elements provide the hidden ground of theology,
when they supply criteria by which evaluations of Biblical material are made,
when they furnish the framework on which Biblical information is arranged,
the result may be Biblical in appearance but unbiblical in its inner substance'
(p. 63).

CHAPTER ONE

Engaging with God in the Old Testament

> He has revealed his word to Jacob,
>   his laws and decrees to Israel.
> He has done this for no other nation;
>   they do not know his laws.
>
> Praise the LORD.
>
> (Ps. 147:19–20)

For many Christians, the Old Testament remains a mysterious and seemingly irrelevant book. At no point does it appear more distant from the needs and aspirations of people in secularized cultures than when it focuses on the temple, the sacrificial system and the priesthood. Yet these institutions were at the very heart of ancient thinking about worship and their significance must be grasped if New Testament teaching is to be properly understood. Most books on Christian worship focus too narrowly on what people said and did in New Testament times. They fail to highlight fundamental beliefs about engaging with God that are common to both sections of the biblical canon.

A theology of worship must consider key themes such as revelation, redemption, God's covenant with Israel and the call for his people to live as a distinct and separate nation. Once the connection between worship and these themes is established and traced through to the New Testament, the distinctiveness of biblical teaching emerges. This becomes even clearer when biblical perspectives are compared with pagan thinking and practice in the ancient world.

What the New Testament says about worship, however, also sometimes stands in stark contrast to the perspectives of the Old Testament. Despite the continuity between the Testaments, the gospel demands a transformation of many of the traditional categories and patterns of worship. History shows that Christians have sometimes wrongly applied Old Testament terms and concepts to the church and different aspects of Christian worship. One of the aims of this book is, therefore, to expose the discontinuity between the Testaments on this subject.

Worship and revelation

Holy places in the ancient world

The great concern of people in the ancient world was to know where the presence of a god could be found and to know the names of gods so that they could be approached and communion with them established. Certain localities came to be identified as the dwelling-places of the gods, and here altars were erected and patterns of worship established. Part of the tradition of the shrine or temple would be the story of how the place had come to be recognized as the abode of the god. If there were several sanctuaries dedicated to the same god, it was recognized that they were but copies of the god's true dwelling-place, like Mount Olympus in Greek mythology, which remained remote from the world of humanity.[1]

Even in cultures where no prominence was given to elaborate temples, knowing the place where a god's presence could be found was still extremely important. The people of Canaan, among whom the Israelites came to dwell, had their own flourishing religion, involving many simple sanctuaries dedicated to the gods Baal, El and Anat. According to the Ras Shamra texts, which reveal much of Canaanite mythology in the fifteenth century BC and earlier, each of these gods is said to have had a dwelling-place on a particular sacred mountain, at some inaccessible point where heaven and earth meet.[2] From such mountains their rule over the land and their influence upon its life were believed to flow.

The covenant-making God of Israel

Against this background, the Old Testament affirms that the one and only creator and lord of the universe had made himself known to the forefathers of Israel at particular times and in particular places. In so doing, he initiated a relationship with Abraham, which was later confirmed with Isaac, Jacob and his descendants, promising to make them into a great nation. They were to pcssess the land of Canaan and be uniquely blessed by God, so that all the peoples on earth might be blessed through them (*e.g.* Gn. 12:1–3, 7; 13:14–17; 15:1–8, 12–16). In this way it was shown that a relationship with the true God could be enjoyed only on the basis of his own self-revelation in history.

It is a distinctive feature of Old Testament religion that when God revealed himself more was involved than displays of power in nature or supernatural phenomena. Words of covenant promise and demand lie at the heart of God's encounters with the patriarchs. Even before God engaged with them in this way, the Bible indicates that those who called upon him and sought to serve him did so within the context of his continuing communication with them (*e.g.* Noah in Gn. 6 – 9).

Abraham, Isaac and Jacob built altars throughout Canaan to mark the sites where God manifested himself to them under various names (*e.g.* Gn. 12:7–8; 13:14–18; 28:10–22). Sacrifice was not offered at any spot which might happen to be convenient, but only at those sites in particular.[3] In this way, it was demonstrated that God's promises were believed by those who received them, that the land actually belonged to him and that he would give it to his people at the appropriate time. Since heaven was recognized as his actual dwelling-place (*e.g.* Gn. 11:5; 18:21; 21:17; 22:11; 24:7; 28:12), it was not considered that God was limited to special holy places but that he had simply chosen to manifest his character and will for his people at such sites. As 'the God of Abraham', 'the God of Isaac' and 'the God of Jacob', he was also linked to certain definite persons, as well as certain

definite places. In short, 'the religion of the patriarchs shows a
real personal communion between men and the deity who acted
as their leader'.[4]

The decisive manifestation of God's glory and power to Israel
was at Mount Sinai, after his mighty act of redeeming them
from Egypt. The exodus had to take place before the promises
made to their forefathers could be fulfilled and further revelation could be given. In drawing the people to that mountain,
God was drawing them to himself (Ex. 19:4). At 'the mountain of God' (3:1; 4:27; 18:5; 24:13), Israel was enabled to
approach God and acknowledge him as rescuer and lord.
Here the terms of the relationship were set out in great
detail and the pattern for acceptable worship was laid down
by God.

In the 'Song of Moses' (Ex. 15:1–18), which celebrates the
victory of the exodus and the anticipated conquest of Canaan,
the whole land promised to Israel is described as the 'mountain'
of God's inheritance, the place chosen by their redeemer for his
dwelling (v. 17, cf. Ps. 78:54). It is 'the sanctuary' where God's
presence may be found and from where 'the LORD will reign for
ever and ever' (v. 18).[5] This concept finds its ultimate expression
in the Old Testament in the choice of Mount Zion as the temple
site and as the place to which, in the prophetic view of the future,
all the nations must eventually come in pilgrimage to Israel's
God (e.g. Is. 2:1–3).

Worship and redemption

The worship of God's people in the Bible is distinctive in that it
is regularly presented as the worship offered by those who have
been redeemed. Acceptable worship does not start with human
intuition or inventiveness, but with the action of God. The
earliest books of the Bible emphasize God's initiative in revealing his character and will to his people, rescuing them from other
lords in order to serve him exclusively, and establishing the
pattern of response by which their relationship with him could
be maintained. Scholars have shown many parallels between
Old Testament religious practices and those of other nations in

26

the ancient world, but what remains unique in the Bible is the theological framework within which the various rituals and institutions were understood and used.

Mount Sinai and the faith of Israel

Fundamental to the faith which united the twelve tribes of Israel was the revelation of God at Horeb or Mount Sinai. This unique encounter explains Israel's sense of God's special presence with them, and indicates why they regarded themselves as his holy people and bound to relate to him in a distinctive way.[6] The book of Exodus is especially important for our study because it establishes a clear connection between Israel's pattern of approach to God and his redemptive purposes for his people. The significance of this portion of Scripture for an understanding of certain New Testament perspectives on worship can hardly be exaggerated.[7]

The early chapters of Exodus suggest that a pilgrimage to meet God at 'the mountain of God' is the immediate focus of the narrative, and that liberation from slavery in Egypt was for the purpose of divine service or 'worship'. Exodus 3 records a prior meeting between God and Moses on the mountain. Here God assured Moses that he would rescue his people from slavery in Egypt and give them possession of the land promised to their forefathers (vv. 7–10). At the same time, Moses was told, 'When you have brought the people out of Egypt, you will worship God on this mountain' (v. 12).[8] The precise meaning of such terminology will be investigated in the next chapter, but a number of requests from Moses to Pharaoh about this meeting with God suggest that it would certainly involve sacrifice and the holding of a religious festival.[9] On that mountain, the special name by which Israel was to call upon God was also revealed (vv. 13–15). It is usually represented in English translations as 'the LORD', but sometimes as 'Yahweh'.

With the redemption from Egypt accomplished and Israel gathered at Sinai, we are told that Moses went up the mountain to meet God. There he was instructed to remind the people of how the LORD had graciously brought them to himself by his mighty acts on their behalf (19:3–4). Moses was then told to declare to the assembled Israelites what it meant to be the people whom God had uniquely drawn into relationship with himself:

> Now if you obey me fully and keep my covenant,
> then out of all the nations you will be my treasured possession. Although the whole earth is mine, you will be for me a kingdom of priests and a holy nation (Ex. 19:5–6).

Such terminology suggests that the engagement with God at Sinai was to inaugurate a total-life pattern of service or worship for the nation. Their salvation had been in fulfilment of the covenant made with the patriarchs and now they were being told how to keep that covenant and live out the relationship it implied.

A common factor in the three terms describing Israel's vocation here ('my treasured possession', 'a kingdom of priests', 'a holy nation') is the note of separation from the nations in order to be uniquely at God's disposal. The Israelites were drawn into a special or sanctified relationship with God from amongst the nations. They were chosen to demonstrate what it meant to live under the direct rule of God, which is actually 'the biblical aim for the whole world'.[10] As such, they were to be the means by which God's original promise to Abraham of bringing blessing to all the nations would be enacted (*cf.* Gn. 12:1–3). As a priestly kingdom, they were to serve the LORD exclusively and thus be a people. through whom his character and will might be displayed to the world. 'Just as a priest is separated from an ancient society in order to serve it and serves it by his distinctiveness, so Israel serves her world by maintaining her distance and her difference from it.'[11]

The giving of the words of God

The remainder of Exodus 19 deals with the special preparations of the Israelites for their encounter with God and the account of the actual theophany or manifestation of God to them. Moses was to set boundaries around the mountain for the protection of the people, with special instructions regarding its approach and severe warnings concerning the breaking of those boundaries.

The people were to be ritually pure so that they could approach God, on his terms, at his holy mountain. The awesomeness of the theophany is then conveyed with imagery that attempts to identify something supernatural and essentially indescribable. Here God in his majestic holiness confronted them and intruded into their lives. Significantly, God spoke to Moses in the midst of this display of his power and glory. Indeed, it is stated that the purpose of this awesome manifestation was to enable Israel always to trust in Moses as the mediator of God's will (v. 9). The outworking of that trust would be obedience to the words of God (*cf.* v. 8).

Exodus 20 reinforces the idea that Israel's relationship with God was not to be at the level of the mysterious and the irrational. They were to enjoy a personal and moral fellowship with the one who gave his ten 'words' or commandments as an integral part of the whole experience of his coming to them. These state the fundamental principles of living in a relationship with the God who had graciously brought them 'out of the land of slavery' and consecrated them to himself. Their call for exclusive devotion to the God who had redeemed them involved not only the avoidance of idolatry, the sanctifying of God's name, and the observance of the sabbath (vv. 1–11), but also obedience to God in the everyday relationships of family and nation (vv. 12–17). The lengthy collection of laws or 'judgments' in Exodus 20:22 – 23:33 functioned as an application of those principles for various aspects of life in the promised land. In this way, the implications of being 'a kingdom of priests and a holy nation' were set forth. A similar mix of moral, social and ritual laws is found throughout Leviticus, Numbers and Deuteronomy, indicating what it meant for Israel to serve the LORD. The idea that acceptable worship is a total-life orientation is not a new discovery by the writers of the New Testament!

The ratification of the covenant is recorded in Exodus 24 in a sequence which begins with the invitation to Aaron, Nadab, Abihu, and seventy of the elders of Israel to 'come up to the LORD' and to 'worship at a distance'.[12] Only Moses was to 'approach the LORD' directly. As a prelude to this promised encounter with God, Moses built an altar and twelve pillars to

represent the twelve tribes, offered sacrifices, recited 'the book of
the covenant' to which the people willingly assented, and sprinkled sacrificial blood on altar and people, asserting that 'this is the
blood of the covenant that the LORD has made' (vv. 3–8). The
meal which this representative group of Israelites shared in
God's presence (v. 11), in the context of this sacrificial ritual,
was a means of confirming the relationship established between
God and his people. Despite their nearness to God, no harm
befell them. The message of the chapter is clear: Israel could
draw near to God in his holiness only because of his gracious
initiative and provision. By means of the exodus event, God
had set them apart from the nations and drawn them to
himself, sealing that relationship with 'the blood of the
covenant',[13] thus confirming the sanctified status of the nation as
a whole.

Worship and the cult

Like other nations in the ancient world, Israel expressed its
relationship with God through sacrifice and ritual, using sacred
enclosures, and depending upon the mediation of priests. In
other words, it had what is technically called a cult. In general
terms this means 'the expression of religious experience in concrete external actions performed within the congregation or community, preferably by officially appointed exponents and in set
forms'.[14] Modern use of the word 'cult' to describe particular
(usually extreme) religious groups should not be allowed to
confuse this issue.

In contrast with the many cults of paganism, one national
cult, with a single sanctuary, is contemplated in Deuteronomy
12. The prophets later condemned any departure from this ideal,
viewing such as a symptom of spiritual decline (*e.g.* 1 Ki. 12:26 –
14:20). The cult had a very important religious and social function, distinguishing between the areas of the sacred and the
profane, integrating the individual within the community of
God's people, and reminding the sanctified community of the
basis and significance of its life in relation to God. In a number
of ways, the Israelite cult corresponded to those of the heathen

world. Yet, given such similarities, it is again important to discern what was not the same in Israel, or what was given new meaning within the framework of God's revelation to his people.

The significance of the tabernacle

The instructions in Exodus 25 – 31 are presented as further revelation to Moses during his time alone with God on the top of Sinai. The Israelites were to bring the finest materials as a free-will offering to the LORD, for the construction of a sanctuary (Hebrew, *miqdāš*, 'holy place', 25:8). They were to make a taber-nacle (*miškān*, 'dwelling', 25:9), with furnishings exactly like the pattern that God would show them, so that God himself might dwell among them (*šākan*). The divine presence in Israel was not to be linked to any kind of image, since they saw 'no form of any kind' when God spoke to them at Horeb out of the fire (Dt. 4:14–20). Nevertheless, God's continuing presence with them was to be proclaimed and expressed by this tent-sanctuary. Exodus 25 then provides the specifications for the ark, which was to be kept inside the tabernacle, and details the items which were to be kept near the ark, namely the table for 'the bread of the presence' and the lampstand.

In some Old Testament contexts the ark, without any men-tion of the tabernacle, is specifically the symbol of God's con-tinuing presence with his people (*e.g.* Nu. 10:33–36; 1 Sa. 4:3–9). Since the ark was a chest containing the tables of the covenant, it clearly also represented God's words to them and therefore his rule over Israel (Ex. 25:10–22; Dt. 10:1–5). God promised to meet with Moses and give him all his commands for the Israelites, 'above the cover between the two cherubim that are over the ark of the Testimony' (Ex. 25:22), and the LORD was later described as the one 'enthroned between the cherubim' (*e.g.* 1 Sa. 4:4; 2 Sa. 6:2; 2 Ki. 19:15). If the ark-cover with its cherubim represented God's throne, the ark itself was regarded as the 'footstool' of God's throne (*e.g.* Pss. 99:5; 132:7–8; 1 Ch. 28:2).[15] Thus God's presence and God's rule were jointly expressed by the placing of these objects in the inner sanctuary of the tabernacle, which was symbolically the throne-room of God in the midst of his people.

The tabernacle was intended to provide a portable expression of God's presence with his people, to be located at the very centre of Israel's life on the march from Sinai to the promised land (*cf.* Ex. 40:36–38; Nu. 2). The covenant relationship graciously established by God contained at its heart the assurance that he would be their God and they would be his people (*e.g.* Gn. 17:7–8; Ex. 6:7). Consequently, he would be uniquely with them, to fulfil his purposes and bring blessing to them (*e.g.* Gn. 28:13–15; Ex. 3:7–8). This truth was to be symbolically represented after Sinai in the cultic provisions for Israel's relationship to God. As with the ark, which was its central feature, the tabernacle was to be, at the same time, the visible representation within Israel of God's presence and God's rule over his people. God's presence in Israel was kingly (Ex. 19:5–6, *cf.* 15:18) and Israel's responsibility was to recognize that in every area of life.

The tabernacle was to stand in the centre of the camp and provide the means by which all of life was to be related to God. With its outer court, inner court, and 'holy of holies' (which only the high priest could enter on the annual Day of Atonement), it represented the holiness of the God who dwelt in their midst. In concrete form it expressed the truth that human beings could not come into his presence on their own terms. The complex provisions for sacrifice in connection with the tabernacle were the cultic means for acknowledging God's kingship or the protocol by which Israel was enabled to approach the Holy One and to live in his presence.[16]

Priesthood, sacrifice and God's glory

God's glory is characteristically linked in the Bible with verbs of seeing (Ex. 16:7; 33:18; Is. 40:5), and appearing (Ex. 16:10; Dt. 5:24; Is. 60:1). Although God is regarded as being invisible, when he makes his presence known or declares himself, Old Testament writers speak of the revelation of 'the glory of the LORD' (*keḇôḏ 'aḏōnāy*). This expression simply refers to his manifest presence.[17] If, in some contexts, this is associated with phenomena such as clouds and lightning and fire, it is not to be thought that God is somehow identified with these things. They serve only to conceal the true power, majesty and magnificence of God, which would destroy anyone to whom he might reveal himself fully (*cf.* Ex. 24:17; 33:20–23). God conceals himself in order to reveal himself to his people in a limited way. The glory of the LORD, veiled in a cloud as at Mount Sinai (Ex. 19:16–18; 24:15–18), would be manifested at the tabernacle (40:34–38), leading Israel all the way to the promised land. The association of God's glory with the tabernacle and later with the temple in Jerusalem (1 Ki. 8:10–11) indicates that the sanctuary was to be the place where God could be known and encountered.

Even though little is said in Exodus about the details of the sacrificial system and its rationale, a significant theological link is provided between the consecration of the priests, the daily burnt offerings and the promise of God to meet with his people and to speak to them through Moses at 'the Tent of Meeting':[18]

> For the generations to come this burnt offering is to
> be made regularly at the entrance to the Tent of
> Meeting before the LORD. There I will meet you and
> speak to you; there also I will meet with the
> Israelites, and the place will be consecrated by my
> glory. So I will consecrate the Tent of Meeting and
> the altar and will consecrate Aaron and his sons to
> serve me as priests. Then I will dwell among the
> Israelites and be their God. They will know that I
> am the LORD their God, who brought them out of
> Egypt so that I might dwell among them. I am the
> LORD their God (Ex. 29:42–46).

The ordinary Israelite was forbidden to enter the holy place, but could meet with God at the entrance curtain of the tabernacle. Only if the sacrificial ordinances of God were carried out according to his decrees would he manifest himself in grace, allowing his glory and his word to dwell among them, to bless them. By means of the ritual outlined earlier in Exodus 29, God consecrated a special priesthood to himself from among the Israelites to enable them to relate to him through the cult. The priests did not derive their authority and function from the community but from God, who set them apart to be his servants, attending to the maintenance of his 'house'. He consecrated the sanctuary in which the priests would operate by allowing his glory to dwell there in the first place, and all this was so that he could continue to reveal himself to his people in his glory. In one sense, then, the priesthood was to be 'a channel for the continual flow of the Word into Israel's life',[19] for the manifestation of the glory of the LORD is intimately connected in the book of Exodus with God's speaking through Moses to his people. In making his presence known among them in this way he would be fulfilling his covenant promise to be 'their God' and his purpose in saving them 'out of Egypt'.

God's name and God's presence

Exodus 24 has been described as the 'ideal end' to the Sinai narrative sequence begun in chapter 19.[20] However, the real conclusion is in Exodus 32 – 34, where there is rebellion in the incident with the golden calf and Moses must plead to God for mercy in the face of his threat to abandon Israel. These chapters give special insight into the way a sinful and stubborn people may continue to relate to God in his holiness. With the making of the calf-idol the Israelites were apparently concerned to provide their own means of securing the presence of the LORD (32:1–6). This is a pagan notion, which is offensive from an Old Testament point of view, because the living and true God cannot be manipulated by his creatures in any way.

As part of the judgment following this incident, the LORD promised to go ahead of Israel in the person of his angel (32:34), but not now to be especially present among them, in case their sinfulness might provoke him to act in terrible wrath against them (33:1–6; *cf.* 32:27–35). God promised Moses that his presence (*pānîm*, 'face') would go with him as intercessor and mediator and give him rest (note the singular pronoun in 33:14). But Moses asked the LORD for his presence to continue with Israel, as a mark of their distinctiveness amongst the nations and this request was granted as a special favour to Moses (33:15–17). He then appealed for a confirmation of God's presence by asking to see a fuller revelation of God's glory (33:18). This request was answered with the promise of another theophany in which the LORD would proclaim his name, parade his goodness before Moses, and reveal his graciousness (33:19–23). Even Moses could not see God's 'face' but God's glory would pass by him and he would see God's 'back'.[21] The promised theophany took place (34:1–9), but with the clear implication that the true glory of God could not be penetrated even by Moses. Yet God was pleased to reveal himself in words, which could be understood and acknowledged by all his people.

God's extraordinary mercy and grace was expressed in the continuation of his covenant commitment, despite their rebellion. These truths are expressed in a propositional form, when the LORD proclaims his 'name' (Ex. 34:6–7),[22] suggesting that Israel could only know God and proclaim his character themselves because of the LORD's initiative (*cf.* 3:1–15; 6:1–8). God confronted his people through the proclamation of his name, which is another way of describing his self-revelation. In this way, he manifested something more of his glory amongst them, specifically in allowing all his 'goodness' to be displayed before Moses (33:19). In view of Israel's rebellion, there was a concentration on God's mercy and grace at this critical moment in the nation's history, though clearly not without recognition of his terrible wrath against sin. Then, as the covenant was renewed, there was an exposition of certain cultic regulations particularly relevant to the maintenance of an exclusive relationship with the God of the covenant (34:10–28).

Exodus 34 concludes with a further play on the word *pānîm* ('face') as the assertion is made that now the Israelites may see the glory of God to some extent reflected in the face of Moses the mediator (vv. 29–35). Israel's access to God was strictly limited by God's design and this would be further expressed in the whole pattern of cultic regulations to be presented in the rest of the Pentateuch. Again and again, the Old Testament makes the point that the Holy One can be approached only in the way that he himself stipulates and makes possible.

In the final analysis, Exodus 32 – 34 indicates that 'Moses was to the people what they wanted the calf to be – a leader and mediator of the divine presence'.[23] This teaching has profound implications for Israel's service to God, for it ultimately means that the law, which has its origin in the revelation given to Moses at Sinai, is the source of the true knowledge of God and therefore of the worship which is acceptable to God. God 'presences' himself through his word' (*cf.* Dt. 4:12, 15).

In this connection, it is significant to recall the role that proclamation of God's character and God's deeds played in the Old Testament, when the people of God met together to renew the covenant and to express their relationship with God (*e.g.* Jos. 8:30–35; 24:1–27; Ne. 8 – 9). Furthermore, the work of teaching God's precepts, which was originally central to the work of the priests and therefore was focused on the sanctuary in Israel (*cf.* Dt. 17:9–11; 33:8–11), preserved the notion that revelation and holy place belong together.[24] Within this framework of thought, with Moses mediating the glory of God, the tabernacle was still to operate as a means by which God's presence amongst his people and his rule over them was dramatically expressed. This is emphasized by the way Exodus concludes with the building of the tabernacle and the account of the coming of God's glory to fill the tent and to remain with Israel during all their travels (40:34–38).

Worship and the sacrificial system

Sacrifice today is often understood in a wholly secular sense to mean renouncing something valuable so that something even more valuable may be obtained. So, for example, many parents make 'sacrifices' of time and money to pay for the education of their children. In common parlance this may have little or nothing to do with God! In the ancient world, however, sacrifice usually involved setting something apart from common usage for the benefit of the gods. Many different forms of sacrifice were used in antiquity, a variety of interpretations being offered to explain their significance. In paganism, all the important processes in the world were thought to be activated by the gods and different gods were regarded as being responsible for particular functions and spheres of life. The object of religion was to secure the goodwill of the gods by faithfully carrying out the prescribed ritual. This was necessary in order to benefit individuals, families, cities and the wider community, or to prevent some disaster from occurring.[25] Yet, however much Israel may have shared the ideas and practices of other ancient religions, the meanings attached to its rituals were often very different.

Sacred festivals

A significant feature of paganism was the extent to which it was concerned to relate human life to the processes of nature. Israel too had its nature festivals, acknowledging the hand of God in the cycle of the seasons and the fruitfulness of the earth, celebrating his goodness with sacrifices and feasting. Thus, the Passover, followed by the seven days of unleavened bread, was connected with the barley harvest (Ex. 12:6; Lv. 23:5–8; Nu. 28:16–25; Dt. 16:1–8); Pentecost, the Feast of Weeks, celebrated the wheat harvest (Ex. 34:26; Lv. 23:10–14; Nu. 28:26–31); and Tabernacles (Booths) was at the same time the Feast of Ingathering, the general harvest festival (Ex. 23:16; Lv. 23:33–36; Dt. 16:13–15).

The spiritual leaders of the nation had a constant struggle to preserve the distinctiveness of Israel's worship from the influences of Canaanite religion. With its orgiastic practices and presumption that the processes of nature could actually be controlled by human rituals, Baalism represented a powerful and attractive alternative to many in Israel. The unique character of Israel's worship, however, is demonstrated not only by what it rejected but also by what it added or affirmed. Thus, the agricultural festivals were all related to the great acts of God by which he brought Israel to himself and to the ordering of life in relation to his covenant.[26] Regularly it was affirmed that the God of creation is the LORD who had revealed himself uniquely to Israel in the saving events of her history.

The Sabbath, which was meant to be a sign of the special relationship between God and Israel (Ex. 31:13–17), was not only a weekly cultic celebration, but was also celebrated as a sabbatical year or year of rest for the land every seventh year (Lv. 25:1–7).[27] The fact that the year was marked by a whole series of festivals is a reminder of the extent to which celebration, praise, and thanksgiving were at the heart of Israelite religion. It would thus be wrong to think of people in Old Testament times being wholly occupied with the business of atonement for sins and to regard their worship as a sombre and dreary necessity. The Psalms especially testify to the joy of the pilgrims journeying to Jerusalem and the longing of the godly to meet with God and his people in the courts of his temple (*e.g.* Pss. 122; 42; 43; 48; 118:19–29).

Clearly the praise of God was not confined to the cult, though many psalms may allude to cultic events (*e.g.* Pss. 5:7; 26:6; 42:4; 68:24–27; 122:1), and praise was a vital aspect of the assembly of God's people (*e.g.* Pss. 22:22–25; 26:6–7; 95:1–7; 122:4; 149:1–4; 150). While some psalms tell of specific acts of God, others praise him more generally for what he is like or what he consistently does in nature or in human history.[28] The praise of God belonged to the whole life of God's people, just as it belonged to the whole life of the individual.

The pattern of sacrifice in Israel

Although the rituals of the Old Testament may have been a highly effective means of communication between God and his people in biblical times, it is not always easy to recover their original meaning. Many are only briefly explained in the Bible, some not at all, so that modern commentators often come up with very different interpretations.[29] Within the compass of this chapter, it is not possible to enter into the scholarly debate about the development of Israel's sacrificial system and the meaning of its constituent parts. Some brief observations, however, will be made about the way the sacrificial system is presented within the structure and theology of the book of Leviticus. Here, the regulations are given as a continuation of the revelation of God to Moses at Mount Sinai (Lv. 1:1; *cf.* 27:34), and therefore as a provision for Israel seeking to live out its role as 'a kingdom of priests and a holy nation' (Ex. 19:6).

Leviticus presents only a selection of material from Israel's cult and focuses on sacrifice as it was institutionalized at the tabernacle and the temple. Many of the details may seem irrelevant to Christian readers, but later chapters will show how a knowledge of such matters gives a better understanding of key passages in the New Testament. The sacrifices are first described in Leviticus in this order: burnt offering (1:3–17), associated cereal offerings (2:1–16), peace offerings (3:1–17), sin offering (4:1 – 5:13) and guilt offering (5:14 – 6:7).

The 'holocaust', or whole-burnt offering of an animal or bird, was totally given up to God, making atonement for the offerer

(1:4) and apparently expressing at the same time complete consecration to God.[30] It was regularly accompanied by the cereal or grain offering, which was partly burned on the altar and partly eaten by the priests. According to Exodus 29:38–41 and Numbers 28:1–8, a whole burnt offering was to be sacrificed every morning and every evening at the LORD's sanctuary, as a community offering. The fellowship or peace offering, which involved burning certain parts of an animal for God, and sharing the remainder in a meal, apparently symbolized the 'peace' between the LORD and his covenant people.[31] Three different types of peace offering are described in Leviticus 7:11–36.

The sin offering and the guilt offering reflected the particular concern in Israelite law for dealing with transgression and its consequences, to maintain the covenant relationship inaugurated by God.[32] Both of these rites of atonement were for those who sinned 'unintentionally' (4:20, 26, 31, 34; 5:16, 18). On the other hand, it should be noted that Leviticus 6:1–7 also offers the possibility of atonement for those who sinned deliberately.[33] Confession of sin is mentioned in connection with both rites (Lv. 5:5–6; Nu. 5:6–8; cf. Lv. 16:21), suggesting that the ritual act had no meaning apart from genuine repentance. Indeed, Judaism regarded the sacrifice of the unrepentant as 'an abomination to the LORD'.[34]

With the consecration of Aaron and his sons to the priesthood (8:1–36), the system was actually inaugurated. A sin offering and a burnt offering were made for Aaron and the priesthood (9:7–14), followed by a sin offering and a burnt offering for the people (9:15–17) and then a peace offering (9:18–21). This appears to be the order whenever the actual operation of the system is in view and suggests a way of understanding the religious significance of these interlocking sacrifices, within the ritual sequence.[35] Emphasis was first placed on sin which needed to be forgiven, to heal any breach of relationship with God. This was followed by an expression of personal consecration in the burnt offering, with its accompanying cereal and drink offerings in many instances. Thus, finally, the peace offering could symbolize the restoration of communion or fellowship with God and with others in the community of his people. Purification and purity were clearly the prerequisites for living in God's presence.

People offering a sacrificial animal would sometimes perform the slaughtering themselves. In many contexts they were required to lay a hand on the head of the victim (Lv. 1:4; 3:2, 8, 13; 4:4, 15, 24; *cf.* 16:21), suggesting not simply identification or ownership, but that the victim was 'a vicarious substitution for the donor himself',[36] or that the worshipper's sins were symbolically transferred to the animal.[37] After the presentation of the victim to the priests, all the activities involved in the actual execution of the offering on the altar were the concern of the priests alone. In the case of the peace offering, the people would share in consuming the meat of the offering with the priests, but otherwise their only responsibility would be to honour the priests with their allotted portions of the sacrifice. At least some of the ritual acts were accompanied by the recital of liturgical texts, explaining the meaning of the ceremony (*e.g.* Dt. 26:1–11).[38]

Cleansing and sanctification

A great concern in the levitical law is to distinguish between 'the holy and the common, and between the unclean and the clean' (Lv. 10:10). Everything that is not holy is common, but common things can be either clean or unclean. Animals are divided into clean and unclean categories (Lv. 11) and various physical conditions are said to make people unclean (Lv. 12 – 15). Cleanness seems to represent normality, so that 'holiness and uncleanness are variations from the norm of cleanness'.[39] Clean things become holy, when they are sanctified, but unclean objects can never be sanctified. On the other hand, clean things can be made unclean, if they are polluted, and even holy items may be defiled and become common, or polluted, and therefore unclean. Holiness characterizes God himself and all that belongs to him, and so he desires that his people should consecrate themselves to him and remain holy (*cf.* Lv. 11:44–45; 19:2; 20:26). The LORD had brought Israel into a special relationship with himself, setting them apart from the nations to be his own, and this truth was to be expressed in the cultic, as well as in the moral, realm (note the mix of cultic and moral laws in Lv. 18 – 27). Pollution and sin were to be avoided in every aspect of life, to maintain this consecrated status.

Sacrificial blood is regularly associated with cleansing and sanctification in Leviticus (*e.g.* 4:5–7; 7:2; 8:11–15, 23–30; 14:6–7). Blood was part of the atonement process in most Israelite sacrifices and a unifying feature of the cult. The sacrificial system reached its climax in the annual day of atonement ritual, when each part of the tabernacle was smeared with blood (Lv. 16:14–16, 18–19), to cleanse it from the effect of the nation's sin. In a very real sense, people and sanctuary were identified in this ancient ritual. The aim was to purify and consecrate both sanctuary and people, making it possible for Israel to draw near to God through the cult and for God to continue to dwell amongst his people. Although in other religions blood was regarded as a source of life-power and was used for healing, for magic and sorcery, or for feeding the spirits, nothing has so far been found that parallels, in any significant way, the treatment of blood in Israel.[40]

The Israelites were expressly forbidden to consume blood, even in the course of eating meat, because God had designated it to be used exclusively for making atonement by means of sacrifice: 'for the life of a creature is in the blood, and I have given it to you to make atonement for yourselves on the altar; it is the blood that makes atonement for one's life' (Lv. 17:10–11, *cf.* Gn. 9:4; Lv. 3:17; 7:26; Dt. 12:16, 23; 15:23). The verb translated here 'to make atonement' (Hebrew *kippēr*) can mean 'to wipe clean' (*cf.* Lv. 4:25; 16:14), where blood is the cleansing agent applied to a polluted object. In non-sacrificial contexts it can also mean 'to pay a ransom' (*cf.* Ex. 21:30), so that a guilty person does not suffer the death penalty demanded by God's holiness in particular situations. It seems best to understand the verb in the latter sense in Leviticus 17:11.[41] The life of an animal, represented by its blood splashed over the altar, is the ransom price for the life of the worshipper: the blood ransoms at the price of a life. Animal blood atones for human sin, not because of some magical quality or life-power in it but simply because God chose and prescribed it for this purpose ('I have given it to you to make atonement').

Although there is a constant concern in the Mosaic law for the proper conduct of sacrifices, it is clear that mere performance of a rite does not make it effective. God promised atonement and forgiveness through the sacrificial system (*e.g.* Lv. 1:4; 4:20, 26,

31, 35), but not simply as the direct physical effect of the rites performed. Cleansing was his gracious gift to those who obeyed his word, seeking his forgiveness in repentance and faith.[42] Indeed, many of the prophets and psalmists highlighted the failure of Israel to engage with God appropriately by means of the cult, and sought to throw the people more directly upon the divine mercy that lay behind its provisions.

Worship and the Jerusalem temple

Both the ark and the tabernacle were more important in early Israel than any other cult object, and the sanctuary where they were located became inevitably 'the foremost sanctuary of Yahweh, and the centre of Israelite federation'.[43] When the LORD anointed David as king over Israel and blessed David's attempts to bring the ark into Jerusalem, the implication was that he was adopting David's city as his sanctuary – the new centre of Israel's life and worship (2 Sa. 6). The link between Jerusalem, or more specifically Mount Zion, as the city of God and the choice of David and his dynasty to be rulers of Israel is clearly made in 2 Samuel 5 – 7 (cf. Pss. 78:68–71; 132:11–14).

The temple and God's purpose for Israel

Although David's suggestion of building a permanent 'house' for God first met with a positive response from Nathan the prophet (2 Sa. 7:3), the LORD then indicated that he would take the initiative himself in the whole enterprise and the temple would be built at the time and in the manner of his choosing (2 Sa. 7:4– 16).[44] It is important to note that there is a play on the word 'house' in this passage. The LORD would establish the rule of David's 'house' over Israel and then David's son would build a 'house' for God.[45] This suggests that the temple was not to be viewed as an automatic consequence of David's political success: it could not simply be understood as a divine endorsement of the king's authority, as was customary in the ancient world. In fact, as the following chapters show, the conquest of Canaan was not yet complete: 'rest' had been given to David (2 Sa. 7:1), and yet there was a 'rest' still to be established (7:11). Only when the promises of the Abrahamic covenant had been fulfilled by God's sovereign action (7:8–11), and David's dynasty had been established as God had decreed (7:12–16), could his son be the temple builder. In this way the temple would more obviously function as the expression of God's kingship in Israel.

The building of the temple in Jerusalem and its subsequent history is a central concern of 1 and 2 Kings. The fulfilment of the 'rest' promised in 2 Samuel 7:10–11 is proclaimed in 1 Kings 5:3–4 (*cf.* 8:56), as a preliminary to the description of the temple in the following chapters (1 Ki. 6 – 7). The notion that God's promise to David had been fulfilled, and thereby 'all the good promises he gave through his servant Moses', is declared when the seven-year building project is completed (1 Ki. 8:14–21, 56–61). Apart from obvious differences in size and magnificence, the design of the temple reflected to a large extent the pattern provided for the tabernacle in Exodus 25 – 27. Like the tabernacle, the temple was to represent God's rule over Israel and to be a reminder of his special presence among them, to bless them and make them a source of blessing to the nations.

The temple as God's earthly 'dwelling-place'

The notion that the exodus traditions were now to be centred on the Jerusalem temple was made very clear at the dedication ceremony (1 Ki. 8:1–21). The ark of the covenant and the tabernacle with all its sacred furnishings were brought in procession to the temple. Then, in language reflecting the tradition about the tabernacle, 'When the priests withdrew from the Holy Place, the cloud filled the temple of the LORD. And the priests could not perform their service because of the cloud, for the glory of the LORD filled his temple' (vv. 10–11; *cf.* Ex. 40: 34–35). This theophany was recognized by Solomon as a sign that the LORD had deigned to make the temple his special dwelling and there to reveal his glory, even though his glory was shrouded 'in a dark cloud' as on Sinai (v. 12). The temple's function as the place where God could be encountered was stressed again by his appearance to Solomon with this assurance:

> I have heard the prayer and plea you have made
> before me; I have consecrated this temple, which you
> have built, by putting my Name there for ever. My
> eyes and my heart will always be there (1 Ki. 9:3).

Many scholars take the statement that God put his name there or that Solomon built the temple 'for the name of the LORD his God' (1 Ki. 5:3, *cf*. 3:2; 5:3–5; 8:44, 48; *cf*. 2 Sa. 7:13) as evidence of a later theological corrective. It was easy for people to make an idol of the temple and to limit God, imagining that the temple was his actual dwelling-place, his palace and his throne.[46] It has been shown, however, that the biblical concept of God putting his name there has parallels in other ancient literature and that it fundamentally means that God is the owner of the sanctuary. This expression does not imply that God was regarded as being remote from the temple, 'for his name, like his face, denotes his presence, and both are extensions of Yahweh's personality'.[47]

The promise that God's 'eyes' and his 'heart' would always be there (1 Ki. 9:3) was a graphic way of affirming that the temple was God's earthly dwelling-place (1 Ki. 8:13; *cf*. Pss. 26:8; 27:4; 43:3–4; 48:1–3; 132:6–9, 13–14). Solomon's dedication prayer questions whether God can really dwell on earth and affirms that 'the heavens, even the highest heaven, cannot contain you. How much less this temple I have built!' (8:27). Nevertheless, Solomon was conscious of praying there in God's presence (8:28, Hebrew, *lᵉpane(y)ka*, literally 'before your face').

The balance between such affirmations of God's presence and the acknowledgment that he cannot be confined to an earthly temple is maintained throughout the dedication prayer with the repeated insistence that, when prayers are directed towards this place, God will answer from heaven, his dwelling-place (8:30, 32, 34, 36, 39, 43, 45, 49). Solomon focused on the temple's function as a place of prayer because the temple was a sign of God's presence and his kingly rule over Israel and the whole created order.[48]

The temple signified that there was a future for Israel as the people of God because the building itself expressed the continuation of God's covenant promise to be with them and bless them

(8:56–61). Even when national sin might reach its ultimate end in exile, prayer directed to the place where God had set his name would bring restoration and forgiveness (8:46–51).

Worship and the future of God's people

Prophetic criticisms of sacrifice and the temple

It was once fashionable to treat the Jewish prophets as essentially critics, even opponents of the cult, and to view them as the only source of everything that was praiseworthy in the faith of Israel. However, modern scholarship sees a much closer link between prophets and priests in the service of God and the temple.[49] There are certainly numerous passages in the writing prophets condemning priests and people for their corruption of the sacrificial system (*e.g.* Am. 4:4–13; Ho. 8:11–13; Je. 7:21–26; Ezk. 16:15–21; 20:25–31). These deal with the introduction of pagan ideas and practices into Israelite worship, or the attempt to worship other gods whilst still claiming to serve the LORD, or the hypocrisy of engaging in the sacrificial ritual without genuine repentance and a desire to live in obedience to God's moral law.

Sometimes, in order to clarify the sort of response the cult was meant to inculcate in God's people, prophecies are worded in a way that appears to be a categorical rejection of the cult (*e.g.* Am. 5:21–27; Ho. 6:6; Is. 1:10–17; 66:1–4; Mi. 6:6–8). However, such passages are condemnations of Israel's abuse of the cult rather than of the cult itself. Moreover, there are texts which speak with approval of future sacrificial activity, portraying a time when God would renew his people and their worship (*e.g.* Is. 19:19–21; 56:6–7; 60:7; Je. 17:24–27; 33:10–11, 17–18; Ezk. 20:40–41). In other words, it is not correct to say that the prophets condemned sacrifice absolutely or that they envisaged the survival of Israel apart from the provision of some form of sacrifice.

It is interesting to note that certain psalms reflect prophetic perspectives. Four almost reach the level of condemning sacrifice (*e.g.* Pss. 40, 50, 51, 69). Yet their intention seems to be to give expression to the true meaning implicit in the sacrificial rituals, insisting that prayer and praise, repentance, confession and obedience, are the essential requirements of God. Worshippers are asked to admit that they cannot give God anything to satisfy his needs and yet he is to be honoured by every expression of faith, gratitude and obedience. What is required of those who would come into God's presence is purity of heart and life (*e.g.* Pss. 15; 24; 119).

Although the prophets could argue that the LORD's presence with his people in his sanctuary on Mount Zion meant that he would defend them against their enemies and bless them (*e.g.* Is. 8:9–10; 31:4–5; 37:33–35), they made it clear that God's protection was not to be regarded as unconditional (*e.g.* Is. 29:1–4; Je. 7:1–15). If Israel remained disobedient to the covenant and neglectful of the worship that was truly honouring to him, terrible judgment would come from the hand of the LORD himself (*e.g.* Is. 1; Mic. 3). If his holiness continued to be desecrated by their corrupt practices, then the temple would have to be destroyed (*e.g.* Je. 7:1–15; Ezk. 7 – 9).

1 and 2 Kings show how the function of the temple was corrupted and diminished, first by the division of the kingdom and then progressively by the faithlessness of leaders and people. When Jerusalem and the temple were destroyed by the Babylonian invaders in 587 BC, and many Jews were taken captive to Babylon (*cf.* 2 Ki. 25), this was seen by the prophets as the inevitable result of the continuing rejection of God's rule by his people. Ezekiel insisted that the loss of the temple meant the departure of God's glory and, with the loss of his presence, the removal of his protection and blessing (*e.g.* Ezk. 9:3; 10:4–5; 11:23; yet note 11:16).

Sacrifice and temple in the prophetic hope

Undoubtedly the preaching of the prophets also enabled Israel to survive this test of faith. They proclaimed that God was acting in judgment but that in due time he would act in forgiveness and restoration, allowing a remnant to return to their homeland (Is. 40:1–11; Je. 31:31–34; Ezk. 20:39–44). Some indicated that the temple would be restored and become the spiritual centre not only of Israel but also a focal point for the nations:

In the last days

the mountain of the LORD's temple will be established
    as chief among the mountains;
it will be raised above the hills,
    and all nations will stream to it.

Many peoples will come and say,
'Come, let us go up to the mountain of the LORD,
    to the house of the God of Jacob.
He will teach us his ways,
    so that we may walk in his paths.'
The law will go out from Zion,
    the word of the LORD from Jerusalem.
        (Is. 2:2–3; 44:28; *cf.* Mi. 4:1–3; Je. 3:17–18)

The coming of the nations, with all their offerings to God, would be the means by which he would adorn his glorious house in the coming age and glorify himself in their midst (Is. 60). Ezekiel's prophecy of the restoration actually included a plan for a new temple (Ezk. 40 – 48). 'Just as the building of the tabernacle completed the Exodus and was its logical conclusion, eschatology is dominated here by the construction of the new temple. Just as the meaning of the Exodus was proclaimed in the "cultic" response of Israel to divine kingship, so here the new temple will function as Yahweh's kingly setting in the new holy city.'[50] The purifying and sanctifying influence of the new temple upon the land would restore it to a paradise situation for God's people (47:1–12; *cf.* Ps. 36:7–9), for God himself would be there (*cf.* 48:35). Although these chapters reflect something of the original exodus structure and its theology, they indicate that God is going to do something totally new in the outworking of his purposes. This temple-plan, with all its marvellous symbolism, combines a number of biblical ideals and points to their ultimate fulfilment, not by some human building programme, but by the sovereign and gracious act of God (*cf.* 20:40–44).

    The rebuilding of the temple after the Babylonian Exile in 515 BC apparently left many with a sense of anticlimax. Instead of being the glorious centre of worship for the nations, Israel was again subjected to a long period of pagan domination, culminating in the Roman occupation just before the New Testament era began. Consequently, the post-exilic prophets pointed to the fulfilment of the hopes associated with the temple and the renewal of its worship in a time that was yet to come.[51]

The idea that a glorious temple would have to be built for a new age persisted in some of the literature of the inter-testamental period (*e.g.* Tobit 14:5; Jubilees 1:15–17, 26–29; *cf.* 25:21; 11QTemple 29:8–10). To this new centre of worship, Jews who were still in exile would return and the Gentiles would come to praise God (*e.g.* Tobit 13:5, 11).[52] In some documents, the restoration of right worship is viewed as the work of the Messiah (*e.g.* in the so-called Psalms of Solomon). Other traditions express the view that God himself must cause his heavenly temple to appear on earth, to replace the corrupted earthly institution (*e.g.* 1 Enoch). The Jewish sect which settled at Qumran set themselves up as the true Israel, 'in the hope of creating a new spiritual centre to replace the desecrated temple until the day when God would finally reveal himself and confirm Israel's victory'.[53] As such, they considered themselves the true temple, 'a sanctuary in Aaron' and 'a house of truth in Israel' (I QS 5:6). These various expectations form an important background for understanding what the New Testament says about the replacement of the temple in Jerusalem.

Conclusion

Decisive for understanding the Old Testament view of worship is the idea that the God of heaven and earth had taken the initiative in making himself known, first to the patriarchs of Israel and then, through the events of the exodus from Egypt and the encounter on Mount Sinai, to the nation as a whole. The book of Exodus proclaims that God rescued his people from slavery in Egypt so that they might serve or worship him exclusively. They were redeemed in order to engage with God, initially at 'the mountain of God', then in the wilderness wanderings, and finally in the land which was to be his gift to them. The ark and the tabernacle were to function as an expression of God's continuing presence with them and his rule over them. The transfer of the ark to Jerusalem and the subsequent building of the temple marked God's choice of Zion as the mountain where he could be known and where his glory would be manifested in the midst of his people. The exodus traditions were thus attached to the city of David and the rule of God was to be expressed through the temple and the Davidic kingship.

The whole system of worship associated with these powerful symbols – the ark, the tabernacle and the temple – was designed to be a means of acknowledging and living in relation to God's royal and holy presence. Obedience to God in cultic observance was to go hand in hand with obedience in matters of everyday life. In one sense, the worship of this 'kingdom of priests' and 'holy nation' could be defined as a faithful observance of all the ordinances of God, in grateful recognition of his mercies towards them. Within this covenant framework, the sacrificial system was the means by which God made it possible for a sinful people to draw near to him, to receive his grace and blessing, without desecrating his holiness and so incurring his wrath against them. By God's provision through the cult the covenant relationship could be maintained.

The failure of Israel to engage with God in the way that he required – in the cult and in everyday life – culminated in the terrible judgment of exile. Yet, the prophetic hope for the restoration of Israel and the blessing of the nations was intimately connected with a vision of renewed worship in a restored temple. By this means God would bring the nations to acknowledge his kingly rule and to be united in his service. The implications of this hope for a Christian theology of worship will be explored in subsequent chapters.

Notes

[1] A classic example of a sanctuary legend in New Testament times is mentioned in Acts 19:35. The great temple of the goddess Artemis at Ephesus in Asia Minor, which in its later form ranked as one of the seven wonders of the world, housed the image of the goddess. The legend that this image, or perhaps a meteorite resembling it, had 'fallen from heaven' was apparently the basis on

which the temple and its cult were established in Ephesus and the city came to be regarded as 'guardian of the temple'.

[2] *Cf.* R. J. Clifford, *The Cosmic Mountain in Canaan and the Old Testament*, HSM 4 (Cambridge, MA: Harvard University, 1972), pp. 34–97.

[3] *Cf.* W. Eichrodt, *Theology of the Old Testament* (ET, London: SCM, 1961; Philadelphia: Westminster, 1967), Vol. 1, p. 102.

[4] R. E. Clements, *God and Temple* (Oxford: Blackwell, 1965), p. 16. Against Clements, it is unnecessary to suppose that because different names for God are used in these narratives the clans descended from the patriarchs worshipped a variety of gods.

[5] The 'mountain' on view here is not yet specifically Mount Zion. *Cf.* R. J. Clifford, *The Cosmic Mountain*, pp. 137–139.

[6] A. S. Herbert, *Worship in Ancient Israel*, Ecumenical Studies in Worship No. 5 (London: Lutterworth, 1959), p. 8, rightly asserts that 'at the heart of Israel's response to Yahweh is gratitude, a gratitude for his decisive act of salvation in the days of Moses, and for its constant renewal in the events of their history'.

[7] Although much scholarship has been devoted to the discussion of the sources of these narratives and to various theories about the development of Israelite religion, it is not possible to examine such matters in a study of this kind. My concern here is simply with the text in its final form, as it influenced Jewish and Christian thinking in the New Testament era.

[8] So also NEB. The Hebrew word *'ābad*, which is used here, and the Greek verb *latreuein* in the LXX translation, both mean literally 'to serve' (so RSV). *Cf.* Ex. 4:23; 7:16; 8:1, 20; 9:1, 13; 10:3, 7, 8, 11, 24, 26; 12:31. The meaning and significance of this terminology is discussed in chapter two.

[9] *E.g.* Ex. 3:18 ('The LORD, the God of the Hebrews, has met with us. Let us take a three-day journey into the desert to offer sacrifices to the LORD our God'); *cf.* 5:3, 8, 17; 8:8, 25–29; and 5:1 ('Let my people go so that they may hold a festival to me in the desert').

[10] W. J. Dumbrell, *Covenant and Creation: An Old Testament Theology* (Exeter: Paternoster; Flemington Market: Lancer; Nashville: Nelson, 1984), p. 87. Dumbrell provides an excellent discussion of Ex. 19:5–6, showing particularly how Israel was to exercise an 'Abrahamic role' (pp. 84–90).

[11] W. J. Dumbrell, *Covenant and Creation*, p. 90. J. I. Durham, *Exodus*, WBC 3 (Waco: Word, 1987), p. 263, similarly argues from this text that Israel is to be 'a display-people, a showcase to the world of how being in covenant with Yahweh changes a people'.

[12] The Hebrew term *hištaḥawâ*, which is used here, and the Greek term *proskynein* in the LXX translation, both convey the sense of paying homage to God as Israel's lord and king. *Cf.* Ex. 4:31; 12:27; 20:5; 23:24; 32:8; 33:10; 34:8, 14. The meaning and significance of this terminology is discussed in chapter two.

[13] The sprinkling of the people with blood may suggest that they are being consecrated like priests (*cf.* Ex. 29:19–21), to fulfil the mandate of Ex. 19:6. W. Eichrodt (*Theology of the Old Testament* 1, p. 157), however, argues on the basis of ancient Arabian practices which accompanied the making of covenants between human parties, that the sprinkling of the altar and the people here indicates the sealing of the covenant relationship between God and his people.

[14] W. Eichrodt, *Theology of the Old Testament* 1, p. 98. While he insists that the cultic and the personal modes of relating to God share a common goal, he acknowledges that it is difficult for the cultic, 'once it has received a particular form, to keep pace with the transformations of the spiritual life within it and to adapt itself to that life with complete flexibility' (p. 101). Thus, a cult may become 'a very real drag on the full development of the content entrusted to it'.

[15] *Cf.* M. Haran, 'The Ark and the Cherubim', *Israel Exploration Journal* 9, 1959, pp. 30–38 and 89–94, for a full discussion of the symbolism of the ark and the cherubim in the light of ancient near-eastern parallels.

[16] *Cf.* W. J. Dumbrell, *The End of the Beginning: Revelation 21 – 22 and the Old Testament* (Homebush West: Lancer; Grand Rapids: Baker, 1985), p. 42. On the connection between kingship and sanctuary see his *Covenant and Creation*, pp. 102–104.

[17] G. von Rad (*TDNT* 2. 238) argues somewhat artificially from the etymology of the Hebrew word *kāḇôḏ* that the glory of the LORD is 'that which makes God impressive to man, the force of his self-manifestation'.

[18] No distinction between the tabernacle and the tent of meeting is to be made here, though some scholars argue for such a distinction elsewhere in the Pentateuch. *Cf.* M. Haran, *Temples and Temple-Service in Ancient Israel* (Oxford: Clarendon Press; Winona Lake: Eisenbrauns, 1978), pp. 260–275, especially p. 272.

[19] G. A. F. Knight, *Theology as Narration: A Commentary on the Book of Exodus* (Edinburgh: Handsel, 1976), p. 179.

[20] J. I. Durham, *Exodus*, pp. 347–348. Such a comment need not imply that Ex. 32 – 34 formed the 'original conclusion to the Sinai narrative sequence' (p. 416).

[21] The Hebrew *'aḥôr* is not the usual term for 'back' in the physical sense and conveys more the notion that, as the LORD presses on ahead, 'Moses can only see *the traces left behind'*, R. W. L. Moberly, *At the Mountain of God: Story and Theology in Exodus 32 – 34*, *JSOTS* 22 (Sheffield: *JSOT*, 1983), p. 82, my emphasis. Moses will see the aftermath of God's glory in goodness, grace and mercy.

[22] Against the view of some scholars that name-theology was a 'demythologizing' of the 'old crude idea' of God dwelling in the shrine (glory-theology), J. G. McConville, 'God's "Name" and God's "Glory" ', *TynB* 30, 1979, pp. 149–163, shows particularly from Ex. 33 that 'there is a theology whose perspective can embrace both the name and the glory' (p. 153).

[23] R. W. L. Moberly, *At the Mountain of God*, p. 109.

[24] *Cf.* W. Eichrodt, *Theology of the Old Testament* 1, pp. 395–396.

[25] *Cf.* R. M. Ogilvie, *The Romans and their Gods in the Age of Augustus* (London: Chatto and Windus, 1969; New York: Norton, 1970). Even where the notion of sacrifice was entirely 'spiritualized' by the philosophers and moralists, its centrality to the religion in question remained clear.

[26] *Cf.* W. Eichrodt, *Theology of the Old Testament* 1, pp. 119–129. Eichrodt presents a view of the historical development of Israel's festivals which ought to be challenged at a number of points. However, he rightly emphasizes the distinctive link between nature festivals and salvation history in Israelite religion. *Cf.* E. D. Isaacs and J. B. Payne, 'Feasts', *ISBE* 2. 292–294.

[27] *Cf.* H. H. P. Dressler, 'The Sabbath in the Old Testament', in D. A. Carson (ed.), *From Sabbath to Lord's Day: A Biblical, Historical, and Theological Investigation* (Grand Rapids: Zondervan, 1982), pp. 22–41, especially pp. 30–31.

[28] C. Westermann, *Praise and Lament in the Psalms* (ET, Edinburgh: T. and T. Clark, 1965; rev. and enlarged edn. Louisville: Westminster John Knox, 1981) classifies psalms that acknowledge some unique act of God as 'psalms of declarative praise' and psalms that acknowledge God's character and deeds more generally as 'psalms of descriptive or narrative praise'.

[29] For a brief survey and critique of various approaches to the interpretation of Old Testament sacrifices see E. E. Carpenter, 'Sacrifices and Offerings in the OT', *ISBE* 4. 260–266. For a comprehensive traditio-historical approach, incorporating the views of post-biblical Judaism, see R. J. Daly, *Christian Sacrifice: The Judaeo-Christian Background before Origen* (Washington: Catholic University Press, 1978), pp. 1–207. *Cf.* also B. S. Childs, *Old Testament Theology in a Canonical Context* (Philadelphia: Fortress; London: SCM, 1985), pp. 84–91, 155–174.

[30] The whole burnt offering was sometimes called the *'ôlâ* in Hebrew, a name which indicates that it 'went up' in smoke to God, sometimes the *kālîl*, to indicate that it was 'wholly' consumed on the altar, and sometimes *'iššeh*, to indicate that it was consumed by 'fire'. *Cf.* H. H. Rowley, *Worship in Ancient Israel* (London: SPCK, 1967), pp. 120–122.

[31] Sometimes these sacrifices are referred to under the Hebrew term *zebahîm*, a general word for sacrifices, sometimes as *šelāmîm*, a term which would seem to be connected with the root from which *šālôm*, 'peace' or 'well-being', was derived, and sometimes by the combination *zebah šelāmîm*. *Cf.* H. H. Rowley, *Worship in Ancient Israel*, pp. 122–126.

[32] The Hebrew term *hattā't* can mean 'sin offering' or, where there is no reference to sacrifice, simply 'sin' (*e.g.* Gn. 4:7; 31:36). Similarly, *'āšām* can mean 'guilt offering', with or without sacrifice (*cf.* 1 Sa. 6:3–4, 8, 17), or simply 'payment' (*cf.* 2 Ki. 12:16 [MT 17]). *Cf.* H. H. Rowley, *Worship in Ancient Israel*, pp. 126–131.

[33] *Cf.* J. Milgrom, 'The Priestly Doctrine of Repentance', *RB* 82, 1975, pp. 186–205. He argues, pp. 195–196, that Nu. 15:30–31 should not be taken absolutely to mean that deliberate wrongdoers were ineligible for sacrificial atonement.

[34] Pr. 15:8; 21:27 (*cf.* Sirach 34:18–19). The Mishnah tractate on the Day of Atonement says: 'If a man say, I will sin and repent, I will sin again and repent, he will be given no chance to repent, If he say, I will sin and the Day of Atonement will clear me, the Day of Atonement will effect no atonement' (*Yoma* 8.9).

[35] *Cf.* Lv. 14:12, 20; Nu. 6:16–17; Ezk. 43:18–27; 45:17b; 2 Ch. 29:20–36. These observations follow the insights of A. F. Rainey, 'The Order of the Sacrifices in the Old Testament Ritual Texts', *Biblica* 51, 1970, pp. 485–488. For a different type of classification see F. M. Young, *The Use of Sacrificial Ideas in Greek Christian Writers from the New Testament to John Chrysostom* (Cambridge, MA: Philadelphia Patristic Foundation, 1979), pp. 35–43.

[36] E. R. Leach, *Culture and Communication* (London and New York: Cambridge University Press, 1976), p. 89. It is significant that Lv. 1:4 attaches this promise

to the requirement: 'and it will be accepted on his behalf to make atonement for him'.

37 G. J. Wenham, *The Book of Leviticus*, NICOT (Grand Rapids: Eerdmans, 1979), p. 62, argues that this view and the view of Leach can both be supported from Scripture and that it is not necessary to decide between them. For an unconvincing argument against such notions see H. H. Rowley, *Worship in Ancient Israel*, pp. 92–94 and F. M. Young, *Sacrificial Ideas*, pp. 51–53.

38 It is widely thought that the book of Psalms preserves a variety of texts designed to help the worshippers enter into the true meaning of the cult. *Cf.* H. H. Rowley, *Worship in Ancient Israel*, pp. 135–139. However, it is too simplistic to say that psalms which relate to a cultic setting reflect the 'inner' side to the 'outer' side of the sacrificial ritual.

39 G. J. Wenham, *Leviticus*, p. 20. Note Wenham's whole discussion of the holy-common, clean-unclean distinctions, pp. 18–25, based on the work of M. Douglas, *Purity and Danger* (London: Routledge and Kegan Paul, 1966).

40 *Cf.* D. J. McCarthy, 'The Symbolism of Blood and Sacrifice', *JBL* 88, 1969, pp. 166–176, and 'Further Notes on the Symbolism of Blood and Sacrifice', *JBL* 92, 1973, pp. 205–210.

41 *Cf.* G. J. Wenham, *Leviticus*, pp. 28, 61–63, 245, following J. Milgrom, 'A Prolegomenon to Leviticus 17:11', *JBL* 90, 1971, pp. 150–151, and B. A. Levine, *In the Presence of the Lord*, SJLA 5 (Leiden: Brill, 1974), pp. 67–68. Conventionally, scholars have taken *kippēr* to mean 'to cover (up/over) sins', but this has been challenged by Levine, pp. 56–63. *Cf.* the criticism of Milgrom's work by B. S. Childs, *Old Testament Theology*, pp. 170–171.

42 *Cf.* B. A. Levine, *In the Presence of the Lord*, pp. 65–66, and H. E. Freeman, 'The Problem of the Efficacy of Old Testament Sacrifices', *Bulletin of the Evangelical Theological Society* 5, 1962, pp. 73–79.

43 R. E. Clements, *God and Temple*, p. 40.

44 *Cf.* R. E. Clements, *God and Temple*, pp. 57–58, for the various ways in which Nathan's prophetic rejection of David's proposal has been interpreted. Against Clements, it is not necessary to suppose that the original prophecy entirely dismissed the idea of building a temple.

45 The Hebrew word *bayit* (Greek, *oikos*) can mean 'temple' in the sense of 'house of God', but it can also function metaphorically to mean 'household' or 'dynasty'. *Cf.* H. A. Hoffner, *TDOT* 2. 111–116. *bayit* is strictly a building or part of a building (*cf. bānâ*, 'to build').

46 The so-called Deuteronomic school is said to have introduced the idea that God was only present by means of his name: the temple was a specially holy site where God could be summoned by name and where he would respond. *Cf.* G. von Rad, *Studies in Deuteronomy*, SBT 9 (London: SCM, 1953), pp. 38–40, and the development of this by Clements, *God and Temple*, pp. 94–99.

47 G. H. Jones, *1-2 Kings*, NCB Vol I (Basingstoke: Morgan and Scott; Grand Rapids: Eerdmans, 1984), p. 155, reflecting the arguments of R. de Vaux, 'Le lieu que Yahvé a choisi pour y établir son nom', in F. Maass (ed.), *Das ferne und nahe Wort*, FS L. Rost, BZAW 105 (Berlin: W. de Gruyter, 1967), pp. 219–228.

48 R. E. Clements (*God and Temple*, pp. 65–67) argues that the decoration of the temple with cosmic symbolism signified 'the cosmic rule of the God who was

worshipped there'. The whole outlook and purpose of the temple was to stress 'his creative and universal action'.

[49] *Cf.* H. H. Rowley, *Worship in Ancient Israel*, pp. 144–175.

[50] W. J. Dumbrell, *The End of the Beginning*, p. 57. He draws a number of parallels between Ezk. 40 – 48 and the Sinai accounts from Ex.

[51] Thus, for example, the prophet Malachi summoned his contemporaries under Persian rule to repentance in view of their neglect of the covenant obligations and their abuse of the temple and its worship (Mal. 1 – 2). Many seemed to have abandoned all hope of a glorious future for Israel, but Malachi reaffirmed that God would suddenly come to his temple. His coming would mean judgment and purification, but he would unquestionably establish a pure worship (Mal. 3 – 4).

[52] Such a hope forms the basis of the prayer to God for the restoration of oppressed and scattered Israel in Sirach 36:11–14. *Cf.* R. J. McKelvey, *The New Temple: The Church in the New Testament* (London and New York: Oxford University Press, 1969), pp. 15–57, for a survey of intertestamental expectations.

[53] B. Gärtner, *The Temple and Community in Qumran and the New Testament*, SNTSMS 1 (Cambridge: Cambridge University Press, 1965), p. 14. From their midst would emerge a priestly Messiah from Aaron's line, to precede the coming of the royal Messiah from the house of David, though some scholars have disputed that the texts actually envisage two separate Messiahs.

CHAPTER TWO

Honouring, serving and respecting God

> Right disposition of the heart and the demonstration
> of this in the whole of religious and moral conduct.
> Here is indeed the true uniqueness of the religion of
> Israel.[1]

In the introduction to this book it was suggested that, from a
biblical point of view, the worship of the living and true God is
essentially an engagement with him on the terms that he proposes and in the way that he alone makes possible. Old Testament teaching on this theme was explored in the last chapter,
with only some attention to the relevant vocabulary. Now it is
time to investigate the meaning and significance of certain key
words and to explore more fully what it meant for people in Old
Testament times to engage with God.

According to the *Oxford English Dictionary*, 'to worship' is 'to
honour or revere as a supernatural being or power, or as a holy
thing; to regard or approach with veneration; to adore with
appropriate acts, or ceremonies'.[2] In English usage, 'worship' is
an attitude of veneration or devotion, or that attitude expressed
in particular actions. The English word 'worship' is thus used to
translate certain Hebrew and Greek terms in Scripture, which
designate a specific bodily gesture, expressing an attitude of
grateful submission, praise or homage to God. More generally,
the same terms may denote activities such as the offering of

sacrifices, going to the temple, or participating in a festival. When this is the case, the word 'worship' in the English translation can be understood to mean engaging in a religious ceremony or series of rituals (*e.g.* 'He went up to worship at the temple'). Of course, the English word can also be understood in an even more general sense, to describe a whole system of thought and activity by which people seek to relate to God (*e.g.* as in the expression 'Jewish worship').

To complicate the matter further, certain other Hebrew and Greek terms are regularly used in Scripture, in parallel with the words already mentioned. These are literally represented in the English versions by 'serve' or 'service', but sometimes more loosely by 'worship'. What is the relationship between such service and our 'worship' of God? Another group of terms encompasses the notion of 'fearing' God and the religious activity which gives expression to that fear.

In preparation for our study of the New Testament, each section of this chapter will focus on the relevant Greek terms, as well as commenting on the underlying Hebrew. This is because the writers of the New Testament appear to have been considerably influenced by the Greek translation of the Old Testament (called the Septuagint, or LXX) and its use of worship terminology. Readers who are unfamiliar with Hebrew or Greek will be pleased to discover that technicalities are confined to the endnotes as much as possible!

The biblical words for worship do not represent discrete concepts but are part of a whole mosaic of thought about the way to relate to God. They are important windows into that structure of thought, but other terms such as faith, love and obedience ought to be considered together with the particular concepts under review. Overall, the aim of this chapter is to gain a better understanding of the theme or doctrine of worship in the Old Testament by looking at the way key words are used in a variety of contexts.

Worship as homage or grateful submission

The word in the Greek Bible most commonly translated 'to worship' is *proskynein*.[3] The early history of the meaning of this verb in Greek literature is obscure and debated by scholars. It is a compound of *pros* ('towards') and *kynein* ('to kiss') and it has been argued that the compound originally referred to a kiss of respect or adoration blown towards one of a higher rank.[4] On the other hand, from earliest times the compound verb in Greek literature expressed the widespread oriental custom of casting oneself on the ground, as a total bodily gesture of respect before a great one, kissing his feet, the hem of his garment or the ground. While some have insisted that *proskynein* only ever implied a gesture of kneeling or prostration, others have argued that there is evidence for some continued association with the gesture of kissing.[5]

In the context of human relationships, kneeling or prostration was a way of greeting people respectfully or of paying homage to them. Falling down before the image of a god or making some literal gesture of homage was a way of acknowledging the god's presence and of expressing devotion. The notion of propitiating the gods by doing obeisance to certain sacred objects and places is more specifically indicated in some Greek literature.[6]

At an early stage *proskynein* came to be used for the inward attitude of homage or respect which the outward gesture represented. Thus, Sophocles has one of his characters say that he would like to handle the bow of Heracles and 'adore it as a god'.[7] This is similar to the metaphorical use of the word 'worship' in English, in expressions such as 'he worshipped the ground on which she stood'. The notion of literal prostration persisted in Greek literature, however, and remained the predominant idea wherever the verb was used in inscriptions. The more general sense prevailed in surviving papyrus documents.[8]

In the Septuagint, *proskynein* was used with much the same range of meaning as in non-biblical literature. Occasionally it translates other Hebrew verbs, but is virtually the only word used to render some form of *hištaʰwâ*. Recent scholarship has suggested that the literal meaning of this verb, which occurs one hundred and seventy times in the Hebrew Bible, is 'bend oneself over at the waist'.[9] That is, in many contexts, the Hebrew indicates more precisely the nature of the gesture in Israelite culture when literal obeisance is in view. The Greek term is still a very apt rendering of the Hebrew, but it should be recognized that bowing or bending over, rather than casting oneself on the ground, is the usual method of expressing homage in the Bible.

Greeting or homage to other mortals or to angels

In some Old Testament passages, a simple greeting with respect is expressed by the use of this terminology (*e.g.* Gn. 18:2; Ex. 18:7; 1 Ki. 1:47).[10] Other contexts suggest that the gesture is more an expression of obeisance or subservience (*e.g.* Gn. 23:7, 12; 33:3, 6–7; 37:7, 9–10). Elsewhere, homage with gratitude is specifically indicated by the context (*e.g.* Ru. 2:10; 2 Ki. 4:36; 1 Sa. 20:41). Occasionally the posture is one of supplication or entreaty before a great one (*e.g.* Ex. 11:8; 2 Sa. 14:4; 2 Sa. 16:4).

A spontaneous response to divine disclosures

The simple translation 'to worship', which is so often found in the English versions where God is the object, may obscure the fact that a specific posture is meant here too. As a general rule, when *hištaḥªwâ* or *proskynein* are used in their primary (postural) sense, adverbial phrases indicating the direction of the physical movement (*e.g.* 'to the earth', 'before the people', 'before God') are employed in the Hebrew and the Greek text. Where these indicators are not present, these verbs may be taken in their secondary (transferred or abstract) sense, namely 'worship, adore, pay homage', though the more literal (postural) sense may still be more appropriate in such contexts.[11]

'Bending over to the LORD' in the Old Testament fundamentally expressed awe and submission to God. In many passages this is specifically motivated by gratitude. Thus, Abraham's servant, sent to find a wife for Isaac, and discovering that his prayer had been wonderfully answered, 'bent over and fell on his face to the LORD' (lit.), saying 'Praise be to the LORD, the God of my master Abraham, who has not abandoned his kindness and faithfulness to my master' (Gn. 24:26–27a; *cf.* v. 52). When the

Israelites in Egypt learned from Moses and Aaron that the LORD was concerned enough about them to rescue them from their misery, 'they bowed down and paid homage' (Ex. 4:31, lit.). This gesture towards God appears to have been an expression of their belief in his promises, their dependence on his power to save them, and their gratitude for the hope he was holding out to them.

Discovering that God would be merciful to the Israelites and forgive them for the episode of the golden calf, Moses similarly 'bowed to the ground at once and paid homage' (Ex. 34:8, lit.). Before he opened his mouth in prayer, he expressed his grateful acknowledgment of the revelation of God's character that had just been conveyed to him (vv. 6–7). When Gideon was given divine assurance of victory over the Midianites, 'he bent over' (NIV 'he worshipped God', Jdg. 7:15), presumably in awe as much as in gratitude. Job's posture in Job 1:20–21 was one of both grief and submission, as he blessed God in the midst of his suffering.

Each of these examples indicates an immediate and spontaneous reaction to events and circumstances. Both the Hebrew and the corresponding Greek verb are to be understood in the physical sense of bending or bowing, as a gesture of awe and surrender to God, often with thanksgiving, in response to some gracious revelation of the LORD in word or deed.

Homage to God in a cultic context

The only command in the Mosaic law to bend over before the LORD was in connection with the presentation of the firstfruits at the sanctuary approved by God (Dt. 26:1–11). Each succeeding generation was to follow the example of those who first took possession of the land and acknowledge that it was the gracious gift of God in fulfilment of his covenant promises. Using the personal form prescribed in the confession of faith ('I declare this day...', vv. 3–10a, RSV), the individual who brought the firstfruits 'acknowledged himself to be the personal recipient of the gift promised centuries beforehand to the patriarchs'.[12] With this confession, and the presentation of the basket of firstfruits in front of the altar (v. 4), bending over before the LORD was an expression of gratitude and humble submission to God as saviour, provider and sustainer. God's goodness in creation was clearly linked in this way with his saving purposes for Israel.

When the Israelites gave generously for the building of the temple, David praised God for his greatness and power, displayed particularly in his goodness to his people (1 Ch. 29:10–19). Then he exhorted the assembly to join him in praising God. 'So they all praised the LORD, the God of their fathers; they prostrated and bent over to the LORD and to the king and offered sacrifices to the LORD' (vv. 20–21a, lit.). A similar posture before God and the king is indicated, with a note of homage and gratitude implied in both cases, but with sacrifice clearly differentiating the response to the kingship of God. Once again, sacrifice is associated with this gesture and with the public expression of praise to God in 2 Chronicles 7:3–4; 29:28–30.

At the great gathering of those returned from the Babylonian exile to hear Ezra read 'the Book of the Law of Moses', 'Ezra praised the LORD, the great God; and all the people responded, "Amen, Amen," with raising of their hands, and they bent over to the LORD and fell on their faces to the ground' (Ne. 8:6, *cf.* 9:3).[13] This was an expression of submission to the will of God, whose commands for his people had been proclaimed afresh (*cf.* Ex. 12:27–28). As their forefathers at Mount Sinai had encountered God through the words spoken by Moses, so this later generation acknowledged his kingly presence and authority. They did this as the Book of the Law of Moses was read and an interpretation was given by the Levites (*cf.* 8:8). Yet the response of the people was also one of tears (8:9) and we read later of them confessing 'their sins and the wickedness of their fathers' (9:2), as they recognized the seriousness of God's demand and their shortfall in meeting it.

✳Kneeling or falling on one's face was sometimes an attitude of prayer in situations of great significance or distress (*e.g.* Nu. 16:22; Dt. 9:18, 25; 1 Ki. 8:54; Ezr. 9:5; 10:1). In such cases, other related Hebrew verbs were used, but not *hištaḥᵃwâ*.[14] This is surprising since the latter certainly describes a posture of entreaty before another person (*e.g.* Ex. 11:8; 2 Sa. 14:4; 16:4). However, when *hištaḥᵃwâ* or *proskynein* indicate a posture towards God, belief, dependence and submission are being expressed, usually associated with thanksgiving rather than supplication.[15]

Worship as a more general and abstract notion

When other verbs denoting bowing or kneeling are absent from the context and there are no other indicators of physical movement, the more general and abstract sense of 'worship' may be understood. Thus, the notion of paying homage to God by an act of sacrifice is intended in passages like Genesis 22:5 (*cf.* v. 2); 1 Samuel 15:25, 30 and Jeremiah 7:2 (compare v. 21), and the translation 'to worship to the LORD' is possible. In Psalm 29:2, which calls upon the heavenly host to 'worship the LORD in the splendour of his holiness', the parallel expression suggests that this homage to God is to be paid by praise, ascribing to the LORD 'the glory due to his name'. However, when similar terminology is used in Psalm 96:9, as part of a summons to the nations to 'ascribe to the LORD the glory due to his name' (v. 8), the preceding expression ('bring an offering and come into his courts') suggests that participation in the temple cult is intended. Perhaps a literal bowing down before God is envisaged, together with the related activities of praise and sacrifice (*cf.* also 1 Ch. 16:29).

Quite often, *histaḥªwâ* is juxtaposed with another Hebrew verb, *'ābaḏ* ('to serve'), in passages forbidding the Israelites to engage in idolatry in any form (*e.g.* Ex. 20:5; 23:24; Dt. 4:19; 5:9), or in contexts describing their disobedience to these commands (*e.g.* 1 Ki. 16:31; 2 Ki. 17:16; 21:3, 21). It is possible to render this combination 'worship and serve', though 'bow down and serve' might be better, since literally bowing or bending over was such a significant expression of devotion to a god.[16] Some such action was a regular part of ancient near-eastern religion (*e.g.* Ex. 32:8; Nu. 25:2; Ezk. 8:16) and it would seem that the act of bending over to honour a god came to represent the cult itself so that in many contexts the customary worship of idols is intended by the use of *hištaḥªwâ* and *proskynein*. God's people were not to pay homage to false gods by engaging in foreign cults and were not to make any idols to represent the LORD. Even though bending over before the LORD at his sanctuary appeared to be like the ritual bowing of pagans before idols, it was simply a recognition of his kingly presence in their midst, without confusing that presence with any image or representation of God (*e.g.* Ex. 24:1; 33:10).[17]

The call of the psalmist for God's people to come regularly 'before his face and bear witness to him' (Ps. 95:2)[18] is followed by an exhortation involving three verbs. The Hebrew means literally, 'let us bend over and stoop down, let us kneel before the LORD our maker' (v. 6). His presence with his people was to be acknowledged by such postures of adoration and homage. This was to take place as testimony to his mighty works in creation and redemption was given in public praise (vv. 1–5). Psalm 95 suggests that God encounters his people in the context of a temple festival as the truth about his character and his dealing with his people is recounted. Their praise then becomes the basis for a challenge to go on listening to his voice, not hardening their hearts in unbelief and disobedience, so that they might enter his 'rest' (vv. 7–11).

Other passages in the Psalms clearly speak of bending over towards the temple in Jerusalem (*e.g.* Pss. 5:7; 138:2) or worshipping 'at his footstool', meaning the ark of the covenant (Pss. 99:5; 132:7). Bending over before God in the forecourt of the temple, turning one's face to the sanctuary, is envisaged as an expression of reverence (Ps. 5:8) or praise (Pss. 99:5; 138:2) to the one whose presence in the midst of his people is affirmed by these institutions. It is important to note, however, that the same psalms affirm God's heavenly rule and encourage his people to acknowledge his kingly presence everywhere.[19]

A number of psalms contain the promise that the nations will one day respond to the LORD and will come and bow down before him (*e.g.* Pss. 22:27, 29; 86:9). This reflects the prophetic view of the future, with its focus on Jerusalem as the divine sanctuary to which the nations must come in pilgrimage (*e.g.* Is. 2:1–3): the LORD will gather the remnant of Israel together as one, to worship him on his holy mountain in Jerusalem (Is. 27:12–13), and all the nations will come and bend over before him (Is. 66:23).[20] The vision of the nations paying homage to Israel's God is expressed with similar terminology in other passages such as Isaiah 45:23 ('Before me every knee will bow; by me every tongue will swear').

Conclusion: worship as homage or grateful submission

In the Old Testament, bowing down or bending over could simply be a respectful greeting, but more often than not it was an expression of inferior status and subservience to another person. Sometimes this obeisance was an indication of gratitude and sometimes it was associated with supplication or entreaty. Whatever the situation, it was a recognition of the total dependence of one party on another for the provision of some need. The same posture was adopted spontaneously by people confronted with sudden disclosures of God's power and grace, in answered prayers, assurances of forgiveness or promises of victory. As such, it was a recognition of God's revealed character and not merely his presence. Sometimes it was associated with an outburst of praise, but sometimes the gesture itself appears to have been sufficient to express the trust and gratitude of those concerned. Even in more formal and cultic contexts, the gesture of bending over to the LORD was regularly a response to some reminder of his character and purposes.

Part of the ritual of worship came to stand for the whole, so that bending over to the LORD came to represent devotion and submission to him as a pattern of life. Particularly by means of sacrifice and praise in the temple cult at Jerusalem, God's dominion over the whole creation, his gracious rule over his chosen people, and his kingly presence in their midst was acknowledged. Such homage to God is essentially what is meant when the English word 'worship' translates *hištaḥ^awâ* and *proskynein* in the Old Testament. The reference is either to spontaneous acts of adoration or to the expression of homage in obedience to his commands.

It would be wrong to conclude from this analysis that a particular posture or gesture is somehow essential to true worship. The culturally accepted way of responding to great ones and benefactors in the ancient world became a means of acknowledging the power and grace of God. But the Old Testament makes it clear that faith, gratitude and obedience are the essential requirements for acceptable worship.

Worship as service

Another verb in the Greek Bible often translated 'to worship' is *latreuein*.[21] In view of its use in non-biblical as well as biblical literature, it is more adequately rendered 'to serve'. It was one of a number of terms in the Greek language for 'service', each of which will be noted and its relevance to our study considered. *Latreuein* was rarely employed in Greek literature until the translators of the Septuagint gave it special prominence, using it to refer exclusively to the service rendered to God or to heathen gods, and especially service by means of sacrifice or some other ritual. While the word-group could mean 'serving for a wage' (*latron*) or for a reward,[22] more often than not it was used in connection with slavery, rather than hired employment. Such terminology could also express the service rendered to the gods, so that Plato could write of divine service (*latreia*) in terms of purifications and sacred rites.[23] It could also refer to Socrates having a service received from and paid to a god, which he discharged by exercising his wisdom.[24] By New Testament times this word-group had come to be used predominantly for religious or cultic duties.

The word more regularly used by Greek writers to refer to the obligations of a slave (*doulos*) to his master was *douleuein*. This meant 'to serve as a slave', with a stress on subjection. Since this verb and its cognates conveyed the notion of total dependence and of obedience without any right of personal choice, it was generally not regarded as an appropriate expression of service to the gods in Greek religion.[25] It is therefore significant that the Greek translators of the Old Testament showed no hesitation in using *douleuein* to describe the bond-service due to the God of Israel, as well as the service due to human masters. In this respect they followed the pattern of the Hebrew text, where the verb *'ābad* with a direct object means 'to serve', in religious and non-religious contexts alike. The writers of the New Testament similarly sensed no difficulty in using *douleuein* in connection with the service of God.[26]

There are about ninety occasions when *latreuein* is employed in the LXX, seventy of which are in Exodus, Deuteronomy, Joshua and Judges. In each case, religious service is implied by the context, and it is this usage that is mostly followed and adapted by New Testament writers. *Douleuein* is generally employed in these books where the reference is to a master-servant relationship in the human sphere,[27] though it occasionally has a religious reference.[28] Such variations in the Greek text are an attempt to convey the different applications of *ʿābad*. In the rest of the Old Testament, however, where *latreuein* occurs very rarely, *douleuein* does double service for both the religious and non-religious applications of the same Hebrew verb. Where *douleuein* or the noun *douleia* ('service') occur in Godward contexts they denote whole-hearted commitment to God expressed in cultic activity (*e.g.* 1 Ch. 25:6; 2 Ch. 30:8).

The service of all Israel

According to the book of Exodus, Israel's redemption from slavery was to release the people for service to God on the mountain where he first revealed himself to Moses (Ex. 3:12). Again and again in the following chapters, Moses demands that Israel be allowed to serve God in the desert.[29] When the parallel expressions 'to sacrifice to the LORD' (*e.g.* Ex. 3:18; 5:3, 8, 17) and 'to hold a festival' (Ex. 5:1) are used, it is clear that Moses is seeking permission from Pharaoh for the Hebrews to 'formalize their relationship with their God by serving him cultically with sacrificial offerings'.[30] Again this term figures regularly in significant contexts in Deuteronomy. When Israel was reminded that God had delivered them from 'the house of slavery' (Dt. 6:12) and was then charged to 'fear' him, to 'serve' him, and to 'swear' in his name alone (Dt. 6:13), it was implied that, the LORD having broken the old ties binding his people to Egypt, 'had thus won the right to call them his vassals'.[31]

Serving the LORD is a comprehensive term for Israel's relationship with God (Dt. 10:12, 20; 11:13). Bowing down and serving aspects of the creation or other gods is strictly forbidden (Dt. 4:19, 28; 5:9; 7:4, 16; 8:19; 11:16, 28; 28:14) and provisions are made for the removal of every temptation to indulge in idolatry (12:2; 13:1–18; 16:21 – 17:7; 29:18[17]). Although cultic service to the living God is clearly involved, some contexts set this service within the broader framework of fearing him, walking in all his ways, and observing all his commands and decrees.

Thus, in Deuteronomy 10:12–13, 'to serve the LORD your God with all your heart and with all your soul' implies a total lifestyle of allegiance to God (*cf.* Jos. 22:5).[32] So also in the book of Joshua, while it is clear that the LORD is to be served specifically 'at his sanctuary', with burnt offerings, sacrifices and fellowship offerings (Jos. 22:27), the call is to 'fear the LORD and serve him with all faithfulness', by rejecting other gods and giving him wholehearted allegiance (24:14–24). The service of God is not possible for those who indulge in a life of sin and rebellion (24:19–20).[33]

The noun *latreia* is used only nine times in the LXX, five times translating the Hebrew *ʿăbōdâ*, and four times appearing in texts for which there is no Hebrew original. It denotes service rendered to other people (3 Macc. 4:14), cultic service to other gods (1 Macc. 1:43), and cultic service to the God of Israel (1 Ch. 28:13). The Passover was a particular 'service' to be observed by Israel, in remembrance of the Lord's redemptive work at the time of the exodus (Ex. 12:25–26; 13:5). When *latreuein* or *latreia* are applied to the service of God they almost always denote the worship of the people as a whole, not the specific work of the priests or Levites.[34]

Priestly service in Israel

When the translators of the LXX wished to specify the priestly role in the cultic service of Israel they chose to use the verb *leitourgein*, the noun *leitourgia*, and related terms. Although this word-group is only found a total of fifteen times in the New Testament,[35] its usage is often quite significant. Of course, the English words 'liturgy' and 'liturgical' are derived from these Greek terms, but this English usage is too narrow to convey the range of meaning of the words in the Greek Bible.

In non-biblical writings this terminology appears to have undergone a considerable development in meaning. It first appears in a technical political sense, with reference to the discharge of specific services to the body politic, either levied by law or rendered voluntarily.[36] This usage is then extended to cover any service to the community and then service in general, such as that of slaves to masters, or of friends to one another.[37] Apart from this wholly secular application of the terminology, there developed a specialized cultic usage in Greek literature and inscriptions. Thus, various cultic and festive acts, such as choruses, hymns, dances, filling the streets with the savour of sacrifices, and wearing garlands, are services said to be sanctioned, commanded and regulated by the gods, and those performing them are 'serving the god'.[38] It is tempting to connect this religious sense with the original political sense of the terminology, viewing service to the gods as a service to the nation. The evidence, however, suggests rather that 'liturgies' were considered as having been imposed by the gods for their benefit. Priests and cultic officials are the representatives of the people but, when this terminology is used, the object of their work is regularly the gods and not the people themselves.

The LXX uses *leitourgein* some 100 times, and generally with specific reference to the service of God in tabernacle or temple by priests and Levites. They were those with a special responsibility to 'minister to the LORD' or 'to serve the LORD',[39] who are also described as serving the altar (Joel 1:9, 13; *cf.* Ex. 28:43), serving in God's sanctuary and so serving 'God's house' (Ezk. 44:11; 45:5; 46:24). The Levites 'ministered their ministry' under the supervision of Aaron and his sons (Nu. 8:22; *cf.* 18:21, 23). Indeed, the Levites were to minister to Aaron (Nu. 3:6), carrying out certain specified functions (*e.g.* Nu. 3:7–9), while he and his sons fulfilled their priestly service. Thus, the service of the Levites to the priests was part of their service to the LORD. According to their respective duties, priests and Levites were 'to offer burnt offerings and fellowship offerings, to minister, to give thanks and to sing praises at the gates of the LORD's dwelling' (2 Ch. 31:2).[40]

As a rule, this Greek verb translates the Hebrew *šērēṯ* (Piel, 'to minister, serve') when the reference is cultic. When other services or relations are on view, different Greek words are mostly used to render this Hebrew verb.[41] Apart from two references to the service of foreign gods (Ezk. 44:12; 2 Ch. 15:16), and occasional non-cultic applications of the terminology (*e.g.* Jos. 1:1; 1 Ki. 1:4, 15; 19:21), we may conclude that *leitourgein, leitourgia*, and related terms were generally employed by the translators of the LXX as technical terms for the ministries of priests to God and of Levites to priests.[42]

There are occasions when the people represented by the priests are explicitly designated as the beneficiaries of the priestly ministry (*e.g.* 2 Ch. 35:3; Ezk. 44:11). However, the nation is served by the priests only to the extent that it is enabled to offer its sacrifices through their mediation. Fundamentally, God is the recipient of all cultic service in Israel.[43] Even so, the Old Testament does not allow that God himself benefits in any material way from the priestly discharge of the 'liturgies' he imposes on his people. Thus, for example, pagan views of sacrifice are dismissed when God says:

> I have no need of a bull from your stall
> or of goats from your pens,
> for every animal of the forest is mine,
> and the cattle on a thousand hills...
> If I were hungry I would not tell you,
> for the world is mine, and all that is in it.
> Do I eat the flesh of bulls
> or drink the blood of goats?
>
> (Ps. 50:9–10, 12–13)

Other Greek terms for service

In Greek literature the *therapeuein* word-group denoted a willingness to serve and to care for someone more powerful or someone in need. In some contexts the meaning was explicitly 'to heal'. The terminology was readily applied to the service of the gods on the understanding that they must be tended or cared for, to gain their favour.[44] The cultivation of the favour of the gods usually took place by means of sacrifice, though some writers stressed the prior importance of moral purity on the part of those offering sacrifices.[45] The LXX rarely uses *therapeuein* in Godward contexts, presumably because of the danger of suggesting that the service of the God of Israel involved the cultivation of his favour.[46] Similarly in the New Testament, this verb is only used once in a religious sense, to bring out the point that the God who made the world and everything in it is not, like the gods of paganism, 'served by human hands, as if he needed anything' (Acts 17:25; *cf.* Ps. 50:9–13).

The *hypēretein* word-group in non-biblical usage denoted service to a superior that involved a willing acceptance of subordination, without prejudice to one's personal dignity and worth. The terminology was applied to every sphere of human life. In a religious sense it could mean devoting one's life to the service of the gods by philosophical endeavour,[47] or by praying and sacrificing to them.[48] Again, it is interesting to observe that in the LXX the *hypēretein* word-group plays next to no role. Apart from the notion that some will serve kings and other great ones (*e.g.* Jb. 1:3; Pr. 14:35; Sirach 39:4), and that certain objects serve human needs (Wisdom 13:11; 15:7), there is the idea that creation serves God (Wisdom 16:21, 24–25; 19:6), or that rulers are accountable to God as servants of his kingdom (Wisdom 6:4).[49]

The *diakonein* word-group was somewhat similar in meaning and indicated 'very personally the service rendered to another', without any notion of subjection.[50] Menial tasks such as serving at table may have been involved in being a *diakonos*, but function, rather than status was denoted by the terminology. There are few instances in Greek literature of *diakonein* referring to the cultic service of the gods, although the expression *diakonos tou theou* ('servant of God') is occasionally found.[51] The verb *diakonein* is not used at all in the LXX. The word-group, however, assumes considerable importance in the New Testament, where certain forms of service may be directed towards fellow human beings and yet, at the same time, be viewed as an expression of service to God.

Conclusion: worship as service

The language of service implies that God is a great king, who requires faithfulness and obedience from those who belong to him. Israel's service in a cultic way was to be understood as a particular expression of the total allegiance due to the LORD, who had set them free from slavery in Egypt to serve him exclusively. The ministry of priests and Levites in the cult was a specialized form of that service to God. As well as having a Godward dimension, the priestly ministry functioned to assist the nation as a whole in its service to God. The Old Testament indicates in several ways that service to God and service to his people are interrelated.

Cultic activity could be either a recognition of the lordship of the God of Israel or a means of dedication to his rivals. Hence the constant challenge in the Old Testament not to compromise the service of God by engaging in foreign cults or by incorporating elements of those cults within the pattern of the temple service. Corruption at the level of the cult was inevitably associated with the corruption of Israel's moral and social life. Cultic activity was meant to be a means of maintaining the holiness of God's people.

More obviously than the language of homage, the terminology of service implies devotion to God as a pattern of life. In modern parlance, the word 'worship' is often applied quite strictly to acts of homage and devotion and is consequently an appropriate translation of *hištaḥªwâ* and *proskynein* in many contexts. 'Bowing down' to God in the Old Testament, however, is ideally an expression of one's desire to 'serve' him. It is therefore necessary to recognize that, from a scriptural point of view, worship involves specific acts of adoration and submission as well as a lifestyle of obedient service. To make this point, it may be helpful to translate words indicating service to God as 'worship'. There is always the danger, however, that readers of the English text will then understand such worship purely in cultic terms! The problem for translation and for theology is that the English word 'worship' is generally used too narrowly.

Worship as reverence or respect

A final word-group to be mentioned in this chapter was much used in non-biblical literature but only to a limited extent in the LXX or in the New Testament. In Greek piety terms based on the stem *seb-* regularly expressed the notion of reverence or respect for the gods. The *seb-* words in the earliest non-biblical texts denote awe, 'whether at a great mistake or at something lofty and sublime'.[52] Not so much fear and trembling, but drawing back with admiring respect, is indicated by these sources. Reverence for the divine, honour for the dead, and respect for parents or rulers, can all be denoted by the use of this terminology.[53]

In due course, however, the common verb *sebomai* and related terms encompassed not only a reverential attitude to the gods but also the cultic activity which gave expression to that reverence. Thus, Herodotus relates how the Spartans, at a shrine dedicated to their dead law-giver, 'pay reverence to him greatly',[54] and Isocrates advises, 'Reverence the gods appropriately, not only by sacrificing but by keeping one's vows'.[55] The true content of piety (*eusebeia*) for the educated Greek was 'reverent and wondering awe at the lofty and pure world of the divine, its worship in the cultus, and respect for the orders sustained by it. It is not being under the unconditional claim of a personal power'.[56]

Although the Old Testament acknowledges that dread, shaking, trembling or terror may be appropriate responses to a divine revelation in certain contexts (*e.g.* Ex. 3:6; 19:16; 20:18–19; Ps. 2:11–12; Is. 2:10, 19, 21), fear of God in the more positive sense of reverence or respect is regularly on view. To fear God is to keep his commandments (*e.g.* Dt. 5:29; 6:2, 24; Ec. 12:13), to obey his voice (*e.g.* 1 Sa. 12:14; Hg. 1:12), to walk in his ways (*e.g.* Dt. 8:6; 10:12; 2 Ch. 6:31), to turn away from evil (*e.g.* Jb. 1:1, 8; 2:3; 28:28; Pr. 3:7), and to serve him (*e.g.* Dt. 6:13; 10:20; Jos. 24:14). Cultic obedience will clearly be one aspect of that service, though this is not normally the focus when the Hebrew verb *yārē'* ('to fear') and its cognates are used. In contrast with the Greek notion of piety, reverence or the fear of the LORD in the Old Testament means specifically faithfulness and obedience to the covenant demands of God and this is synonymous with true religion (*e.g.* Gn. 20:11; Ex. 18:21; Ps. 25:14; Mal. 3:16; 4:2). The LXX clearly prefers the *phoboun* word-group to render the various meanings of this Hebrew terminology.[57]

The verb *sebomai* occurs infrequently in the Greek Old Testament, translating *yārē'* and its cognates only five times. Occasionally the reference is to cultic acts directed towards idols (Jos. 24:33 [LXX only]; *cf.* Wisdom 15:16; Bel and the Dragon 3, 4, 23), and occasionally the reference is to Israel's cultic worship or to Jewish ritual observance more generally (Jos. 22:25; Is. 29:13; *cf.* 3 Macc. 3:4; 4 Macc. 5:24). Elsewhere, the more general sense of reverence or fear of God expressed by total lifestyle is implied by the context. Thus, Joshua declared that the purpose of the exodus deliverance was to reveal God's might to the nations and to enable Israel always to 'fear the LORD' (Jos. 4:24), Jonah described himself as one who fears 'the LORD, the God of heaven, who made the sea and the land' (Jon. 1:9) and, within the Wisdom literature, Job is given as an outstanding example of one 'who fears God and turns away from evil' (Jb. 1:8, RSV).[58] It cannot always be assumed that *sebomai* was chosen to indicate specifically the cultic expression of reverence for God.

In the New Testament, the notion of fearing God emerges at a number of points with the employment of *phoboun* or *phobos* (*e.g.* Acts 9:31; 2 Cor. 5:11; 7:1; Col. 3:22; 1 Pet. 1:17; 2:17). The *seb*-words are mostly not used of Christian believers in their relationship with God.[59] Apart from this, the noun *eusebeia* ('piety, godliness') and related words are applied to Christians in only a few particular contexts.[60]

Conclusion: worship as reverence or respect

The biblical concept of the fear of the LORD differed considerably from Greco-Roman notions of piety. In the Old Testament, reverence or respect for God is essentially a matter of walking in his ways and keeping his commandments. Worship in the sense of obedience to the cultic demands of God can be designated in the LXX by the common Greek word *sebomai*, but this is rare. Worship in the sense of a lifestyle of reverent obedience is more often in view, but even this use of the terminology is rare in the Greek Bible. Preference for the *phoboun* word group to render the relevant Hebrew terms suggests that the translators were seeking to highlight the distinctiveness of the scriptural view of reverence.

Conclusion

From one point of view, worship in the Old Testament is an attitude of homage or adoration to God as a great king. It could be expressed in silence or by a simple gesture. It could be indicated by that gesture in association with praise or the offering of sacrifices. In the final analysis, it is the attitude of the heart that really matters. Such responses were made spontaneously, in recognition of some new disclosure of God's character and will, or in the course of some regular pattern of ritual activity.

Adoration was not a form of intimacy with God or an indication of special affection towards him,[61] but rather an expression of awe or grateful submission – a recognition of his gracious character and rule. This is consistent with my interpretation of the tabernacle, the ark and the temple as symbols of God's kingly presence in the midst of his people. The ritual associated with these institutions was consequently the cultic means of acknowledging God's power and presence.

From another point of view, acceptable worship in the Old Testament is service rendered to God. With the use of such terminology, the focus is again on the acknowledgment of his divine kingship in national and personal life. Moreover, Scripture indicates that it was only possible to serve the LORD acceptably because of his gracious initiative, rescuing his people from bondage to other masters, and revealing his will to them. The service of God demanded obedience and faithfulness in every sphere of life, with cultic activity being viewed as a particular expression of Israel's dependence upon and submission to God. The service of priests and Levites within the prescribed cult was designed to facilitate the service of all Israel to God.

Reverence or the fear of the LORD in the Old Testament means faithfulness and obedience to all the covenant demands of God. While this found expression in cultic activity, the reference was normally to the honouring of God by total lifestyle. When Christians imply that reverence is essentially a matter of one's demeanour in church services, they show little understanding of the Bible's teaching on this subject!

Thus, acceptable worship in Old Testament terms involves homage, service and reverence, demonstrated in the whole of life. A common factor in these three ways of describing Israel's response to God is the assumption that he had acted towards them in revelation and redemption, to make it possible for them to engage with him acceptably. By contrast, the worship activities of the nations are considered to be offensive to God, because they are human inventions, arising from misconceptions about God and ignorance about what pleases him.

The overlap of meaning between these concepts may be somewhat imperfectly represented as in the diagram below.

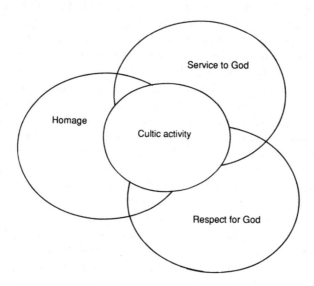

Notes

[1] H. Strathmann, *TDNT* 4. 61, commenting particularly on the notion of service to God in the Old Testament.

[2] *The Oxford English Dictionary*, Vol. XII V-Z (Oxford: Clarendon Press, 1933), pp. 320–321. A number of obsolete uses of the noun and the verb are noted in this dictionary, relating mainly to the showing of respect or honour to a person or thing. An address like 'your worship' to someone like a mayor remains as an example of this ancient usage.

[3] This verb occurs no less than 60 times in the New Testament, but is better rendered in some contexts 'to bow down' or 'to pay homage'. The noun *proskynetes* ('worshipper') occurs once, in Jn. 4:23.

[4] *Cf.* H. Greeven, *TDNT* 6. 758–759, following J. Horst, *Proskynein. Zur Anbetung im UrChristentum nach ihrer religionsgeschichtlichen Eigenart* (Gütersloh: Neutestamentliche Forschungen 3.2, 1932), pp. 4–6. The oldest use of *kynein* in Homer (*e.g. Iliad* 6, 474; *Odyssey* 23, 208) points in this direction.

[5] *Cf.* B. M. Marti, 'Proskynesis and Adorare', *Language* 12, 1936, pp. 272–282. Perhaps the word became a technical term for adoration of the gods because those who wished to honour the underground gods of primitive Greek religion had to stoop to kiss the earth or the image of a god (so, H. Greeven, *TDNT* 6. 759, again following J. Horst, *Proskynein*, 18, 24. So also H. Schönweiss, *NIDNTT* 2. 876).

[6] *E.g.*, Sophocles, *Electra* 1374: *Philoctetes* 776, 1408; Aeschylus, *Prometheus* 936; Plato, *Republic* 451a, 469a.

[7] *Proskysai th ' hōsper theon* (Sophocles, *Philoctetes*, 656–657). Earlier, Philoctetes summons Neoptolemus to 'salute' or 'show respect' for his home as he departs (*proskysante tēn esō aoikon eisoikēsin*, 533–534).

[8] Two interesting applications of this terminology occur together in a papyrus letter from the first or second century AD, cited in G. H. R. Horsley (ed.), *New Documents Illustrating Early Christianity*, 1 (Sydney: Macquarie University, 1981), pp. 56–57.

[9] The root is *ḥ-w-y* ('curl up'), rather than *š-ḥ-w* ('sink down, subside'), as older scholars supposed (*cf.* M. I. Gruber, *Aspects of Nonverbal Communication in the Ancient Near East*, Studia Pohl 12/1 [Rome: Biblical Institute, 1980], pp. 90–95, H. D. Preuss, *TDOT* 4. 249–250, H.-P. Stähli, *THAT* 1. 530–531). The other Hebrew verbs rendered by *proskynein* are *sāgaḏ*, 'to bow down' (Is. 44:15, 17, 19, and the corresponding Aramaic verb in Dn. 2:46; 3:5–7, 10–12, 14–15, 18, 28 [95]); *kāraʿ*, 'to kneel down' (Est. 3:2, 5); *nāšaq* 'to kiss' (1 Ki. 19:18); *zûāʿ* 'to tremble' (Dn. 6:27 [26]); and *ʿāḇaḏ* 'to serve' (Ps. 97 [96]:7). H. Greeven (*TDNT* 6. 760, n. 23) discusses the few instances where *hištaḥ^awâ* is not rendered by *proskynein*.

[10] H. Greeven (*TDNT* 6. 761) reads too much into the text when he argues that in such verses 'there is always expressed in the act a recognition that the one thus honoured is God's instrument'.

[11] This is a modified version of the position of M. I. Gruber (*Nonverbal Communication*, pp. 96–97). Against Gruber, when the Hebrew pairs *hištaḥ^awâ* with another verb meaning 'to bow down' (as, for example, in Ex. 4:31), *hištaḥ^awâ* is more logically read in a semi-technical or transferred sense, namely 'to worship, adore, pay homage' (*i.e.*, They 'bowed down and paid homage').

¹² J. A. Thompson, *Deuteronomy, TOTC* (London: IVP; Grand Rapids: Eerdmans, 1974), p. 256.

¹³ Translation of M. I. Gruber (*Nonverbal Communication*, p. 130), who comments that the 'raising of the hands' accompanying the exclamation 'Amen, Amen' is a gesture of affirmation, 'an extension of the oath gesture from the judicial sphere to the cultic' (p. 130, n. 1).

¹⁴ Sacrifice, prayer and bending over to the LORD are obviously closely linked in Scripture. Yet, the gesture of bending over cannot simply be equated with prayer. For a comprehensive study of postures for prayer and the relevant Hebrew terminology *cf.* M. I. Gruber, *Nonverbal Communication*, pp. 90–151.

¹⁵ Moses' posture in Ex. 34:8–9 was certainly a preliminary to intercession, but it was primarily a response of awe and gratitude to the revelation of God's grace that he had just received (vv. 5–7). Supplication may be implied in 1 Sa. 1:19, but the reference is more likely to be quite generally to participation in the sacrificial ritual at Shiloh (*cf.* 1:3). 2 Ch. 20:18 has been taken to refer to a posture of entreaty to God, but it is more obviously an expression of grateful submission to the will of God, as proclaimed by the prophet (vv. 14–17).

¹⁶ It is strange that the translators of the RSV and NIV prefer to translate *hištaḥᵃwâ* 'bow down' in contexts where *ʿābad* is juxtaposed, rendering the latter 'to worship', rather than 'to serve'. Yet these versions translate *hištaḥᵃwâ* 'worship' where the Hebrew text has more obvious indicators that a specific physical gesture is in view.

¹⁷ What the elders of Israel actually 'saw' in their encounter with God in Ex. 24 was only the glory that was 'under his feet' (v. 10). Their response was to eat and drink in God's presence (v. 11), expressing the reality of their acceptance by God in the covenant relationship he had established (*cf.* Gn. 31:46, 54). Later, whenever the people saw the pillar of cloud standing at the entrance of 'the tent of meeting', 'they all stood and worshipped, each at the entrance to his tent' (Ex. 33:10), yet this response was an acknowledgment that God was speaking to Moses (vv. 8–9), not a form of adoration directed to the tent or the cloud.

¹⁸ This is the more literal rendering of A. Weiser, *The Psalms* (ET, London: SCM; Philadelphia: Westminster, 1962), p. 625. RSV has 'Let us come into his presence with thanksgiving' and NIV 'Let us come before him with thanksgiving'.

¹⁹ The Israelites were taught to offer praise 'in the joyous hope of the coming of the righteous rule of their God over the whole world' (A. Weiser, *The Psalms*, p. 643). *Cf.* Ps. 99:1–3.

²⁰ The same fundamental notion of universal worship is expressed differently by Zp. 2:11 (every nation 'in its own land') and Zc. 14:16–17 (in Jerusalem, 'year by year').

²¹ This verb occurs some 21 times in the New Testament, with the cognate noun *latreia* ('worship') being found 5 times, in Jn. 16:2; Rom. 9:4; 12:1; Heb. 9:1, 6.

²² *E.g.* Solon 13. 47–48 (*latreuein*); Pindar, *Olympian Odes* 10. 28 (*latrion*). I am indebted to the comprehensive study of the serving terms in Greek usage from Homer (where applicable) to the end of the New Testament era, provided by Mark Harding, *The Terminology of Respecting and Serving God in the New Testament Era*, M. A. Dissertation (Sydney: Macquarie University, 1987). *Cf.* H. Strathmann, *TDNT* 4. 58–59.

23 Plato, *Phaedrus* 244E. *Cf. Euripedes, Ion* 128, 151–152 *(latreuein); Phoenician Maidens* 221 *(latris);* Plutarch, *The Oracle at Delphi* 407E *(latreuein).*

24 Plato, *Apology* 23C *(hē tou theou latreia).* Serving wisdom is the notion in Sirach 4:14 *(cf.* Philo, *On the Sacrifices of Cain and Abel* 84).

25 *Cf.* K. H. Rengstorf, *TDNT* 2. 261–265, 268–269, noting the influence of eastern religions on later Greek usage. *Douleuein* in the sense of dependence and subordination in service was regarded as debasing and contemptible *(cf.* Epictetus, *Dissertations* 4, 1, 7 ff.).

26 *Cf.* the use of this verb in Mt. 6:24; Lk. 16:13; Acts 20:19; Rom. 7:6, 25; 12:11; 14:18; 16:18; Eph. 6:7; Col. 3:24; 1 Thes. 1:9. Rom. 6:16–23 offers a particularly striking picture of servitude to God using related terms.

27 *E.g.* Ex. 14:5, 12; 21:2, 6; Dt. 15:12, 18; Jdg. 3:8, 14; 9:28, 38. *Latreuein* is never used in this sense. *Cf.* H. Strathmann, *TDNT* 4. 60.

28 *E.g.* Ex. 23:33; Dt. 13:5 (Codex A); 28:64; Jdg. 2:7; 10:6, 10, 13, 16 (Codex B).

29 *E.g.* Ex. 4:23; 8:1 [LXX, 7:26]; 8:20 [LXX, 8:16]; 9:1, 13; 10:3, 7, 24, 26.

30 D. J. A. Clines, *The Theme of the Pentateuch, JSOTS* 10 (Sheffield: *JSOT*, 1978), p. 48.

31 P. C. Craigie, *The Book of Deuteronomy, NICOT* (Grand Rapids: Eerdmans, 1976), p. 173. The Hebrew brings out this connection between the verses more obviously than the Greek version. In Mt. 4:9–10 / Lk. 4:7–8, the basis of Jesus' response to Satan's temptation is Dt. 6:13, expressing his determination to serve God alone.

32 Craigie observes that the various expressions in Dt. 10:12–13 have a common theme, which is 'allegiance to the God of the covenant' *(Deuteronomy,* 204). In Dt. 10:20, the words 'and you shall keep close to him' are added, the language indicating a very close and intimate relationship, such as between a man and his wife *(cf.* the same verb in Gn. 2:24; Jb. 19:20). Philo *(On the Special Laws* I, 300) expounds Dt. 10:12–13 to show that service to God is not exhausted by cultic activity. *Cf.* also H. Ringgren *TWAT* 5. 994.

33 In the inter-testamental book of Sirach the terminology is used in a transformed sense to refer to the service of wisdom through morality: 'those who serve *(hoi latreuontes)* her render a cult *(leitourgēsousin)* to the holy' (4:14). So also in the reflections of later Judaism on texts like Dt. 11:13 and Dn. 6:11, 16, it was observed that prayer and the study of Torah were service to God. *Cf.* Wisdom 18:21 and the evidence presented by R. Meyer, *TDNT* 4. 222–225.

34 1 Esdras 4:54 and 1 Ch. 28:13 appear to be exceptions to this rule.

35 Lk. 1:23; Acts 13:2; Rom. 13:6; 15:16, 27; 2 Cor. 9:12; Phil. 2:17, 25, 30; Heb. 1:7, 14; 8:2, 6; 9:21; 10:11.

36 *E.g.* Isocrates, *Against Callimachus* 58, 64. The older form of the word is *lēitourgein,* indicating that it is a combination of *lēitos* 'concerning the people or national community', and the root *erg. Cf.* H. Strathmann, *TDNT* 4. 215–219 and N. Lewis, '*Leitourgia* and Related Terms', *Greek, Roman and Byzantine Studies* 3, 1960, pp. 175–184; 6, 1965, pp. 227–230.

37 *E.g.* Aristotle, *Politics* III, 5, p. 1278a, 12; Plutarch, *On a Multitude of Friends* 6 (II, 95e); Lucian, *The Dance* 6.

38 *Lētourgōn tō theō* (Demosthenes, *Against Meidias* 56. The divine authorization of these activities is mentioned in 51–52). *P. Lond.,* 33 (161 BC) describes those engaged in cultic duties associated with the Serapeion at Memphis as rendering

liturgies in the temple (*hai leitourgousai*). Again, *P. Tebt.*, 302:20 (AD 70–71) describes priests at Tebtunis performing liturgies with respect to the gods (*hai tōn theōn leitourgiai*). *Cf.* H. Strathmann, *TDNT* 4. 218–219.

39 *Leitourgein kyriō* (2 Ch. 11:14; *cf.* Ezk. 45:4; Joel 2:17).

40 The LXX version of 2 Ch. 31:2 makes *leitourgein* the last verb in the verse and thus associates it with the particular ministry of the Levites in this context. This is possibly also the implication of the Hebrew syntax.

41 H. Strathmann (*TDNT* 4. 219–221) gives some important examples. He also notes that *leitourgein* can be used to translate other Hebrew verbs such as *'ābad* when they have a cultic reference. For the differences between *'ābad* and *šērēt* in the Hebrew text *cf.* C. Westerman, *THAT* 2. 1019–1022.

42 The noun *leitourgia* occurs some 40 times in the LXX, almost always for the Hebrew *'abōdâ* Usually only a cultic *'abōdâ* is rendered *leitourgia*. In other cases, a variety of Greek words is used to translate the Hebrew noun. *Cf.* H. Strathmann, *TDNT* 4. 221.

43 M. Harding (*Respecting and Serving God*, p. 80) takes issue with the argument of Strathmann (*TDNT* 4. 222) that the LXX translators chose *leitourgein* to denote the levitical duties because this word captured the sense of the benefit to Israel which the people enjoyed, following the older official or technical political use of the terminology. Harding argues, p. 73, that in the LXX, as in Greco-Roman literature, this terminology is used in cultic contexts to describe the work of discharging 'liturgies' imposed by the gods. However, he acknowledges that the Old Testament resists the notion that the priests of Israel benefit God in any way. *Cf.* G. E. Wright, *The Old Testament Against its Environment* SBT 2 (London: SCM, 1950), Part III.

44 Xenophon, *Memorabilia* 2. 1. 28 (*therapeuteon tous theous*). A brief catalogue of the kinds of activities and dispositions comprehended by *therapeia* is offered by Plato, *Euthyphro* 13A-C.

45 *E.g.* Plato, *Laws* 716D; Isocrates, *To Nicoles* 20. The religious significance of the terminology is more common in the inscriptions and papyri (*cf.* H. W. Beyer, *TDNT* 3. 128–129).

46 Moses is certainly called God's *therapōn* (Ex. 4:10; Nu. 12:7; Dt. 3:24; 1 Ch. 16:40 [LXX only]) and the Israelites are designated *hoi therapeuontes kyrion* in Is. 54:17, instead of the more usual *douloi theou*. Judith 11:17 speaks of Judith serving God day and night, doubtless by ritual observance (*cf.* Sirach 35:16), and the Letter of Jeremiah 25 uses the terminology to refer to the cultic honour paid to idols (*cf.* Dn. 3:12–13 [LXX only]).

47 *E.g.* Plato, *Apology* 30A; Epictetus, *Discourses* 3. 22. 82.

48 *E.g.* Plato, *Euthyphro* 14D (*cf.* also 13B). *Cf.* K. H. Rengstorf, *TDNT* 8. 530–532.

49 The verb *hypēretein* occurs in the New Testament only in Acts 13:36; 20:34; 24:23. The noun *hypēretēs* is more widely used to describe someone who is the instrument of another person's will (*e.g.* Mt. 5:25–26; 26:58; Lk. 4:20; Acts 13:5), including those who are specifically designated as servants of Jesus (*e.g.*, Jn. 18:36; Acts 26:16; 1 Cor. 4:1; *cf.* Lk. 1:2).

50 H. W. Beyer, *TDNT* 2. 81. J. N. Collins, 'Georgi's "Envoys" in 2 Corinthians 11:23', *JBL* 93, 1974, p. 89, note 4, confirms this and shows from a variety of texts that *diakonos* could indicate the function of a courier, an agent, an intermediary, or one waiting in attendance on another.

[51] *E.g.* Epictetus, *Discourses* 3. 22. 69; 3. 24. 65; 3. 26. 28; 4. 7. 20; Josephus, *Jewish War* 3. 354; 4. 626 and the inscriptions cited by H. W. Beyer, *TDNT* 2. 92. Josephus (*Antiquities* 3. 155; 7. 365; 10. 72) uses *diakonein* to designate cultic service to the God of Israel.

[52] W. Foerster, *TDNT* 7. 169. He argues that the stem *seb-* means originally 'to fall back before'. W. Burkert, *Greek Religion* (Cambridge, MA: Harvard University, 1985), p. 273, puts it this way: 'To designate the awe that spreads from the gods the root *seb-* appears; etymologically it too points back to danger and flight, yet in Greek, reverence and admiration come to the fore.'

[53] *E.g.* Sophocles, *Antigone* 777 (the divine), 780 (the dead); *Oedipus at Colonus* 1377 (parents); *Ajax* 667 (kings). Words in the *seb-* group include, *sebomai, sebazomai, sebasma, eusebeō, eusebeia, eusebēs, theosebeia, theosebēs, asebeia, asebēs.*

[54] *Sebontai megalōs* (Herodotus, *Histories* 1. 66). So also Dionysius of Halicarnassus (*Roman Antiquities* 1. 30. 3) writes of the 'divine rites' of the Etruscans (*ta theia sebasmata*); and an inscription from Delphi (dated 189 BC) insists that the Roman consuls and senate have always paid reverence to (*sebesthai*) and honoured (*timan*) the gods (W. Dittenberger, *Sylloge Inscriptionum Graecarum* [Leipzig: Hirzel, [3]1920], #611. 24). *Cf.* Josephus, *Antiquities* 12. 253.

[55] *Eusebei ta pros tous theous* (Isocrates, *To Demonicus* 13). A variety of texts insist that the reverence of the gods is not to be restricted to the cultic sphere, *e.g.*, Dio Chrysostom *Discourses* 36. 54; Epictetus, *Discourses* 1. 16. 15–18; *P. Oxy.*, 215. 7–8, 16.

[56] W. Foerster, *TDNT* 7. 178.

[57] The verb *phoboun* is used some 291 times in the LXX to translate *yārē'*. *Cf.* G. Wanke, *TDNT* 9. 197–205. For a helpful summary of biblical teaching on the fear of God and a discussion of the relevant terminology see G. A. Lee, *ISBE* 2. 289–292.

[58] Jb. 1:9 has *sebetai ton theon*, whereas Jb. 1:1 uses the adjective *theosebēs* to translate the same Hebrew expression. The verb *sebomai* is used quite generally to convey the attitude or life-orientation of reverence to God in Is. 66:14; Dn. 3:33, 90 [LXX only]; 2 Macc. 1:3.

[59] Indirectly, Christianity is dismissed as a way 'to worship God contrary to the law' (*para ton nomon...sebesthai ton theon*) in Acts 18:13. Otherwise *sebomai* is used of non-Christians in Mt. 15:9 / Mk. 7:7 (= Is. 29:13); Acts 13:43, 50; 16:14; 17:4, 17; 18:7; 19:27. *Cf.* the variant *sebazomai* in Rom. 1:25; the noun *sebasma* in Acts 17:23; 2 Thes. 2:4.

[60] *Eusebeia* is found in Acts 3:12; 1 Tim. 2:2; 3:16; 4:7–8; 6:3, 5–6, 11; 2 Tim. 3:5; Tit. 1:1; 2 Pet. 1:3, 6–7; 3:11; *eusebēs* in Acts 10:2, 7 (Cornelius); 2 Pet. 2:9; and *eusebōs* in 2 Tim. 3:12; Tit. 2:12. *Cf. eusebein* in Acts 17:23 (pagan worship) and 1 Tim. 5:4 (the religious duty of Christian widows).

[61] G. Kendrick, *Worship*, pp. 23–24, following the argument of H. Schönweiss and C. Brown, *NIDNTT* 2. 875–876, wrongly supposes that *proskynein* conveys the notion of intimacy. Old Testament usage, rather than any supposed etymology of the word, must be the interpreter's guide.

CHAPTER THREE

Jesus and the new temple

The centre of the new religious community was not
an institution located in buildings or at a place – not
even in Jerusalem, nor was it a hierarchy or ruling
organization, nor yet a new ideal or way of life; it was
simply and entirely the person, Jesus Christ.[1]

How did the writers of the New Testament use and adapt Old
Testament worship themes? In particular, what happened to
Jewish hopes for the renewal of worship in a restored temple?
How does the New Testament employ the key worship terms
reviewed in the last chapter? Turning first to the gospels, we will
be concerned in the following two chapters to discern Jesus'
teaching about the traditions of Israel and their fulfilment in the
messianic era. Jesus provided no systematic instruction about
such matters, but certain sayings and actions reflect his radical
perspective. The gospels are also important because they show
how the evangelists and the early Christian communities viewed
the significance of Jesus' coming. They illustrate the extent to
which Jesus had stimulated a whole new way of thinking about
worship.[2]

The gospels are firmly set within the framework of first-
century Jewish piety. The sacrificial rituals continue to be maintained by the official priesthood in the temple at Jerusalem.
Godly Israelites gather there for prayer in association with the

daily offerings or make special pilgrimages to the holy city for the celebration of great festivals. In addition we are shown the importance of the synagogue as a centre for prayer and the study of the Scriptures. The home and the family continue to be centres for the propagation and celebration of the faith. The ministry of Jesus is intimately connected with each of these institutions, yet Matthew and John in particular develop a picture of Jesus as the fulfilment of everything that the temple stood for and the focus of worship under the new covenant.

The temple, like its predecessor the tabernacle, was regarded as a meeting-point between heaven and earth, the place where the transcendent Lord of all was pleased to manifest his glory in the midst of his people Israel. As a representation of God's presence with them and a sign of his rule over them, the temple was to be a reference point for the life of the nation. The ritual conducted in connection with this holy place was the God-ordained way of maintaining the covenant relationship that he had established with them. It was supposed to enable Israel to live out its destiny before the nations as 'a kingdom of priests and a holy nation'. Consequently, it is not surprising to find various expressions of the hope for a new temple at the centre of Jewish thinking about the future. With the promise that God would dwell forever in the midst of his people, in a new and unparalleled way, went the belief that the nations would somehow be united in the worship of the one true God. Matthew and John highlight the fulfilment of these expectations in a number of distinctive ways.

Matthew's perspective

God with us

The New Testament begins with the assurance that all history has been moving towards Jesus Christ as its goal and that he is the final and definitive manifestation of God's presence with his people. Matthew's genealogy and narrative of the conception and naming of Jesus are introduced with the words 'a record of the origin of Jesus Christ, the son of David, the son of Abra-ham'.[3] The genealogy points to the rise and fall of the house of David in the history of Israel and implies the re-establishment of Davidic rule in the person of Jesus. As the son of David, he is the promised messianic ruler, who will rescue and restore Israel (*e.g.* Is. 11:1–11; Je. 23:5–6). Specifically, he comes to deliver his people 'from their sins' (Mt. 1:21). As the son or offspring of Abraham he is the one through whom God's promise of univer-sal blessing for the nations will be effected (*e.g.* Gn. 12:3; 17:7; 22:18; *cf.* Mt. 28:16–20).

Although these affirmations are vital for understanding Jesus in the light of Jewish expectations, Matthew moves immediately to a motif of divine sonship, to indicate the full significance of the central character in his gospel.[4] God's intervention through the Holy Spirit in the conception and birth of Jesus, as revealed and interpreted by an angel of the Lord, marks a radically new development in the line of David (compare v. 16 with vv. 18–21). As David's son Jesus is also God's son in a unique way. His conception signals the fulfilment of Isaiah 7:14, with its promise that the birth of a certain Davidic prince would be the sign of God's continuing presence with his people and therefore an assurance of the continuation of his covenant relationship with Israel:[5]

> All this took place to fulfil what the Lord had said
> through the prophet: 'The virgin will be with child
> and will give birth to a son, and they will call him
> Immanuel' – which means, 'God with us'
> (Mt. 1:22–23).

The point is not that Jesus ever bore Immanuel ('God with us') as an actual name, but that this title indicates the deepest significance of his coming.

The theme of the divine sonship of Jesus runs like an unbroken thread through the early chapters of Matthew, 'becoming ever more visible and thus alerting the reader to the manner in which Matthew would have him comprehend the person of Jesus'.[6] In the remainder of this gospel, the confession of Jesus as Son of God is obviously central to Matthew's view of discipleship (*cf.* 14:33; 16:16; 27:54; 28:19). The 'Son' theme incorporates the notion that Jesus is the one who fulfils the role and destiny of the true Israel (*cf.* 2:15; 4:3), as well as the notion that he is the promised king of Israel (*cf.* 3:17; 16:16; 17:5; 26:63) and the one who uniquely manifests the power and presence of God amongst his people (*cf.* 8:29; 14:33). The claim that Jesus is the Messiah might also have indicated to some of Matthew's original readers that he is the one to build the eschatological temple. On the other hand, the claim that he is 'God with us' suggests that in him is to be found the reality towards which the temple pointed. How these themes are expressed and inter-related remains to be explored.

The first gospel does not explicitly declare Jesus to be the new temple, even though there are pointers to the truth that in him the promises regarding the temple in the End-time are fulfilled. In the debate with the Pharisees about Sabbath-keeping Matthew alone records the claim of Jesus that 'one greater than the temple is here' (12:6).[7] Jesus reminds his opponents that the law of Moses provided for the priests in the temple to 'desecrate' the Sabbath by fulfilling their duties and yet to remain 'innocent' (12:5; *cf.* Nu. 28:9–10; Lv. 24:8). The recognition that temple duties took precedence over Sabbath regulations was an accepted Rabbinic argument,[8] which Jesus took a step further. If the service of the temple could legitimate certain work on the Sabbath, how much more could 'one greater than the temple'. In short, Jesus asserts that he represents God's royal presence and authority more fully than the temple.

Jesus claims to be superior both to David and the temple, and as the Son of Man is 'Lord of the Sabbath' (12:8). The Sabbath controversy is not merely an isolated struggle against one aspect of Jewish legalism but raises the question of Jesus' true identity and the nature of his authority.[9] It is not surprising, therefore, that the evangelist goes on to develop that theme. He shows that the uniqueness of the person and work of Jesus is linked to his possession of the Spirit and that a recognition of this truth is of eternal significance (12:18–21, 25–28, 30–32; *cf.* 3:16–17). With the transfiguration of Jesus, a veil is withdrawn, and three disciples are briefly allowed to see something of the true glory of the Son of God (17:1–8). Israel's hope of God tabernacling amongst his people again in a mighty way appears to be in the process of fulfilment. The challenge to the disciples is to go on listening to Jesus, since he enshrines the true revelation of God.

Jesus' commissioning of the disciples forms a climax to Matthew's presentation of the 'God with us' theme (28:16–20). Jesus appears to the eleven disciples and they acknowledge him as the risen Lord (v. 17). He commands them to make disciples of all nations because he is the one to whom 'all authority in heaven and on earth has been given'. By virtue of his resurrection, the exalted Christ has become the one through whom all God's authority is mediated to the nations. This new stage in redemptive history should impel his disciples forward to 'a universal ministry he himself never engaged in during the days of his flesh, "except in reluctant anticipation" '.[10] Thus, Matthew suggests that the acknowledgment of the divine sonship of Jesus and the proclamation of his heavenly rule are at the heart of discipleship. With these final verses, the evangelist returns to the theme of his opening chapter. The blessings promised to Abraham, and through him to all peoples on earth (Gn. 12:3), are now to be enjoyed in Jesus the Messiah. His promise to be present always, 'to the very end of the age' recalls the central idea of the covenant in the Old Testament, indicating that the covenant is renewed and consummated in Jesus, in whom God's presence is perfectly manifested.

Homage to Jesus

Apart from the book of Revelation, Matthew's Gospel employs the verb *proskynein* more frequently than any other New Testament writing, with Jesus as its object on ten occasions (2:2, 8, 11; 8:2; 9:18; 14:33; 15:25; 20:20; 28:9, 17). Significantly, it occurs first in a narrative introducing a number of other important Matthean themes. Magi from the Gentile world express a desire to pay homage to the one born king of the Jews (2:2). Herod the Great, who had been made king of Judea by the Roman Senate and who had consistently crushed all opposition to his rule, is represented as similarly seeking to honour the child, while in reality plotting to destroy him (2:8). Supernaturally guided to the place where the baby lay, the Magi 'fell down and paid homage to him' (*pesontes prosekynēsan autō*), opening their gifts

(2:11). A physical expression of homage is implied by the combination of these two verbs.

Although some English versions view this action as 'worship' (AV, RSV, NIV), the statement of the Magi in verse 2 suggests that the meaning is homage paid to royalty rather than the worship of deity (so Phillips, NEB; cf. 1 Sa. 25:23; 2 Ki. 4:36).[11] Of course, Matthew's opening chapter has pointed to Jesus' divine sonship and the evangelist no doubt intended his readers to discern that this homage had a greater significance than the visitors from the East could have imagined. Their attitude to Jesus anticipated the submission of the nations to the risen Lord, which is the essence of discipleship, according to Matthew 28:16–20. The immediate context in Matthew 2, however, does not demand that worship of Jesus as Son of God is yet in view.

On four occasions Matthew portrays persons in need approaching Jesus with a form of homage and entreaty (8:2; 9:18; 15:25; 20:20). Since *proskynein* in these verses is not accompanied by the verb 'to fall down', most translations understand that the posture was either kneeling down (RSV, NIV, Phillips) or, more accurately in view of our study of Old Testament usage, bowing low (NEB). Despite the fact that these incidents reveal exemplary trust in Jesus and a dawning recognition of his true identity, it is doubtful that the posture should be viewed as 'worship' (AV), implying a recognition of his divine sonship.[12] As suppliants in the Old Testament expressed their total dependence on kings and other authority figures by bowing before them and begging for help (*e.g.* 1 Sa. 2:36; 2 Sa. 14:4; 16:4), so these people recognized the extraordinary power and authority of Jesus to meet a variety of needs.[13] Furthermore, if Old Testament usage is any guide, when *proskynein* means 'worship' it usually implies humble submission to the will of God or grateful acknowledgment of his gracious initiative to those concerned, not primarily supplication.

Similar to the spontaneous reaction of people in the Old Testament to divine disclosures is the response of the disciples to Jesus when he walked on the water and stilled the storm, and 'those who were in the boat worshipped him, saying, "Truly you are the Son of God" ' (Mt. 14:32–33; *cf.* Lk. 5:8). Matthew alone records the invitation to Peter to walk on the water (14:28–31) and offers a more positive conclusion to the incident than Mark (14:33; cf. Mk. 6:51–52). Associated with this confession of divine sonship, the response of the disciples in Matthew's account can be aptly described as worship. In making this judgment, it is not necessary to suppose that the evangelist was reading into an earlier stage of the disciple's experience an estimate of Christ's person which actually emerged at a later juncture, either at Caesarea Philippi (16:16) or after the resurrection (28:9, 17).

The important claim of Jesus in Matthew 11:27 ('No-one knows the Son except the Father, and no-one knows the Father except the Son and those to whom the Son chooses to reveal him') brings the whole of Christ's ministry under the head of revelation. The Father's revelation of the Son is inextricably bound up with the Son's revelation of the Father. Since 'the entire history of Christ has been in the nature of a divine revelation which the disciples, with greater or lesser clarity, and with admixture of doubt and bewilderment, have come to comprehend',[14] Matthew 14:33 and 16:16 represent different stages in the subjective apprehension by the disciples of the revelation being made to them. Whatever the precise understanding of the disciples on this occasion, Matthew surely intended his post-resurrection readers to recognize Jesus here as 'the one who has dominion over chaos and evil, the one whom the church confesses and worships as the Son of God, "God with us" '.[15]

In recording the mock homage of the soldiers, Matthew does not use the word *proskynein*, as Mark does (Mt. 27:28–30, cf. Mk. 15:19). Presumably this is because he wishes to retain the term as an indicator of the right sort of approach to Jesus. As the gospel draws to its climax, there is no doubt that the approach in question should ultimately be identified as 'worship' in the sense of acknowledging the presence and authority of the risen Lord. The response of the women to an appearance of Christ (28:9) and the response of the eleven disciples when they meet him on the mountain (28:17)[16] is the same expression of grateful and reverent homage found in 14:33. Indeed, the final encounter with the resurrected Christ involves an unmistakable declaration of his divine kingship ('All authority in heaven and on earth has been given to me') and the implication of the charge that follows is that the disciples are to call upon people everywhere to express the same homage to Christ as they disciple the nations.

A consideration of the concluding scene of Matthew's gospel reveals the 'affective response' which the narrative as a whole seeks to produce. 'The proper response to the risen Lord is worship (28:17) and confidence (28:20) derived from the sure knowledge that all authority has been granted to Jesus the Messiah. The narrator expects the readers to worship Jesus as the risen Lord and to be confident that he is present to the church until the close of the age.'[17] Indeed, the great commission is 'not an ending but a beginning, which invites the reader to discipleship and the evangelization of the nations'.[18] Because worship and confidence hinge upon the person of Jesus, the plot of Matthew's gospel is largely concerned with the recognition of his true identity.

In short, Matthew develops a picture of Jesus as the one to whom 'every knee should bow' (cf. Is. 45:22–23; Phil. 2:10). At the most basic level, suppliants come to him for life and health and even for a place of honour in his kingdom. At the most profound level, he is to be acknowledged as the one who, in his earthly life, was truly 'God with us' and is now the resurrected Son of God. We may infer that unbelievers begin to worship Christ when they recognize his true identity and turn to him, yielding themselves in grateful obedience to the Saviour and Lord of the nations. Matthew's presentation of Christ is designed to elicit such worship. Disciples continue in the worship of Christ as they confess him, obey his teaching, proclaim his heavenly rule, and bring others to acknowledge him too.

The cleansing of the temple

As in the other synoptic gospels, the final visit of Jesus to Jerusalem to preach in the temple courts and celebrate the Passover with his disciples is shown in Matthew to be the visit of ultimate importance, both for Judaism and Jesus (Mt. 21:1 – 26:30; cf. Mk. 11:1 – 14:26; Lk. 19:28 – 22:38). It is the focus of Jesus' attention and teaching in the central section of each of these gospels, as he leads his disciples to that last, fateful encounter with the Jewish authorities and ultimately his death (Mt. 16:21 – 20:34; Mk. 8:31 – 10:52; Lk. 9:22 – 19:27).

Mark prefaces the narrative of the cleansing of the temple with a report of Jesus cursing a fig tree (Mk. 11:12–14) and follows this up with a note about the fig tree having withered in response to his word (11:20–21). Matthew combines the two parts of this story into one and records it after the visit to the temple. Mark's structure makes the cursing of the fig tree and the cleansing of the temple more explicitly a commentary on each other. This prophetic-type action, using a traditional symbol for Israel's fruitfulness or lack of fruitfulness before God (*e.g.* Je. 8:13; 29:17; Ho. 9:10, 16; Joel 1:7; Mi. 7:1–6), dramatizes the judgment that is about to fall on Jerusalem and the temple. Just as the leaves of the tree concealed the fact that there were no figs to eat, so the temple and its activities concealed the fact that Israel was not producing the fruit of obedience demanded by God from his covenant people. Mark presents the cleansing of the temple more obviously as an acted parable of the judgment to come, though that theme is not absent from the context in Matthew (21:18–19, 33–44) and Luke (19:41–44; 20:9–18).[19]

It would seem from rabbinic evidence that the establishment of markets in the temple forecourt, where pilgrims could buy objects for sacrifice and change their Roman money to pay the annual half-shekel temple tax (*cf.* Ex. 30:13–16), was a shocking innovation introduced by the high priest Caiaphas in about AD 30.[20] At one level, Jesus' violent expulsion of the merchants could simply have been understood as an expression of the deep indignation shared by others in his day at this abuse of the temple and its sacred precincts.[21] However, Jesus' use of Isaiah 56:7 ('My house will be called a house of prayer for all nations'), in combination with a phrase from Jeremiah 7:11 ('but you are making it "a den of robbers" '), suggests a deeper significance to his actions. The designation of the temple as a house of prayer for God's people recalls Solomon's dedication in 1 Kings 8:28–30. In Isaiah the Lord affirms his intention to allow foreigners who 'bind themselves to the LORD' (Is. 56:6) and hold fast to his covenant to share in the blessings of his house:

> These I will bring to my holy mountain and give
> them joy in my house of prayer. Their burnt offerings
> and sacrifices will be accepted on my altar; for my

house will be called a house of prayer for all nations
(Is. 56:7; *cf.* 2:1–4; 1 Ki. 8:41–43).

The omission of the words 'for all nations' in Matthew and
Luke has been taken as an indication that these evangelists were
playing down this aspect of Jesus' challenge.[22] Since it was the
outer 'court of the Gentiles' that he cleared, however, the theme
is really implicit in these accounts. Jesus' contemporaries had
obscured the temple's true function as a place where God's
holiness was to be revealed and where pure worship was to be
offered. In particular they had prevented Gentiles from using the
one place set aside for them to pray, by turning it into a 'den of
robbers'. This phrase was no doubt designed to suggest a link
with Jeremiah's temple sermon (Je. 7:1–11), in which the
prophet warned his contemporaries about the danger of believing that the temple guaranteed their security, no matter how
they behaved. Implicit in Jesus' challenge is the suggestion that
'the Jews were not simply robbing one another; they were robbing God'.[23] Unless the temple functioned in Israel's life as God
intended, the Abrahamic promise could not be fulfilled and
Israel could not be the means by which God's blessing extended
to all the nations.

It is not possible to explore all the different nuances in the
various gospel accounts of the cleansing of the temple. Jesus
appears to some extent as a prophetic reformer, challenging
Israel to face afresh the fundamental question of what it means
to be the people of God. He briefly takes possession of the temple
as a basis for teaching the people and preaching the gospel (Mt.
21:23 – 24:1).[24] In his teaching, however, he offers no hope for
Israel because of its corrupt leadership (Mt. 21:33–44 and parallels), condemning the hypocrisy of the teachers of the law and
Pharisees without denouncing the law, the temple or the customs
of Judaism themselves (Mt. 23:1–36). Since the religious leaders
have persistently resisted and persecuted the messengers of God
and now seek to turn the people away from Jesus, he predicts the
judgment of God upon that generation, involving the desolation
of Jerusalem and its 'house' (Mt. 23:37–39, *cf.* Lk. 13:34–35;
19:41–44; 23:28–31).

Israel and the temple have not functioned according to God's plan and so the gospels indicate that Jesus is to become the centre of salvation and blessing for the nations (*e.g.* Mt. 28:18–20; Lk. 24:46–49; Jn. 12:20–33). The tearing of the curtain of the temple from top to bottom at the moment of Jesus' death (Mt. 27:51; Mk. 15:38; Lk. 23:45) could be taken as an expression of the judgment of God, anticipating the more drastic events to come in AD 70, but also as a symbol of the opening of a new way to God through the death of Jesus.

Jesus' prediction of the destruction of the temple

Before Jesus could be condemned correctly under Jewish law the agreement of two witnesses had to be obtained (*cf.* Nu. 25:30; Dt. 17:6; 19:15). Matthew indicates the difficulty the authorities had in finding such witnesses, until two gave testimony that he had said, 'I am able to destroy the temple of God and rebuild it in three days' (Mt. 26:59–61). The parallel in Mark 14:57–59 expands the charge, claiming that Jesus said, 'I will destroy this man-made temple and in three days will build another, not made by man.'[25] Matthew says the Sanhedrin was looking for 'false evidence' and that many 'false witnesses' came forward but does not, like Mark, dismiss this particular testimony as false. In both gospels Jesus refuses to comment on such a charge, which leads the high priest to demand if he is truly the Christ. This was logical, since any suggestion of replacing the temple might have been understood as a messianic claim. On the basis of his response to this question Jesus was condemned to death for blasphemy. Although the evidence of the witnesses may have been inconsistent and distorted, the question remains whether it was a complete fabrication or whether it was a misrepresentation of a genuine saying of Jesus.[26]

Jesus certainly foretold the abandonment of Jerusalem by God and the destruction of the temple. After his denunciation of the teachers of the law and the Pharisees for their hypocrisy and resistance to the truth, Matthew marks the climax of Jesus' public teaching ministry with these words:

O Jerusalem, Jerusalem, you who kill the prophets
and stone those sent to you, how often I have longed

to gather your children together, as a hen gathers her
chicks under her wings, but you were not willing.
Look, your house is left to you desolate. For I tell
you, you will not see me again until you say, 'Blessed
is he who comes in the name of the Lord' (Mt.
23:37–39; cf. Lk. 13:34–35; 19:41–44).

Jerusalem represents the nation, condemned by Jesus for its
treatment of the messengers of God, and unwilling to repent. He
speaks as one who has been exercising the divine function of
gathering Israel to himself, but who has been rejected. While the
word 'house' might refer to Israel as a whole (cf. 10:6; 15:24), the
immediate context suggests that the temple is specifically in view
(cf. 24:1–2). In any case, Israel, Jerusalem and the temple are all
closely connected in biblical thought and rise and fall together.
The declaration 'your house is left to you desolate' speaks 'not so
much of the physical condition of the temple, as of the fact that
God has departed from it' (cf. Ezk. 10:18–19; 11:22–23).[27] In
other words, the temple is abandoned because the relationship
with God which it symbolizes is broken (cf. Je. 12:7). Jesus
implies that what Israel does with him, and not with the temple,
determines the nation's fate. This saying falls short, however, of
any suggestion that Jesus himself might be responsible for the
destruction of the temple and its replacement with another.

Each of the synoptic gospels presents an eschatological discourse delivered by Jesus to the disciples, as a last piece of
instruction before they prepare to celebrate the Passover
together. In each case, remarks about the magnificence of the
temple buildings provoke him to predict that 'not one stone here
will be left on another; every one will be thrown down' (Mt. 24:2;
cf. Mk. 13:2; Lk. 21:6).[28] Apart from the fact that this prophecy
and all that follows is delivered to the disciples in private,
however, the form of words can hardly be taken as the basis for
the charge by the witnesses at his trial. No utterance of Jesus
except the saying recorded in John 2:19 can account for the
development of that garbled testimony.[29] This important text
will be discussed later in this chapter.

Gathering in Jesus' name

Temple imagery is not explicitly transferred to the Christian
community in Matthew's gospel, though it is easy to see how
that application could later be made. The well-known saying in
18:20 identifies Jesus himself with the divine presence and promises his presence to the most insignificant gathering of two or
three in his name.[30] The broader context is a discourse from
Jesus on relationships in the messianic community and the
immediate setting is his teaching about the treatment of a
'brother' who sins against another member of 'the church'
(18:15–17).[31] Various instructions about how to deal with such
difficulties are given, culminating in the promise of Jesus 'I tell
you the truth, whatever you bind on earth will be bound in
heaven, and whatever you loose on earth will be loosed in
heaven' (v. 18). The future perfect construction in the Greek here
(literally, 'will have been bound...will have been loosed')
implies that when disciples unite to rebuke or to forgive in such a
case, their action will carry the prior endorsement of heaven!
How is it possible for disciples to be so in touch with the will of
God?

The word 'again' (*palin*) in verse 19 appears to introduce
intercessory prayer as a new subject ('Again, I tell you that if
two of you on earth agree about anything you ask for, it will be
done for you by my Father in heaven'). A link is maintained with
what has gone before, however, by the repetition of the promise
that decisions on earth will be ratified in heaven. Prayer expressing agreement on earth about difficult relationships or any
other matter will be answered in heaven by the one whom Jesus
uniquely calls 'my Father' (*cf.* 11:25–27). Such agreement is
possible where disciples are gathered in Christ's name. This will
not simply refer to any gathering that is remotely connected with
the name of Christ but to disciples united in their desire to obey
his teaching and reflect his character in their lives together.[32]
Wherever such union occurs, Christ is truly present, enabling
disciples to know the will of heaven and to seek for the Father's
will to be done. In the final analysis, it is Christ's promise to be
present with his people that makes possible the fulfilment of the
other promises in this passage.

Two or three engaged in evangelism are just as much assured of Christ's presence with them as those meeting for prayer, to study the Scriptures, or to resolve some problem of relationships in the Christian assembly (*cf.* 28:18–20). Jesus' teaching here invites comparison with the assertion of the Rabbis that 'when two sit together and words of the Law (are) between them, the Shekinah (God's presence) rests between them'.[33] In the final analysis, the New Testament proclaims that Jesus Christ in union with his church is the new temple, where God dwells in or through the Spirit (*e.g.* 1 Cor. 3:11–17; Eph. 2:18–22).

John's perspective

God with us

The fourth gospel has even more to say about the way in which Jesus replaces the Old Testament institutions of worship. The divine presence is no longer bound to the temple, but the Word who was with God 'in the beginning' and who in fact 'was God', has become flesh and taken up temporary residence or 'pitched his tent among us' (1:14, lit.: *eskēnōsen en hēmin*). This terminology recalls the instruction to Israel to make a tent-sanctuary (Ex. 25:8–9, *skēnē*), as the site of God's localized presence on earth, and the later teaching about God's presence in the temple or on Zion, his holy hill. The prophets indicated that in the End-time God would 'make his dwelling' (*kataskēnoun*) in the midst of his people for ever (Joel 3:17; Zc. 2:10; *cf.* Ezk. 43:7) and John proclaims the fulfilment of that promise in the incarnation of the eternal Word.[34] John 1:14 goes on to record the testimony of those true Israelites, who 'received him' and 'believed in his name' (*cf.* vv. 11–13): 'We have seen his glory, the glory of the One and Only [Son], who came from the Father, full of grace and truth.'

In Jesus, the believing community has seen the glory of God, which in the Old Testament was associated with Mount Sinai (Ex. 24:15–16), the tabernacle (Ex. 40:34) and then the temple in Jerusalem (1 Ki. 8:10–11; Is. 6:1–4) and which, it was believed, would be revealed to 'all mankind' in the new age (Is. 40:5). Ezekiel's vision of the glory of God filling the restored temple (Ezk. 44:4) has been witnessed in Christ. God has pitched the ultimate tabernacle in the flesh of Jesus and in this way made his glory visible! Yet, 'it is not only his glory, his name or *sh^ekhînāh*, but God himself, God the Word, who dwells with his people. Now at last the longstanding tension between the transcendence and the immanence of God is resolved.'[35]

As in Matthew's gospel, the notion of God's presence among his people is closely tied to the divine sonship of Jesus: literally, the glory is 'as of a father's only [son]'.[36] The 'Son' theme in the fourth gospel incorporates the same ideas as in the synoptics, but John goes beyond the other gospels in bringing out more clearly the essential identity of 'the Son' with the Father (*e.g.* 14:9–11), at the same time pointing to the complete dependence of the Son on the Father (*e.g.* 5:19–23). The evangelist demonstrates from the material that he records how 'any meanings so far given to the name "son of God" are far transcended by the reality which is in Jesus'.[37]

As the one who is 'full of grace and truth' (Jn. 1:14), the Son supremely manifests that divine mercy and faithfulness proclaimed to Moses on Sinai at the renewal of the covenant (Ex. 34:6), and associated with the promise of God's continuing presence with his people. The giving of the law through Moses was an expression of God's enduring love, but 'from the fulness of his grace' Christians have received 'grace upon grace' (RSV) through Jesus Christ, who is the embodiment of grace and truth (Jn. 1:16–17). Not even the greatest representatives of Israel such as Moses and Isaiah actually saw God, but 'God the only [Son], who is at the Father's side, has made him known' (1:18).[38] Thus, as a climax to a chapter of confessions about the person and work of Christ, Jesus tells Nathaniel, 'I tell you the truth, you shall see heaven open, and the angels of God ascending and descending on the Son of Man' (1:51). Despite the complexity of this verse, its allusion to the dream of Jacob in Genesis 28:12 is clear and suggests that Jesus as the Son of Man is the new Bethel ('the house of God...the gate of heaven', Gn. 28:17), the new point of contact between earth and heaven.

The emphasis on the presence of God in the person of Jesus

has an important outcome in the teaching of John's gospel about the Spirit. Jesus is the one who baptizes in Holy Spirit (1:33) and through the Spirit makes the benefits of his saving work available in the present age (3:5–8; 6:63; 7:37–39). Through the gift of the Spirit, the glorified and exalted Lord Jesus continues to dwell in and with his disciples (14:15–20). The Counsellor, whom the Father sends in Christ's name, teaches and guides the community of believers through the apostolic word, reminding them of everything the earthly Jesus said (14:26; 16:13–15). Then, through their testimony, the Spirit convinces or convicts the unbelieving world (16:8–11; cf. 15:26–27) and enables disciples to fulfil their missionary charge (20:21–23). 'The Spirit is thus the eschatological *continuum* in which the work of Christ, initiated in his ministry and awaiting its termination at his return, is wrought out.'[39]

Jesus' prediction of the temple's replacement

Although John's narrative of the cleansing of the temple (2:13–22) is similar enough to the synoptic tradition concerning the visit of Jesus at the end of his ministry, there are some important differences.[40] Chapters 2 – 4 portray Jesus as the one in whom the religion of the Jews finds ultimate fulfilment, and it would seem that the evangelist has placed the cleansing narrative at this early stage in his gospel to assist in the development of this theme.[41] Jesus reveals something of his true identity and purpose at the temple site, first by his authoritative action and then by his saying about the raising up of a new temple. John's interpretation makes it clear that Jesus becomes the true temple, the house of prayer for all nations, by means of his death and resurrection.

As in the synoptic accounts, Jesus' cleansing of the temple in John 2 is at one level a prophetic-type protest against the profanation of God's house. To those who sold doves he said, 'Get these out of here! How dare you turn my Father's house into a market!' This recalls the prophecy of Zechariah 14:21 ('There shall no longer be a trader in the house of the LORD of hosts on that day', RSV) and suggests that Jesus was taking action to bring about the fulfilment of that End-time vision, in which God is to be glorified by the pure worship of his people.[42] The immediate context in the fourth gospel also suggests that the action was a specifically messianic sign, pointing to the replacement of the temple by Jesus. At the wedding in Cana of Galilee (2:1–12), Jesus changed the water in the six stone jars used by the Jews for ceremonial washing into wine and thus 'revealed his glory' to his disciples. This is the first of a series of signs indicating that Jesus is the one sent by the Father to replace the customs and feasts of Judaism. Jesus does this by bringing in the blessings of the messianic era, here signified by the abundance of choice wine.[43] By cleansing the temple, he further revealed himself as the one sent to replace the institutions of the Mosaic covenant.

Although the witnesses at Jesus' trial and the bystanders at the crucifixion charged Jesus with saying, 'I will destroy this temple', John 2:19 records that he actually said, 'Destroy this temple' (*lysate ton naon touton*), using the imperative in an ironical way, as if to suggest to the authorities, 'Go ahead and destroy this temple and see what happens!' Apart from other minor differences, the synoptic reports use the verb 'to build' (*oikodomein*), which is applicable only to another edifice such as the existing temple, whereas John's report uses 'to raise up' (*egeirein*), which may refer to a building or to the resurrection of Jesus' body. On the surface, this pronouncement refers simply to the Jerusalem temple and could have been taken as a claim by Jesus to be the builder of the eschatological temple ('Destroy the existing temple and I will raise it again in three days'). The insight that this saying referred to his resurrection body came only after he had been raised and the disciples 'believed the Scripture and the words that Jesus had spoken' (2:22).[44] The expression 'in three days' ('after three days' in the synoptics) meant a short, but indefinite time (*cf.* Ex. 19:11; Ho. 6:2; Lk. 13:32) and hinted at a miraculous establishment of the new edifice. Hence the response of the Jews: 'It has taken forty-six years to build this temple, and you are going to raise it in three days?' (2:20).

The Scripture that the disciples 'believed' (Jn. 2:22) was probably Psalm 69:9 (cited in Jn. 2:17). John emphasizes the typological or predictive aspect of this psalm about a righteous sufferer by substituting the future tense ('Zeal for your house will consume me') for the past tense. As a prophecy of Jesus' death, it suggests that Jesus' concern to establish the purpose of God for Israel, Jerusalem and the temple would destroy him! Because of this zeal, the Jewish leaders would bring about his death, but Jesus would take up his life again. John indicates that the glory of God is ultimately manifested in the death of Jesus on behalf of God's flock, so that he might raise them up to share the new life of the kingdom with him (*cf.* 10:14–30). The incarnation makes possible a manifestation of the glory of God surpassing anything experienced in the Old Testament, but the hour of the Son's death is the hour of his ultimate glory and the moment when he completes the task of glorifying the Father, opening the way for believers from every nation to enjoy eternal life (*cf.* 2:4; 12:23–26; 17:1–5).

The temple stood for revelation and purification: it was both the meeting-place of heaven and earth and the place of sacrifice for purification from sin. Thus, it found fulfilment in the incarnation and the sacrifice of Christ. The coming of the 'Greeks' to Jerusalem marked the beginning of the predicted pilgrimage of the nations to Zion and was the signal to Jesus that the hour of his glorification through death had come (12:20–33). His 'lifting up' from the earth would be the means by which he drew the nations to himself. The temple of the new age in John's gospel is not the church but the crucified and resurrected Son of God.[45]

Worship in spirit and truth

The teaching on worship in John 4 forms an important part of the evangelist's total picture of the fulfilment of Old Testament institutions in the person and work of Christ. John moves from the idea of Jesus as the true tabernacle (1:14) and the true temple (2:19) to suggest that he fulfils the ideal of the holy mountain where God can be encountered (4:20–24). Having exhibited the sort of knowledge which suggested that he was a prophet (4:18–19), Jesus was asked by the Samaritan woman to settle a controversial question: 'Our fathers worshipped on this mountain, but you Jews claim that the place where we must worship is in Jerusalem' (4:20). With such a question, the woman was not simply seeking to avoid the issue of her own moral and spiritual condition. The Samaritans expected a *Taheb* (lit., 'the one who returns'), who would be a prophet like Moses (*cf.* Dt. 18:15–18), rather than a Davidic messiah. Amongst other things, he was expected to settle such controversies and to restore proper worship.[46]

Jesus shifted the focus from the place of worship, which was such an issue between Jews and Samaritans, to the manner of worship (4:21, 'Believe me, woman, a time is coming when you will worship the Father neither on this mountain nor in Jerusalem'). When he says 'You... worship what you do not know; we worship what we do know, for salvation is from the Jews' (4:22), he asserts that Samaritan worship, based as it was on an inadequate knowledge of God, was false. However, despite the implication that Jewish worship was truly based on divine revelation and therefore honouring to God, it is to be superseded:

> Yet a time is coming and has now come when the
> true worshippers will worship the Father in spirit and
> truth, for they are the kind of worshippers the Father
> seeks. God is spirit, and his worshippers must
> worship in spirit and truth (Jn. 4:23–24).

With the expression 'the time is coming and has now come', Jesus continues to develop the idea introduced in verse 21 that his ministry initiates a totally different way of relating to God. In the fourth gospel the coming 'time' or 'hour' signifies the hour of his death, resurrection and return to the Father (*e.g.* 2:4; 7:30; 12:23; 13:1; 17:1). With these events the new temple is raised up (2:19) and then the Spirit is given (7:37–39). But, even before the cross, the period of true worship is present and operating in advance in the person and ministry of Jesus.[47] Such worship can take place only through him, since he is the ultimate temple (2:19–22).

The word 'true' (*alēthinoi*) in the expression 'true worshippers' (*hoi alēthinoi proskynētai*) means 'real and genuine', in contrast with the symbolic and typical.[48] Old Testament worship was not false, as Samaritan worship was false, but it was, in effect, only 'a shadow of the good things to come' (Heb. 10:1, RSV), pointing forward to the reality which has come in Jesus. True worship is defined as being 'in spirit and truth' (*en pneumati kai aletheia*).

Jesus does not simply contrast the old external and cultic pattern of worship with a new inward and universal spirituality. 'Neither Jews nor Greeks were in need of enlightenment about the superiority of a spiritual form of worship over a cultic form of worship.'[49] 'Spirit' and 'truth' are closely connected in John's portrait of Christ. No-one can see the kingdom of God or experience the blessings of the End-time without being born again by the Spirit (3:1–8). Thus, in slightly different language, the Father begets true worshippers through the Spirit, whom Jesus makes available by means of his saving work (*cf.* Rom. 8:15–16). The primary reference in John 4:23–24 is not to the human spirit but to the Holy Spirit, who regenerates us, brings new life, and confirms us in the truth (*cf.* 15:26–27; 16:13–15). 'Spirit' and 'truth' are God's gifts through Jesus, by which he sustains us in genuine relationship with himself.

Jesus is the truth (14:6), who uniquely reveals the character of God and his purposes (8:45; 18:37).[50] So the true worshippers will be those who relate to God through Jesus Christ (*cf.* 17:3). The coming hour is already present because Jesus draws attention to himself as the giver of living water (4:10, 14; *cf.* 7:37–39), using a metaphor which combines both ideas: he gives the ultimate revelation and provides the life-giving Spirit.[51] The Father seeks those who would relate to him in this way because such 'worship' accords with his nature (4:24).[52] Jesus is not the focus or object of worship in 4:23–24 but the means by which the Father obtains true worshippers from every nation (*cf.* 12:32).

At the beginning of this dialogue, *proskynein* clearly refers to the customary worship of God, as practised by Jews or Samaritans (*cf.* 12:20). As the discussion proceeds, however, it is used in conjunction with other terms to describe the relationship with God, which Jesus alone makes possible, in the present, eschatological hour. This is not a relationship that is tied in any way to any earthly 'place' (4:20) or cult, for the prophetic hope of the temple as the centre for the universal worship of God in the End-time has been fulfilled in the person and work of Jesus. Such worship is only possible for those who recognize the true identity of Christ (4:25–26, 42) and yield him their allegiance (*cf. prosekynēsen autō*, 9:38). In effect, the exalted Christ is now the 'place' where God is to be acknowledged and honoured. He, rather than a renewed temple in Jerusalem or on some other holy mountain, is the 'place' of eschatological pilgrimage for all the nations. The Father cannot now be honoured unless Jesus is given all the honour due to him as the Son (*cf.* 5:22–23; 8:49).[53]

While this text may suggest that Christian worship should be largely independent of outward forms, locations and ceremonials, it actually has something more profound and positive to say than that. The fundamental teaching of this fascinating passage is lost when we rush too quickly to apply it to our congregational activities. Indeed, it is easy to become quite arbitrary in the use of John 4 and to argue, for example, that there is no place for the slipshod, the flippant and the frivolous, in our approach to God,[54] or to establish that spiritual gifts combined with musical skill facilitate true worship![55] New-covenant worship is essentially the engagement with God that he has made possible through the revelation of himself in Jesus Christ and the life he has made available through the Holy Spirit. The implications of such teaching for the Christian gathering remain to be explored as this book progresses.

Jesus and the Jewish festivals

John 5 – 10 is dominated by Jesus' actions and discourses on the occasion of several Jewish festivals, suggesting that in some way he offers a replacement for them all. On the Sabbath feast (Jn. 5), as he exercised the powers of life and judgment entrusted to him by the Father, he made available the blessings of the new age to which the Sabbath pointed. At Passover (Jn. 6), Jesus multiplied bread as a sign that he is the true bread from heaven. At Tabernacles (Jn. 7 – 9), the indication was given that the water and light ceremonies were replaced by Jesus, who provides 'streams of living water' and is 'the light of the world'. At the feast of the Dedication (Jn. 10), celebrating the reconsecration of the altar and the temple in the Maccabean era (*cf.* 1 Macc. 4:41–61), Jesus referred to himself as the one who had been truly consecrated by God and whose death would secure eternal life for the flock of God.[56] Thus, with a surprising array of images, and with much terminology suggestive of Old Testament teaching, the fourth gospel presents Jesus as the centre of life and worship for the End-time.

Conclusion

The gospels of Matthew and John are particularly concerned to stress that God's presence and God's glory, so intimately connected with the tabernacle and temple under the Mosaic covenant, and consistently at the centre of Jewish expectations for the messianic era, are fully and finally experienced in Jesus Christ. The prophetic hope of a new temple is realized in and through his ministry, culminating in his death, resurrection and ascension. These saving events establish and reveal the true nature and extent of his divine kingship. At the same time, they make it possible for him to become the source of eternal life and the means of sanctifying the nations in a new relationship with God. Jesus did not come to destroy Judaism, but to bring it to its destined end in the worship of the new age.

Jesus appears to have shared some of the thinking of the Old Testament prophets and inter-testamental writers regarding the temple in the plan of God. However, his view of the future did not involve the restoration of the existing temple in a new and more glorious form. In effect, he did as the Qumran community had done and transferred the significance of the temple from the building in Jerusalem to another entity. Yet, for Jesus, the replacement of the temple was not primarily to be in the messianic community but in his own person and work. Only by implication may we discern from his teaching that the new fellowship with God that would be set up through his death and resurrection would in some respects function as the new temple. The presence of God, which was more fully manifested in the person of Jesus than it had ever been in the tabernacle or temple, would eventually be linked with those whom he had gathered to himself.

Jesus replaces the temple of Jerusalem as the source of life and renewal for the world and as the centre for the ingathering of the nations. He does this because he is the ultimate meeting point between God and humanity, by virtue of his incarnation, death and exaltation. In his own person and in his saving work he does all that the temple was meant to do for Israel and for the nations in the prophetic view of the End-time. He is, at one and the same time, the ultimate means of relating to God and is himself the object of homage or worship. These two perspectives belong together and will be further explored in subsequent chapters.

The most important practical consequence of all this is the need for Christian teaching and preaching to centre on the person and work of Jesus Christ. Unbelievers will become 'true worshippers' only when they recognize who he really is, turn to him as Saviour and Lord, and receive from him the life that he offers. God brings people to himself as they come to know his Son through the proclamation of the gospel and yield themselves to him through the work of his Spirit in their lives. Such exclusive claims inevitably provoke hostility and hostility brings with it the temptation to modify the message. But evangelism that falls short of sharing these truths and urging people to respond to them will be less than biblical in its content and aim. In a world characterized by relativism and religious pluralism, Christians need every encouragement to keep pointing to Jesus as the one in whom alone the nations can be united in worship.

Moreover, genuine discipleship can be fostered only by a continuing focus on the character of Jesus, his promises and commands, and his achievements for us. Jesus and his words must remain at the heart of the Christian life, for individuals, families and congregations. The reading, teaching and application of that Spirit-inspired testimony to Jesus we call the New Testament must surely have pride of place in any ministry amongst Christians. Neither sacramentalism, nor the development of the inner life, nor a preoccupation with issues of social justice, can rightly usurp it. Matthew and John also indicate that Christians need to know and understand the Old Testament. We need to be shown how Jesus fulfils the hopes of Old Testament writers and replaces all the provisions for engaging with God that were laid upon Israel. Such teaching would be a healthy corrective to some of the strange views about the church and its functions that bedevil many Christian traditions today.

Notes

[1] H. W. Turner, *From Temple to Meeting House: The Phenomenology and Theology of Places of Worship*, Religion and Society 16 (The Hague, Paris and New York: Mouton, 1979), p. 134. Turner explores the phenomenon of the temple or sacred place in ancient religions to show what happens to these categories in the New Testament teaching about the new temple.

[2] The gospels will be examined in their final, canonical form, without engaging in traditio-historical study of the text.

[3] The expression *biblos geneseōs* probably embraces the whole of chapter one, since the word *genesis* occurs again in v. 18 in a resumptive sense and vv. 18–25 appear to be explaining the strange statement about the birth of Jesus in v. 16. *Cf.* R. E. Brown, *The Birth of the Messiah* (London: Chapman, 1977; New York: Doubleday, 1979), pp. 58–59.

[4] R. E. Brown (*Birth of the Messiah*, p. 135, n. 9) rightly points out that although the title 'Son of God' does not appear in 1:18–25 the theme of divine sonship is present there. 'Before Jesus has ever raised the problem, Matthew in the infancy narrative has told the reader that, although the messianic king is David's son, David can call him "Lord" (Mt. 22:41–46)' (p. 137).

[5] *Cf.* J. A. Motyer, 'Context and Content in the Interpretation of Isaiah 7:14', *TynB* 21, 1970, pp. 118–125 and J. Jensen, 'The Age of Immanuel', *CBQ* 41, 1979, pp. 220–239.

[6] J. D. Kingsbury, *Matthew: Structure, Christology, Kingdom* (Philadelphia: Fortress, 1975), p. 17. However, Kingsbury's assertion that Son of God is the christological category under which all other titles of Christ are to be subsumed, cannot be sustained. *Cf.* D. Hill, 'Son and Servant: an Essay on Matthean Christology', *JSNT* 6, 1980, pp. 2–16.

[7] The neuter *meizon* ('greater') in Mt. 12:6 is best taken as a reference to the person of Jesus, since that is the meaning of the neuter expressions in the comparisons with Jonah and Solomon in 12:41–42. For a discussion of alternative interpretations see D. A. Carson, 'Matthew', in F. E. Gaebelein (ed.), *The Expositor's Bible Commentary* Vol 8 (Grand Rapids: Zondervan, 1984), pp. 281–282.

[8] *Cf.* Mishnah, *'Erubin* 10:11–15; *Pesahim* 6:1–2.

[9] R. A. Cole, *The New Temple*, Tyndale Monograph Series (London: Tyndale, 1950), p. 13, argues that in this incident 'the whole doctrine of the manner of God's presence amid his people is ultimately at stake'. The wider question of Jesus' attitude to the Mosaic law will be faced in the next chapter.

[10] D. A. Carson, 'Matthew', p. 595, citing Stendahl. *Cf.* Mt. 15:21–28 for an example of what is meant by Jesus' 'reluctant anticipation' of the discipling of the nations.

[11] The presentation of gifts to Israel's royal son (v. 11) reflects the hope of Ps. 72:10–11 (*cf.* also Is. 60:3–7) and confirms that homage to the messianic ruler is the primary notion. *Cf.* D. A. Carson, 'Matthew', pp. 86, 89.

[12] R. H. Gundry, *Matthew: A Commentary on his Literary and Theological Art* (Grand Rapids: Eerdmans, 1982), p. 139, argues, for example, that whereas Mk. 1:40 has the leper 'beseeching (Jesus) and falling on his knees', Mt. 8:2 has the leper 'approaching' Jesus (*proselthōn*) and 'worshipping' (*prosekynei*). But it is

reading too much into the terminology at this stage of the gospel to suggest that Matthew views this as worship. The developing recognition of Jesus' divine sonship in Matthew's presentation comes at certain obvious and significant moments, to be highlighted below.

[13] H. Greeven (*TDNT* 6. 763–764) oversimplifies the evidence by implying that *proskynein* regularly implies 'true adoration' for Matthew. The absurdity of his approach is particularly obvious when he treats Mt. 18:26 allegorically as the worship of God in the person of the king.

[14] N. B. Stonehouse, *The Witness of Matthew and Mark to Christ* (Grand Rapids: Eerdmans; London: Tyndale, 1944), p. 216. He goes on to make some helpful remarks about the difference between Matthew's and Mark's conclusions to this narrative. *Cf.* D. A. Carson, 'Matthew', pp. 345–346.

[15] J. D. Kingsbury, *Matthew: Structure, Christology, Kingdom*, p. 66.

[16] The words 'but some doubted' in 28:17 indicate that there were still some for whom the move from unbelief and fear to faith and joy was a hesitant one. *Cf.* the discussion of alternatives by D. A. Carson, 'Matthew', pp. 593–594. On the significance of obeisance to Jesus for Christology see C. F. D. Moule, *The Origin of Christology* (Cambridge, London, New York and Melbourne: Cambridge University Press, 1977), pp. 175–176.

[17] F. J. Matera, 'The Plot of Matthew's Gospel', *CBQ* 49, 1987, p. 242. The infancy narrative prefigures these affective responses: the angel assures Joseph that God is present to his people through Jesus who is Emmanuel (1:23; *cf.* 28:20), and the Magi pay homage to the infant King of the Jews (2:11; *cf.* 28:17).

[18] *Ibid*, p. 252.

[19] C. H. Giblin, *The Destruction of Jerusalem according to Luke's Gospel*, AnBib 107 (Rome: Biblical Institute, 1985), argues that Luke takes greater pains to draw attention to Jesus' prophetic words concerning the devastation in store for the city of Jerusalem, rather than the temple, because he wishes his readers to see the destruction of Jerusalem as a 'type' of what will happen to every God-rejecting society.

[20] *Cf.* V. Eppstein, 'The Historicity of the Gospel Account of the Cleansing of the Temple', *ZNW* 55, 1964, pp. 42–58.

[21] The preferred term in the gospels for the temple complex is *to hieron* (*Cf.* W. von Meding, 'Temple', *NIDNTT* 3. 781–785). Luke uses *naos* in 1:9, 21–22; 23:45 to distinguish the holy place from the temple in general or the temple courts (*cf. naos* in Mt. 23:16, 17, 21, 35; 26:61; 27:5, 40; Mk. 14:58; 15:29, 38; Jn. 2:19–21). Since Jesus' action took place in the outer Court of the Gentiles, it cannot be interpreted as an attack on the temple cult itself.

[22] *Cf.* J. A. Fitzmyer, *The Gospel According to Luke X-XXIV*, AB 28A (Garden City, New York: Doubleday, 1985), p. 1261.

[23] R. J. McKelvey, *The New Temple*, p. 65. *Cf.* W. L. Lane, *The Gospel According to Mark*, *NICNT* (Grand Rapids: Eerdmans, 1974), p. 407, for an alternative interpretation of the word 'robbers' in this context.

[24] This is most obvious in Luke, where an editorial note in 19:47–48 follows immediately upon the evangelist's much abbreviated account of the cleansing of the temple (19:45–46), suggesting that the sanctuary is purified in order to become the centre for the revelation of God to Israel once more. An inclusion is formed by the repetition of a similar editorial note in Lk. 21:37–38, indicating

that all the intervening material was delivered in the context of the temple and that the people came regularly to hear him in that context.

25 The words *cheiropoiēton* and *acheiropoiēton* suggest some connection with a developed system of catechesis running through the New Testament and associated with such terms (*e.g.* Acts 7:48; 17:24; Heb. 9:11). *Cf.* R. A. Cole, *The New Temple*, pp. 23–27 and C. F. D. Moule, 'Sanctuary and Sacrifice in the Church of the New Testament', *JTS* 1, new series, 1950, pp. 29–41. The word *naos* is consistently used in all the gospel sayings about the destruction of the temple attributed to Jesus. *Cf.* note 21 above.

26 The accusation of the crowds at the scene of the crucifixion reflects again the supposed claim of Jesus to destroy the temple and rebuild it in three days (Mt. 27:39–40; Mk. 15:29–30) and adds further weight to the suggestion that this charge may have been based on some genuine claim by Jesus. Note that in Mt. 27:40 and Mk. 15:29 the present participles *ho katalyōn…oikodomōn* may imply a repeated claim by Jesus.

27 R. T. France, *The Gospel According to Matthew, TNTC* (Leicester: IVP; Grand Rapids: Eerdmans, 1985), p. 332. 'Its physical destruction (24:2) is only the outward completion of God's repudiation of it, which will be symbolized in 24:1 when Jesus leaves it, never to return.'

28 Matthew omits the story of the widow's offering, thus linking these words more closely with Jesus' prediction of the desolation of Jerusalem's 'house' (23:37–39).

29 Against R. T. France, *Matthew*, p. 336. So R. A. Cole (*New Temple*, pp. 21–22) argues that the saying of Jn. 2:19 must be authentic because it alone can account for the charge of the witnesses and the emergence of a whole pattern of Christian teaching about Jesus and the temple. C. H. Dodd, *Historical Tradition in the Fourth Gospel* (Cambridge, London and New York: Cambridge University Press, 1963), pp. 90–91, argues that there is no evidence that John's form of the saying is part of an independent tradition.

30 Despite the fact that the gathering of the whole community (*ekklēsia*) to make judgments in such matters is mentioned in v. 17, it is the agreement of two or three that assures the presence of Christ in vv. 19–20.

31 On the use of the word *ekklēsia* in Mt. 16:18 and 18:17 and whether Jesus intended to found a church, see the discussion by G. Maier, 'The Church in the Gospel of Matthew: Hermeneutical Analysis of the Current Debate', in D. A. Carson (ed.), *Biblical Interpretation and the Church: Text and Context* (Exeter: Paternoster; Grand Rapids: Baker, 1984), pp. 45–63.

32 J. D. M. Derrett, ' "Where two or three are convened in my name…": a sad misunderstanding', *ExpT* 91, 1979–80, pp. 83–86, overstates the case when he argues that v. 19 does not deal with prayer at all, but he rightly emphasizes that the focus of the passage is two or three members of the church coming to an agreement concerning some friction or dispute. 'It means that unofficial dispute-settlers, peacemakers, perform a divine function.'

33 Mishnah *Aboth* 3:2. Note also the references given by G. F. Moore, *Judaism in the First Centuries of the Christian Era: The Age of the Tannaim* (Cambridge, MA: Harvard University Press, 1927), I, p. 436.

34 For a different way of expressing the fulfilment of that same Old Testament hope see Rev. 21:3. In the symbolism of the new Jerusalem, 'coming down out

of heaven from God', the point is made that God will locate himself personally and corporately in believers and the community of the new age.

[35] R. J. McKelvey, *The New Temple*, p. 76.

[36] *hōs monogenous para patros*. Although the word 'Son' is not actually used in Jn. 1:14, and *monogenēs* by itself simply means 'the only one of its kind', when this word is used in relation to father 'it can hardly mean anything other than only (-begotten) son', C. K. Barrett, *The Gospel According to St John* (London: SPCK; Louisville: Westminster John Knox, [2]1978), p. 166.

[37] J. Howton, ' "Son of God" in the Fourth Gospel', *NTS* 10, 1963–64, p. 237. *Cf.* C. H. Dodd, *The Interpretation of the Fourth Gospel* (Cambridge, London and New York: Cambridge University Press, 1953), pp. 250–262; G. E. Ladd, *A Theology of the New Testament* (Grand Rapids: Eerdmans, 1974), pp. 246–251.

[38] On the variant readings and possible meanings of this text see R. E. Brown, *The Gospel According to John I-XII*, AB 29 (Garden City, NY: Doubleday, 1966; London: Chapman, 1971), p. 17. 'At the Father's side' implies an active and vital relationship. The present participle *ho ōn* ('the one who is') may imply that the earthly Jesus, the Word-become-flesh, was with the Father at the same time that he was on earth.

[39] C. K. Barrett, *The Gospel according to St John*, p. 90.

[40] D. A. Carson, *The Gospel according to John* (Leicester: IVP; Grand Rapids: Eerdmans, 1991), pp. 177–178, shows that there are better reasons for believing that Jesus cleansed the temple at the beginning and at the end of his ministry than scholars generally allow. *Cf.* L. L. Morris, *The Gospel According to John*, NICNT (Grand Rapids: Eerdmans, 1971), pp. 189–191. R. E. Brown (*John I-XII*, pp. 116–118) attempts a compromise position.

[41] *Cf.* C. K. Barrett, *John*, pp. 195–196.

[42] *Cf.* R. H. Hiers, 'The Purification of the Temple: Preparation for the Kingdom of God', *JBL* 90, 1971, pp. 82–90. It is simplistic to say that 'by throwing the sacrificial animals and birds out of the temple Jesus proclaims that the worship of Israel is at an end' (R. J. McKelvey, *The New Temple*, p. 78).

[43] *Cf.* the imagery of the new age in Mk. 2:19–22. O. Cullmann, *Early Christian Worship*, SBT 10 (ET, London: SCM, 1953), pp. 46–59, rightly indicates the necessity for discerning a double meaning in so much of the Johannine tradition. However, his exegesis is uncontrolled allegory when, p. 69, he interprets the wine in Jn. 2:1–11 as 'a pointer to the wine of the Lord's Supper, i.e. the blood, which Christ shed for the forgiveness of sin'. This suggests three layers of meaning in the text! *Cf.* R. E. Brown, *John I-XII*, pp. 109–110.

[44] O. Cullmann's suggestion of a eucharistic, sacramental symbolism in the 'body' of Jesus after the reference to the wine (= blood) of Jesus at Cana (*Early Christian Worship*, p. 74) is again fanciful. *Cf.* note 43 above and R. E. Brown, *John I-XII*, p. 125.

[45] R. Bultmann, *The Gospel of John. A Commentary* (ET, Oxford: Blackwell; Philadelphia: Westminster, 1971), pp. 127–128, n. 6) rightly argues against Cullmann that it is impossible that the body of Christ here should refer to the community of believers in a Pauline sense, since the object of *luein* and *egeirein* in Jn. 2:19 must be one and the same.

[46] *Cf.* J. Bowman, 'Early Samaritan Eschatology', *JSS* 6, 1955, p. 63. Even

though the more familiar Jewish expectation of Messiah is expressed by the woman in v. 25, the sequence in vv. 19–20 suggests that she is basically operating within the framework of thought outlined by Bowman.

[47] The anticipated effects of Jesus' 'hour' upon his disciples are beginning to be felt as Jesus talks to the Samaritan woman (*cf.* 5:25; 16:32). *Cf.* R. E. Brown, *John I-XII*, pp. 517–518.

[48] R. E. Brown, *John I-XII*, pp. 500–501. The word is used to contrast OT types and NT realities, thus Jesus is the 'true light' (1:9), 'the true bread' (6:32) and 'the true vine' (15:1).

[49] R. Bultmann, *John*, p. 190, n. 4, where references are given to Jewish and pagan sources expressing such notions.

[50] He 'sanctifies' believers in the sense that they are 'taken out of this worldly existence and set in the eschatological existence (17:17, 19)' (R. Bultmann, *John*, p. 191).

[51] R. E. Brown, *John I-XII*, pp. 178–179. However, G. R. Beasley-Murray, *John* WBC 36 (Waco: Word, 1987), p. 60, rightly suggests that we should interpret Jesus as 'both the living water and he who gives water of life to believers'.

[52] The expression 'God is Spirit' does not define God's essential nature in Jn. 4:24 but his mode of action and working with us (so R. Bultmann, *John*, pp. 191–192). Consequently, there can be no true relationship between man and God 'unless it first be grounded in God's dealing with man'. *Cf.* D. A. Carson, *John*, p. 225.

[53] The word *timan* in Godward contexts can mean 'to pay honour' by means of cultic activity, and so 'to worship' (*e.g.* Xenophon, *Memorabilia* 4. 3. 16–17; Dn. 11:38 [LXX]; 2 Macc. 3:2; 13:23; Josephus, *Antiquities* 3. 250). However, Dio Chrysostom (*Discourses* 36. 54) and Philo (*On Noah's Life as a Planter* 126, 131) show how good deeds and appropriate words can be the means of honouring the gods. *Cf.* Mt. 15:4 / Mk. 7:6 (= Is. 29:13).

[54] *Cf.* R. P. Martin, *The Worship of God*, p. 19.

[55] *Cf.* R. Sheldon (ed.), *In Spirit and in Truth: Exploring directions in music in worship today* (London: Hodder & Stoughton, 1989), pp. vii–x.

[56] R. E. Brown, *John I-XII*, pp. 104, 411. A Guilding, *The Fourth Gospel and Jewish Worship* (Oxford: Clarendon, 1960), argues that John is so interested in showing the fulfilment of Jewish worship in Christianity that he has constructed his gospel as a commentary on the Old Testament lectionary readings, as they were arranged for the synagogue in a three-year cycle. This is not a theory that has been widely accepted by scholars, but Guilding's work shows many interesting links between John and the Jewish Festal calendar.

CHAPTER FOUR

Jesus and the new covenant

> The forgiveness of sins is the gift of the time of
> salvation. A greater gift than a share in the
> redeeming power of his death Jesus could not give.
> Through the appropriation of the forgiveness of sins
> the disciples become the redeemed community of the
> End time.[1]

Salvation, temple, covenant and acceptable worship are intimately linked in biblical theology. Consequently, when the gospels indicate that the temple has been replaced by the person
and work of Jesus and that the messianic salvation has been
accomplished by his death and resurrection, the implication is
that a new covenant has been inaugurated. Jesus only talked
openly in such terms at the Last Supper, when he interpreted the
cup as 'the new covenant in my blood' (Lk. 22:20; *cf.* 1 Cor.
11:25). Amongst other things, these words point to the fulfilment
of the promises of Jeremiah 31:31–34. Yet there are also sugges-
tions earlier in the gospel narratives that his ministry would
bring about a profound change in God's dealings with his
people.

This chapter begins with some observations about the way
Jesus expressed his own relationship with God. To some extent,
he is portrayed as a model 'worshipper' – a pious Jew, participating in activities associated with the temple or synagogue,

fervent in prayer, and constantly seeking to discern and do the Father's will. Nevertheless, his teaching raises questions about the continuing role of the Mosaic law and the whole system of approach to God associated with the Sinai covenant. Jesus implies that his ministry opens up a new way to engage with God, which he finally describes in terms of the fulfilment of Jeremiah's promises. By means of his faithfulness and obedience to the Father, even to the point of death, Jesus accomplishes the messianic salvation and makes available the blessings of the new covenant.

The worship of Jesus

During his testing in the wilderness, Jesus was tempted to acknowledge the devil as the one whom 'all the kingdoms of this world' now serve. To win the allegiance of the nations he was challenged to yield himself to Satan. This compromise with the devil is presented as a challenge to 'fall down and worship' (RSV) God's rival (*ean pesōn proskynēsēs moi*, Mt. 4:8–10 = Lk. 4:5–8). The combination of these two verbs, as elsewhere in the gospels, suggests some form of literal homage. As noted in chapter two, however, when the initial act of bending over to honour a god was prolonged into permanent submission, *proskynein* came to mean adoration or devotion to that god. So here some decisive act of loyalty to God's great adversary would amount to a new allegiance for Jesus and thus the worship of Satan as a pattern of life.

Without hesitation, 'the ideal of world political domination is rejected by the one who will serve God and mankind by his humble obedience and suffering'.[2] Having already dedicated himself at his baptism to do the Father's will, he renews that commitment in the wilderness. Jesus' command for Satan to depart is accompanied by a quotation from Deuteronomy 6:13 ('Worship the LORD your God, and serve him only'),[3] which demanded the exclusive loyalty of Israel to the Lord, in the face of every temptation to follow other gods. With these words Jesus affirms the fundamental requirement of the Sinai covenant for unconditional submission and service to the Lord

God. Yet, as we shall see, his teaching and actions continually raise a question about how that worship is to be offered to God. In one sense, the rest of the gospel narratives are an illustration of what it meant for Jesus to fulfil the ideal of Deuteronomy 6:13. Jesus offers the perfect pattern or model of acceptable worship in his obedient lifestyle. Yet Jesus' life is more than an example of sacrificial service. His obedience proves to be the means by which the messianic salvation is achieved.[4]

Discerning and doing the Father's will

Luke alone among the evangelists records the boyhood visit of Jesus to the temple, where he was found sitting among the teachers, listening to them and asking them questions (2:41–50). Together with the earlier note about Jesus' circumcision and presentation in the temple (2:21–40), this incident marks him out as a faithful and obedient Jew, travelling every year with his godly parents to Jerusalem to celebrate the Feast of the Passover.[5] It is in this context that Jesus' first declaration about his relationship to God is presented ('Did you not know that I must be in my Father's house?' 2:49, RSV).[6] This unique relationship prompts him to seek the Father's will in the temple – the place traditionally associated with the self-revelation of God to his people. Discerning the Father's will for Israel, the Messiah and the nations, as set out in Scripture, was doubtless a continuing aspect of his devotion to the Father.

Luke also highlights Jesus' personal communion with the Father in prayer at a number of points in his narrative. Jesus often withdrew to lonely places and prayed (Lk. 5:16; *cf.* Mk. 1:35). Sometimes he prayed for himself (*e.g.* Lk. 22:40–46; 23:46) and sometimes for others (*e.g.* 22:32; 23:34). Yet most of Luke's references are far from being incidental. They point to the significance of Jesus' prayers in the progress of his ministry and in the fulfilment of the purposes of his Father. For example, Jesus is pictured at prayer on the occasion of his baptism, when he dedicated himself to fulfil the role of the Servant-Messiah (3:21). Jesus prayed before he chose the twelve apostles, who were to play such a key role in the propagation of his message (6:12), and before asking his disciples what conclusion they had come to about his identity (9:18–20). Again, Jesus is at prayer when he is transfigured (9:28–29), and as he prepares for his arrest, trials and suffering (22:40–46). Even on the cross he expresses his faithfulness to the Father in prayer (23:34, 46).[7]

In each of the gospels, Jesus' obedience to the will of the Father clearly culminates in his death. Officially organized opposition to his ministry will not deflect him from completing the task that he believes he has been given (*e.g.* Mt. 12:14–21; Lk. 13:31–35). The narrative of his last journey to Jerusalem is punctuated in the synoptics by his predictions of impending rejection and death (*e.g.* Mk. 8:31; 9:30–32; 10:32–34, 45, and parallels). Yet Jesus continues resolutely on his way. In John's gospel, laying down his life for his 'sheep' is a command he has received from the Father (Jn. 10:17–18; *cf.* 4:34), so that the 'hour' of his death is the climax towards which his ministry moves (Jn. 12:23–33). Under the dread of death, Jesus resists the temptation to avoid the approaching anguish and suffering, and rededicates himself to do the Father's will, allowing himself to be delivered into 'the hands of sinners' (Mt. 26:36–46; Mk. 14:32–42; Lk. 22:39–46). The redemptive significance of this obedience will be considered shortly.

Jesus and the synagogue

The synoptic gospels draw attention to Jesus' involvement in the synagogues of Galilee. There he had opportunity to teach, to heal, and to debate informally with the scribes and other leaders of the people (*e.g.* Mt. 4:23 = Mk. 1:39 = Lk. 4:44; Mt. 12:9–14; 13:54–58).[8] The word *synagōgē* was used in Greek for various kinds of gatherings, but became a technical term for a Jewish assembly or congregation. Like the word 'church' in Christian circles, in time 'synagogue' came to be applied to the building where the gathering took place, and then came to be regarded as a symbol for the religion of Judaism itself.[9] Jewish tradition ascribes the origin of this institution to the time of Moses, but most contemporary scholars hold that it derives from the period of the Babylonian exile in the sixth century BC. It is argued that the exiles met spontaneously to sustain their faith in the absence of the temple cult, and that these meetings were consolidated into institutional form in due course, after the return to Palestine.[10]

Unlike the temple, synagogues were lay led, with a president and a caretaker, and a group of elders in charge of their affairs. No sacrificial ministry was carried out within the services. The primary object of the synagogue was instruction in the law of God, which meant the study of Scripture, together with the oral law, which in Talmud and Midrash, finally became written down. An endeavour was made to educate the whole community in its faith, applying the words of God to every area of life, working out the implications of covenant obedience. This was done, not merely through Sabbath gatherings, but through the use of synagogues more generally as places for elementary education and more advanced studies. The synagogue services consisted of the recital of the *Shema'* (based on Dt. 6:4–9), prayer, the reading of the Law (the Pentateuch) and the Prophets, and the Blessing. The Law was read in Hebrew and explained in Aramaic, with the readings being arranged over the course of time into Sabbath portions for a three-year cycle.[11] Only if a priest were present, would the priestly blessing (Nu. 6:24–26) be pronounced to conclude the proceedings.[12]

The synagogue actually represents 'a new type in the phenomenology and history of religion that we may call the meeting-house, *a house for the meeting of the people of God,* rather than a house for the god himself'.[13] So long as temple and synagogue existed together, the latter remained a supplement to the other. The synagogue readings and prayers, however, were linked with all the great festivals at the temple and effectively provided a substitute for these services for the very large number of Jews who could rarely, if ever, travel from distant places to Jerusalem. In time, God's presence was associated by the rabbis with any meeting of Israelites for prayer and with the faithful community gathered around the law.[14] After the destruction of the second temple by the Romans in AD 70, synagogues became even more obviously substitutes for the temple and centres for the religious and community life of Jews scattered throughout the world.

Undoubtedly there are ways in which synagogue ideas and practices influenced the pattern of early Christian gatherings.[15] Nevertheless, it is clear from Jesus' own preaching that he sought to establish a new centre for Israel, in himself and the salvation he proclaimed (*e.g.* Lk. 4:18–21), rather than in the synagogue, the temple, the law or the inherited customs of his people.

Jesus and the law of Moses

Jesus' attitude to the Old Testament law is a complex issue, requiring detailed study of many key passages. What follows is a reflection on his teaching concerning just some of its provisions. None of the gospels presents Jesus as offering a sacrifice in the temple, though his instruction to his disciples to prepare the Passover would have involved sacrificing a lamb in anticipation of their meal together. He clearly takes the sacrificial system and the associated cult as a given (*e.g.* Mt. 5:23–24; Mk. 1:44; 12:41–44). Yet his teaching is generally more concerned with the ethical than the cultic. He often stands with the Old Testament prophets in condemning the cultic practices and traditions of his contemporaries, without criticizing the law itself. Those traditions were often designed to protect the pious from infringing the commandments of God. Yet so radical is Jesus' challenge concerning such traditions that he raises questions about the continuing role of the law itself. The impression is given 'of a life neither geared to nor drawn up against the Law, but one that is *moved by quite different considerations*, yet to which observance of the Law can indirectly be made to bear witness'.[16]

Cleanness and uncleanness

The discourse on ritual uncleanness, which is found in Mark 7:1–23 and Matthew 15:1–20, is particularly significant in this regard. The Pharisees and scribes complained that Jesus' disciples defiled themselves by not observing 'the tradition of the elders' about ritual washing before taking food. This custom was apparently grounded in the Old Testament requirements for the priests to wash their hands and feet prior to entering the tabernacle.[17] The Pharisees, however, had extended priestly regulations to the laity in an attempt to sanctify the ordinary acts of life. Mark refers to their traditions more generally (7:2–4), to prepare for Jesus' condemnation of the whole Pharisaical attitude to tradition. 'You have let go of the commands of God and are holding on to the traditions of men', Jesus insists (7:8; *cf.* Mt. 15:3). His challenge includes a quotation from Isaiah 29:13 ('These people honour me with their lips, but their hearts are far from me. They worship me in vain; their teachings are but rules taught by men'). This is followed by a pointed example of how they rejected God's commandments in order to keep their own tradition (Mk. 7:9–13; *cf.* Mt. 15:3–6).

In a subsequent address to the crowds, Jesus widens his response even further to confront the issue of the true source of defilement, by saying, 'Nothing outside a man can make him "unclean" by going into him. Rather, it is what comes out of a man that makes him "unclean" ' (Mk. 7:15; Mt. 15:11). This claim, and the explanation to the disciples that accompanies it, does not attack Old Testament laws about ritual cleanness directly. 'It moves in a different realm altogether, for it expresses an entirely new understanding of what does and does not constitute defilement.'[18] True purity before God cannot be obtained by scrupulous observance of cultic laws because rituals are unable to deal with the defilement that comes from within, from a rebellious and corrupt 'heart' (Mk. 7:17–23; Mt. 15:16–20; recalling Is. 29:13). The prescriptions of the Mosaic covenant for ritual cleansing were a sign of the need for purification in a more profound and complete sense. Jesus' teaching raises a question about where such cleansing might be found. The immediate context provides no answer, though his teaching about the significance of his death ultimately offers a solution to this problem.

Mark's editorial note draws out the implications of Jesus' teaching for the benefit of his readers: 'in saying this, Jesus declared all foods "clean" ' (7:19). Mark regards the Mosaic food-laws as no longer binding on those to whom his gospel was addressed.[19] The further implication would be that Old Testament prescriptions about defilement and purification are transcended by something new. Mark's statement recalls the vision given to Peter in Acts 10:9–16, with its assurance that the purity laws of the Mosaic covenant were no longer applicable. When Peter rejected the suggestion that he should eat what was previously regarded as unclean, the Lord told him 'Do not call anything impure that God has made clean' (Acts 10:15).

How and why such changes came about remains to be explored. Here it is sufficient to note that Jesus' criticism of scribal traditions and their attitude to the law of God revealed the need for a change of heart towards God – in effect, the writing of God's law on their hearts – and a new means of cleansing from the defilement caused by sin. In short, Jesus' teaching points to the need for the promises of the new covenant in Jeremiah 31:31–34 to be fulfilled.

Prophesying before the fall of Jerusalem in 587 BC and the exile of the Jews to Babylon, Jeremiah was convinced that the nation had irrevocably broken the covenant made by God with their forefathers and that God himself would therefore bring them to ruin (*e.g.* Je. 11:1–17). Since God was the initiator of the original covenant, he alone could restore it by an act of sovereign grace (Je. 31:31–34). The time was coming when he would re-establish a united people ('the house of Israel' and 'the house of Judah'). He would forgive their wickedness and 'remember their sins no more'. He would place his law within them, enabling them all to know him ('from the least of them to the greatest'), giving them the desire and ability to do his will and live as his renewed people. Jeremiah's language stresses the novelty of this alliance, despite the obvious continuities with the past.[20] God alone could create the conditions necessary for the restoration of relationships with such a rebellious people.

Sabbath observance

In the various controversies between Jesus and his opponents over Sabbath-keeping, the gospels reveal that he and his disciples once again offended against Pharisaical rules and regulations, rather than breaking any particular Old Testament law. Jesus' response to their challenges, however, raises the wider issue of his authority and the relation of the law's provisions to his own person and work.

This is illustrated most clearly in the narratives about the disciples picking ears of corn and eating them on the Sabbath (Mt. 12:1–8; Mk. 2:23–28; Lk. 6:1–5). In answer to the charge that his disciples were doing 'what is unlawful on the Sabbath', Jesus pointed to certain Old Testament precedents. These arguments were apparently designed to raise questions about his identity and the nature of his authority, rather than to justify the behaviour of the disciples. As noted in the last chapter, Matthew's account makes this christological focus to the encounter more obvious by recording Jesus' claim to be 'one greater than the temple' (12:6). Again, in Matthew alone, Jesus brings the words of Hosea to bear on the situation: 'If you had known what these words mean, "I desire mercy, not sacrifice," you would not have condemned the innocent' (12:7; *cf*. Ho. 6:6). At first glance it might appear that this simply claims a priority for the moral over the ceremonial demands of the law. Here and in Matthew 9:13, where the same text is cited, however, the Pharisees are being challenged more fundamentally to consider the mercy of God at work in the ministry of Jesus. His practice of eating with the outcasts of Jewish society (9:10–13), and the way he interprets the law for his disciples (12:1–8), suggest that, through Jesus, God is working in a new way to draw people into relationship with himself.

All three gospels record the statement that 'the Son of Man is Lord of the Sabbath' as a climax to their narratives of this decisive incident. In the face of various interpretative problems relating to this verse, I would argue that it is most natural to read it as an indirect claim by Jesus (speaking of himself as 'the Son of Man' in the third person) to be the one who has the authority to determine the kind of behaviour that is suitable on the Sabbath.[21] An examination of those narratives in which Jesus is condemned by his opponents for healing on the Sabbath reveals a similar perspective (*e.g.* Mt. 12:9–14 and parallels; Lk. 13:10–17; 14:1–6; Jn. 5:1–47). What Jesus takes up in all these incidents is 'not a particular orientation towards the sabbath-law, but the demand that the sabbath be oriented towards, interpreted by, and obeyed in accordance with, his own person and work'.[22] This interpretation is confirmed by the charge laid at his trial. Jesus was counted worthy of death, less because he was a sabbath-breaker in the eyes of his contemporaries but more because of his claims about himself. The law was not abrogated or rejected by Jesus. It was transcended and fulfilled in his teaching and practice, ultimately in his death.

The gospels and Jesus' death

The redemptive significance of Jesus' ministry

Each of the gospels presents a broad framework of teaching about the saving significance of Jesus' life and ministry. Thus, for example, the opening chapter of Matthew interprets Jesus' name to mean that 'he will save his people from their sins' (Mt. 1:21), Luke soon makes it plain that the promised messianic salvation involves the forgiveness of sins (Lk. 1:77), and John identifies Jesus from the beginning as 'the Lamb of God, who takes away the sin of the world' (Jn. 1:29). In the synoptic gospels, however, it is not until the narrative of the Last Supper that Jesus' death is explicitly identified as the means of effecting that salvation from sins. Matthew alone includes the words 'for the forgiveness of sins' in Jesus' saying about the cup ('This is my blood of the covenant, which is poured out for many for the forgiveness of sins', Mt. 26:28). Luke, however, makes it clear that 'the new covenant' is inaugurated by Jesus' death, thereby implying the definitive forgiveness of sins predicted by the prophet Jeremiah (Je. 31:34; *cf.* Lk. 22:20; 1 Cor. 11:25).

Prior to Jesus' teaching at the Last Supper, his most pointed saying about the redemptive significance of his death occurs in Matthew 20:28 and Mark 10:45. There he claims that 'the Son of Man did not come to be served, but to serve, and to give his life as a ransom for many'. James and John had sought precedence and rank in the kingdom which they believed Jesus would soon establish. Jesus responded by telling them that they did not know what they were asking. There was a cup which he must drink and a baptism with which he must be baptized before he could enter into his glorious reign as the Christ (Mt. 20:22–23; Mk. 10:38–40). The implication of this challenge was that they could not share in the suffering which he alone must endure. When they brashly asserted that they could drink from the same cup and share in Jesus' baptism, he conceded that they would, 'but to sit at my right or left is not for me to grant. These places belong to those for whom they have been prepared' (Mk. 10:40).

In the Old Testament, the cup of wine is a common metaphor

for suffering experienced as a divine judgment for sin (*e.g.* Ps. 75:8; Is. 51:17–23; Je. 25:15–28). Jesus' application of that image to himself here and in his prayer to the Father in Gethsemane (Mt. 26:39, 42; Mk. 14:36) suggests that he viewed his death in such a way. This is indeed a paradox, since the gospels present him as one who was consistently faithful and obedient to the Father, not as one deserving his wrath. The image of Jesus' death as a baptism (*cf.* Lk. 12:50) indicates that it was to be an overwhelming disaster for him and should be taken as a parallel to the image of the cup.[23] When he applies the same imagery to James and John, he is prophesying that they too will endure great tribulation and suffering for the sake of the kingdom. The idea that there is something unique and unrepeatable about his suffering, however, becomes clear as the narrative draws to a close.

Jesus contrasts the conduct of pagan rulers with the submission to service and sacrifice which is appropriate to his disciples, presenting himself as a model to be followed. He concludes, 'whoever wants to become great among you must be your servant, and whoever wants to be first must be your slave – just as the Son of Man did not come to be served, but to serve, and to give his life as a ransom for many' (Mt. 20:27–28). The reference to his life being given 'as a ransom for many' (*lytron anti pollōn*) suggests that he viewed his death as a substitutionary atonement for the benefit of others. Such terminology implies that the 'many' are held in a captivity from which only the sacrifice of Christ can release them. The wider context of Jesus' teaching indicates that this captivity is caused by sin.

The expression 'to give his life' signifies the voluntary nature of his death and recalls Isaiah 53:10–12, which speaks of the Servant of the LORD offering his life as a compensation or payment for the sins of his people. Another link with that prophecy is provided by the word 'many', a term used to describe the beneficiaries of the Servant's sacrifice (LXX, *pollois, pollōn*).

The word *lytron* in Matthew 20:28 and Mark 10:45, meaning 'payment for loosing' or 'ransom price', does not occur in the Greek translation of Isaiah 53:10, but is a possible rendering of the Hebrew word *'āšām* in that text.[24] Jesus could also have had in mind Isaiah 43:1–4, where different terminology is used to affirm that a ransom will be provided by God to redeem Israel. If both texts are drawn together by Jesus' saying, we may conclude that he viewed himself as the ultimate 'guilt offering' for the sins of his people and the ransom to redeem them from judgment and death.[25] Jesus' whole life was a ministry to others, designed to serve (*diakonēsai*) their needs. But ultimately his service to them meant offering himself in death, in perfect obedience to the will of his Father, as a payment for their sins. Although the language of worship is not specifically used in this context, the notion of Jesus' death as an atoning sacrifice is close at hand. The link between service to God and service to his people in the Old Testament was noted in chapter two.

Luke uses the terminology of salvation more frequently and with a wider application than any other gospel writer. A number of key passages reveal that the salvation offered by Jesus is equivalent to the eternal life of the coming reign of God. But its blessings can be enjoyed in anticipation by those who receive forgiveness from Jesus, bringing true peace with God (*e.g.* Lk. 7:36–50; 19:1–10, *cf.* Acts 2:38–40; 5:31–32; 13:38–39). The call to proclaim to the nations repentance and forgiveness of sins in Jesus' name is closely related to his suffering and resurrection (Lk. 24:44–48). The necessity for his suffering and death as a prelude to his glorification is highlighted in a number of passages and is viewed as the fulfilment of Scripture (*e.g.* 9:22; 17:24–25; 18:31–33). The redemptive significance of his death, however, is really made plain only in the context of the Last Supper (22:14–22, 37). In Acts the salvation offered by Christ and his messengers is again linked to his death and resurrection, although atonement theology is not explicitly given in the apostolic preaching (*e.g.* 3:18–21; 4:10–12; 5:30–32; 10:42–43; 26:22–23).[26]

There is no parallel to Matthew 20:28 and Mark 10:45 in the third gospel. Nevertheless, on the eve of Jesus' death, Luke has him making an explicit identification of himself with the Suffering Servant, providing the only formal quotation from Isaiah 53 by Jesus in any of the gospels:

It is written: 'And he was numbered with the transgressors'; and I tell you that this must be

fulfilled in me. Yes, what is written about me is
reaching its fulfilment (Lk. 22:37; *cf.* Is. 53:12).

The wording of this verse makes the strongest possible assertion that the prophecy in question must be fulfilled in him.
Indeed, there is no reason to doubt that the whole of Isaiah 53,
with its presentation of the vicarious suffering of the Servant is in
view, not simply the particular verse quoted. The phrase 'he was
numbered amongst the transgressors' shows that Jesus was 'preoccupied with the fact that he, who least deserved it, was to be
punished as a wrongdoer'.[27]

The Last Supper

The so-called eucharistic words of Jesus occupy 'the central
place in Jesus' self-disclosure, and therefore they offer a crucial
key to understanding his person and work'.[28] There are differences of emphasis in the various gospel accounts, but each one
points to the fact that it was in the context of a traditional
Passover meal that Jesus enjoyed his last supper with his disciples.[29] The Passover was an annual celebration of the way in
which God had fulfilled his covenant promises in the time of
Moses, rescuing Israel from bondage in Egypt in order to establish them as his own distinctive people in the promised land
(*cf.* Ex. 12:1–30). According to Jewish tradition, the blood
of the lambs sacrificed at the time of the exodus had redemptive
power and made God's covenant with Abraham operative.[30]
When families or groups of friends gathered in Jerusalem to
eat the Passover meal, they were reminded in a very personal
way of the whole basis of their relationship with God and their
existence as a people. Additionally, the Passover had become
an occasion for Israelites to express their confidence in a
future redemption by God, associated with the coming of the
Messiah.[31]

Jesus' longing to celebrate this last Passover with his disciples
is especially emphasized in Luke's account:

He said to them, 'I have eagerly desired to eat this
Passover with you before I suffer. For I tell you, I
will not eat it again until it finds fulfilment in the

kingdom of God' (Lk. 22:15–16; *cf.* 22:18).

Yet his hope of celebrating it anew, when it would be fulfilled 'in the kingdom of God', is expressed in each of the gospels (*cf.* Mt. 26:29; Mk. 14:25). The notion of fulfilment indicates that for Jesus the Passover had a typological significance. In other words, he was endorsing the Jewish tradition that this rite pointed forward to an eschatological deliverance of God's people and the subsequent possibility of enjoying the messianic banquet together in the End-time (*e.g.* Is. 25:6–7; Lk. 14:15; 22:30). The context makes it clear that his approaching death would be the event to accomplish that deliverance. The Lord's Supper, which has its origin in Jesus' teaching at the Last Supper (*cf.* Lk. 22:29–30; 1 Cor. 11:26), is not itself to be regarded as the fulfilment of the Passover. In some respects, the Lord's Supper functions as a Christian substitute for the Passover, focusing on Jesus' death, rather than the exodus from Egypt, as the means by which God's people are saved and brought to share in the blessings of the inheritance promised to them.

Theologically, the Passover came to an end with its final celebration by Jesus. We cannot say with certainty that he identified himself explicitly with the Passover lamb on this occasion, but that link was soon made by early Christian writers (1 Cor. 5:7–8; *cf.* 1 Pet. 1:18–19).[32] Jesus himself took the unusual step of accompanying the distribution of the bread and at least one of the Passover cups with his own words of interpretation. In this way, the food was presented to the disciples as a symbol of his approaching death and of the salvation he would accomplish. Their eating and drinking appears to be an anticipation and symbolic reception of the benefits to be obtained by his death: 'Jesus uses the grace before and after eating to give his disciples one after another the additional personal assurance that they share in the kingdom because they belong to the many for whom he is about to die.'[33]

Some commentators interpret the bread-word and the cup-word differently, since they were separated by the main course of the meal and each saying was meant to be complete in itself. Thus, 'this is my body' is taken to refer to Jesus' person – the bread broken and distributed is to be a pledge of his continuing presence with them[34] – and 'this is my blood' is taken to refer to his sacrificial death. However, even though the two sayings were originally separate, 'we must surely grant that Jesus intended the two sayings to be in some way complementary to each other. If, then, the second saying speaks of Jesus' sacrificial death, we should expect something similar to be present in the former saying.'[35] With mention of the fact that his blood is to be 'poured out' as a sacrificial offering 'for many' (Mt. 26:28 = Mk. 14:24; Lk. 22:20 has 'for you'), there are allusions again to the role of the suffering Servant of Isaiah 53, who 'poured out his life unto death, and...bore the sin of many' (Is. 53:12; *cf.* Mt. 20:28 = Mk. 10:45; Lk. 22:37).

Most significant for our present study is the fact that the cup-word speaks of the inauguration of a new covenant by Jesus' blood. In the version of the saying in Matthew 26:28 and Mark 14:24, the strange expression 'my blood of the covenant' occurs. This recalls Exodus 24:8, where the covenant established by God at Mount Sinai is said to have been sealed by means of animal sacrifice. Only the version of the saying in Luke 22:20 and 1 Corinthians 11:25 mentions explicitly that Jesus had in view the new covenant promised in Jeremiah 31:31–34. Jeremiah said nothing about sacrifice or blood, but pointed to a definitive and permanent solution to the problem of Israel's sin as a basis for the renewal of God's relationship with his people. Yet, it is obvious even from the words 'my blood of the covenant' that Jesus envisaged some renewal of the covenant with Israel, effected by his death. Since Matthew 26:28 indicates that Jesus' death was specifically 'for the forgiveness of sins', the link with Jeremiah 31:34 is clear. Thus, the various forms of the cup-word in each of the gospel narratives express materially the same meaning.

> This is my blood of the covenant, which is poured out for many for the forgiveness of sins (Mt. 26:28; *cf.* Mk. 14:24).

> This cup is the new covenant in my blood, which is poured out for you (Lk. 22:20; *cf.* 1 Cor. 11:25).

Jesus' death not only served to replace the temple and its sacrificial system in the plan and purpose of God (*cf.* Jn. 2:19–22) but also to re-establish the underlying covenant with Israel on a new basis. A new or renewed covenant was effected by his shed blood, fulfilling the typology of Exodus 24:8 and the prediction of Jeremiah 31:31–34. Jesus' allusion to Isaiah 53:12 implies also that his blood shed as the Servant of the LORD was the means of atonement 'for many'. Indeed, the idea of a covenant established through the death of a human being, rather than through the shedding of animal blood, probably stems from the Servant passages in Isaiah. The Servant is made by God 'a covenant for the people and a light for the Gentiles' (Is. 42:6; 49:8). These passages indicate that the restoration of a right relationship between Israel and the LORD will also mean the ultimate fulfilment of that ancient promise to Abraham to bring blessing to all peoples on earth (*cf.* Gn. 12:2–3). Through the death of Jesus, Jews and Gentiles will experience atonement and consecration to God as his people.

The idea that the Twelve would sit with Jesus in the table-fellowship of his kingdom, forming the nucleus of this new people of God, is expressed in Luke's narrative of the Last Supper:

> You are those who have stood by me in my trials.
> And I confer on you a kingdom, just as my Father
> conferred one on me, so that you may eat and drink
> at my table in my kingdom and sit on thrones,
> judging the twelve tribes of Israel (Lk. 22:28–30).

Jesus' promise to give his followers the kingdom by way of a new covenant means 'making them the people of the Kingdom of God or the people of God who are to share his rule over the world (*cf.* also Lk. 12:32; Rev. 3:20–21)'.[36] Thus, the culmination of his preaching of the kingdom of God is his Last Supper promise about his death being the atoning and covenant-establishing sacrifice through which the kingdom is to become a reality. The implication is that only those who take advantage of his sacrificial death share in the kingdom and its benefits.

Eating and drinking at Jesus' table

Did Jesus intend to institute a new 'cult' at the Last Supper? The word 'cult' is used here, as in chapter one, with reference to 'the expression of religious experience in concrete external actions performed within the congregation or community, preferably by officially appointed exponents and in set forms'.[37] Converts to Christianity from paganism were accustomed to participating in a great variety of cultic meals and sacrificial rituals in honour of the gods of the Greco-Roman world. The Jews also had their system of rituals and cultic meals associated with the great annual festivals at Jerusalem. The Dead Sea Scrolls community regularly shared meals together at which grace was said by a priest and the participants looked forward to the time when the Messiah would be present with them at such meals.[38] Was Jesus, then, instituting for Christian believers anything comparable to these practices?

The command to 'do this in remembrance of me' is found only in Luke 22:19 (after the bread-saying) and in 1 Corinthians 11:24–25 (after both sayings). The present tense of the Greek imperative (*poieite*) implies the need to repeat Jesus' actions, together with his words of interpretation, to eat and drink in remembrance of him. The cup-saying in 1 Corinthians 11:25 even more emphatically indicates a pattern to be followed ('Do this, whenever you drink it, in remembrance of me'). Paul goes on to say, 'as often as you eat this bread and drink the cup (alluding to the bread and the cup of the Last Supper), you proclaim the Lord's death until he comes' (11:26, RSV). Some explanation is necessary for the fact that Matthew, Mark, and some manuscripts of Luke, have no command to repeat the rite.[39] But Paul's account makes it clear that such teaching was part of the earliest tradition communicated to his churches (11:23).

Jesus was not instituting a new version of the Old Testament ritual calendar. If the Passover analogy is to be followed at all, the remembrance meal he inaugurated was to be a celebration in a household context, loosed entirely from any preliminary ritual at the temple and taking its meaning from his once-for-all sacrifice on the cross. It might be argued again from the Passover analogy that the head of a Christian household or community would be expected to officiate at such meals, but not in a priestly role. Sometimes the words 'in remembrance of me' (*eis tēn emēn anamnēsin*) are taken to mean 'as a memorial before God', suggesting that Jesus inaugurated a sacrificial rite.[40] But the Passover meal was a memorial *for Israel's benefit* (*cf.* Ex. 12:14), not an offering to the Lord. Jesus indicates that believers under the new covenant should likewise celebrate in the form of a meal the great benefits won for them by their Saviour (*cf.* 1 Cor. 11:26).

Taking bread, giving thanks to God, breaking and distributing it, was the normal method of saying grace and beginning a meal in Jewish culture. Similarly, a host would indicate the formal end of a meal together by taking a cup of wine, giving thanks to God and sharing it with all present. These were not new customs introduced by Jesus and they were certainly not cultic acts to be performed by 'officially appointed exponents'. Nevertheless, by means of a spoken grace, such meals became 'an association under the eyes of God'.[41] Church history shows that there soon developed the notion of a Christian cult, focusing on the celebration of the Lord's Supper, incorporating Old Testament concepts of priesthood and sacrifice in a Christian guise. The reasons for this are complex and the investigation of such matters falls outside the scope of this work. What evolved was far removed from the simple message of the Last Supper, leading Christians to be profoundly divided over an activity which was meant to be an expression of their unity!

In a sense, Jesus' reinterpretation of familiar parts of the ancient paschal liturgy could give a redemptive and eschatological significance to any future experience of table-fellowship amongst his disciples. The Last Supper was the climax of a series of meals shared with his disciples and with the religious and moral outcasts of his day. The scribes and Pharisees protested vehemently about this practice (*e.g.* Mt. 9:10–13; Lk. 15:1–2), but Jesus continued to use table-fellowship as a means of expressing the forgiveness, acceptance and companionship that belong to the messianic salvation (*e.g.* Lk. 19:5–10). Such meals were an anticipation of the kingdom of God. At the Last Supper, Jesus was clarifying the theological significance of eating and drinking together as the community of the Messiah. He did this by means of the words of interpretation, challenging disciples to remember the basis of their relationship in his redemptive death and the certainty of their hope of feasting together in his kingdom.

The recital of the words of institution might be necessary to highlight the significance of a meal together, but eating and drinking together in Christ's name would be the heart of the event. With such 'concrete external actions' the reality of life under the new covenant would be expressed, and the benefits of Christ's sacrifice would be enjoyed by faith, in the fellowship of the redeemed. Only in this very modified sense could it be said that Jesus instituted a 'cultic' meal for his disciples.[42] However, there is nothing in the Last Supper narratives to suggest that such table-fellowship would be tied to sacred times and sacred places or be bound by the ministrations of any priesthood.

Jesus as the bread of life

The Gospel of John does not record Jesus' words about the bread and wine at the Last Supper. The foot-washing incident is provided where an account of the institution of the Lord's Supper might have been expected (Jn. 13:1–17). This narrative points to Jesus' humility and self-sacrificing service, proceeding from a love for 'his own'. It is a symbolic action prefiguring the crucifixion and pointing to the meaning of his death for the disciples: 'the act of washing is what the crucifixion is, at once a divine deed by which men are released from sin, and an example which men must imitate'.[43] The theme of discipleship then dominates Jesus' teaching in the context of the meal that follows (Jn. 13 – 17).

Some commentators have argued that Jesus' teaching about eating his flesh and drinking his blood in John 6:51c–58 is the evangelist's way of highlighting the eucharistic implications of the feeding of the five thousand.[44] Others propose that these verses are a later editor's way of introducing teaching about the Lord's Supper where John had none. Although such views are widely held, there are good reasons for challenging them. First, the verbal and thematic links between these verses and the rest of the chapter are much more detailed and significant than the critics have allowed.[45] Secondly, Jesus himself is the focus of the whole discourse and the accent is on the need to believe in him (6:29, 35, 36, 40, 47, 64, 69). The bread in the feeding of the five thousand (vv. 1–15) and the manna in the discussion that follows (vv. 25–35) are contrasted with and are symbols of Jesus, not of the Lord's Supper. He is 'the bread of God... who comes down from heaven and gives life to the world' (v. 33). When verses 51–58 are compared with verse 35, it is clear that 'eating' and 'drinking' Christ are vivid metaphors for coming to him and believing in him as the bread of life:

> I am the bread of life. He who comes to me (= eats
> my flesh) will never go hungry, and he who believes
> in me (= drinks my blood) will never be thirsty (Jn.
> 6:35, with elements of v. 53).

So why does the imagery change from eating the bread of life (vv. 48–51b) to eating the flesh of Christ and drinking his blood (vv. 51c–58)? According to John, such language was offensive to Jesus' listeners and even caused some to turn back from following him (vv. 52, 60–66). It would have been similarly offensive to Jewish and Gentile readers of John's gospel. Fundamentally, this imagery stresses that Christian faith is belief in the Son of Man who became flesh and blood and was a real human being. At the same time, the sacrificial connotations of the phrase 'flesh and blood'[46] make it clear that the one who comes down from heaven must give himself in death to bring eternal life to the world. Those who want to be raised up at the last day and live with him for ever must come to the crucified Messiah and believe in the necessity of his atoning death for their salvation (*cf.* 1:29; 3:14–16; 12:31–33). An important clue for understanding the figurative nature of the language is given at the end of the discourse:

> Aware that his disciples were grumbling about this,
> Jesus said to them, 'Does this offend you? What if
> you see the Son of Man ascend to where he was
> before! The Spirit gives life; the flesh counts for
> nothing. The words I have spoken to you are spirit
> and they are life' (Jn. 6:61–63).

Jesus makes it clear that 'eating' and 'drinking' of his flesh and blood is only possible because the crucified Son of Man ascends to the Father and pours out his Spirit. By this means, people are enabled to believe the word about his incarnation and sacrificial death and to receive the eternal life he makes possible. Eating his flesh and drinking his blood means taking advantage of the benefits of his death by faith. It would be totally out of character with Jesus' teaching in the rest of this chapter and elsewhere in the gospels to suggest that participation in the Lord's Supper was essential for eternal salvation. Yet that must be the implication of a strictly sacramental reading of verse 53 ('Unless you can eat the flesh of the Son of Man and drink his blood, you have no life in you'). Jesus is not talking about a physical eating of the Son of Man in his earthly state, or saying that eternal life is bound up with eating the Lord's Supper. The words of Jesus must be 'consumed' so that the glorified Christ might live in us and we in him. When Simon Peter confesses, 'You have the words of eternal life' (v. 68), the implication is that Jesus' words 'deal with the subject of eternal life, and convey eternal life to those who believe'.[47]

If in any way John 6 seeks to relate Jesus' claim to be the bread of life to early Christian thinking about the Lord's Supper, the passage must surely be a warning against literalistic interpretations of the Supper:

> Eating and drinking the elements of the Lord's
> Supper vividly represents the act of coming to and
> believing in Jesus and the resulting eternal life
> through union with him, but in the actual reception
> of that life the eucharistic elements are of no avail,
> they play no part; in the event it is the Spirit who
> gives life, and he does so primarily through the words
> of Jesus.[48]

Conclusion

At one level, Jesus is presented in the gospels as a pious Jew, attending the festivals in Jerusalem, teaching in the temple courts, or participating in the activity of the Galilean synagogues. By his words and actions he often endorsed the Old Testament law, sometimes condemning the interpretations and practices of his contemporaries, but not criticizing the law itself. Yet so radical was his challenge concerning the traditions of the scribes and Pharisees that he raised questions about the continuing role of the law in the messianic era. The law was not abrogated or rejected by Jesus, but fulfilled and transcended in him.

Jesus' whole life was an example of sacrificial service to God and his people. Yet obedience to the Father ultimately led him to offer himself in death, as the final and perfect expression of uncompromising worship. Jesus interpreted his death as a fulfilment of what was written in the Scriptures about the Christ and especially identified himself with the portrait of the Servant of the LORD in Isaiah. He offered himself as 'a ransom for many' and as a perfect sacrifice for sins, thus inaugurating the new covenant. The implication is that the Old Testament sacrificial system has been fulfilled and replaced by means of his atoning death.

Application of the terminology of sacrifice to the death of the righteous in Jewish writings did not make the overthrow of the temple cult a logical necessity for Judaism. Jesus' unique connection between his sacrificial death and the idea of a new covenant, however, apparently had such an effect on early Christianity. The New Testament shows the emergence of a 'religion' without any earthly cult in the traditional Jewish or Greco-Roman sense. The bringing together of ideas such as atonement through the blood of Christ, covenant, the people of God, and the kingdom of God elsewhere in the New Testament (*e.g.* Heb. 9:14–15; 12:22–24; Rev. 1:5–7; 5:9–10), suggests the profound influence of Jesus' sayings at the Last Supper on early Christian thought.[49]

Jesus pointed to the bread and the cup at the Passover meal as symbols of his approaching death and of the salvation he would accomplish. The invitation to the disciples to eat and drink implies that only those who take advantage of his sacrifice for sins share in the kingdom. But it would be a gross misunderstanding of Jesus' teaching to suggest that participation in what was later called 'the Lord's Supper' is somehow essential for eternal salvation. Believing what he proclaims in a variety of contexts about the significance of his death and responding to his invitation to enjoy its benefits is at the heart of true discipleship.

From the narratives of the Last Supper preserved by Luke and Paul, it seems clear that Jesus intended his disciples to recall and celebrate the benefits of his saving work in the context of a community meal. No direction is given about the frequency of such meals and Christians throughout the centuries have varied in their response to this liberty. Even for churches where the Lord's Supper is held irregularly, however, there are guidelines in the Last Supper narratives about what should lie at the heart of every Christian gathering. With one eye on the past and what Jesus has done for us, we need to express our gratitude to God for his grace towards us and reach out together to experience afresh the forgiveness and restoration he has promised us. With another eye on the future and what it will mean for us to share with Christ in his coming kingdom, we need to encourage one another in this hope and to learn what it means to live as the redeemed community in the present. These gospel perspectives can be obscured in liturgical and non-liturgical traditions alike. Only effective biblical teaching can transform what we do, and give the appropriate point and purpose to our meetings.

Notes

[1] J. Jeremias, *The Eucharistic Words of Jesus* (ET, London: SCM; Philadelphia: Trinity, 1966), p. 236.

[2] D. Hill, *The Gospel of Matthew*, NCB (London: Oliphants, 1972; Grand Rapids: Eerdmans, 1981), p. 102.

[3] *proskynēseis kai autō monō latreuseis* (Mt. 4:10; Lk. 4:8) replaces *phobēthēsē kai auto latreuseis* ('you shall fear him and serve him', Dt. 6:13 LXX) because the challenge to Jesus has come from Satan specifically with the words *ean pesōn proskynēsēs moi*.

[4] B. Gerhardsson, 'Sacrificial Service and Atonement in the Gospel of Mat-

thew', in R. J. Banks (ed.), *Reconciliation and Hope*, FS L. L. Morris (Exeter: Paternoster; Grand Rapids: Eerdmans, 1974), pp. 25–35, seeks to relate these two ideas together in an interpretation of Matthew.

⁵ R. E. Brown (*Birth of the Messiah*, pp. 267–268, 453) points out that a certain 'temple piety' dominates Luke's opening chapters, suggesting to his readers that 'if opposition arose between the Temple / priesthood and the following of Jesus, it was not because there was an inherent contradiction between Christianity and the cult of Israel'. It is those who were 'observing all the commandments and ordinances of the Lord' (1:6) who were first receptive to Jesus and not opposed to him.

⁶ The Greek expression *en tois tou patros mou* in Lk. 2:49 could also mean '(involved) in my Father's affairs' or even 'among those people belonging to my Father', namely, among the teachers of God's law. Most modern commentators, however, take this phrase to be a reference to Jesus' presence in the temple as God's 'house' (*cf.* Lk. 19:46; Jn. 2:16). *Cf.* J. A. Fitzmyer, *The Gospel According to Luke I-IX*, AB 28 (Garden City, New York: Doubleday, 1979), pp. 443–444; J. Nolland, *Luke 1– 9:20*, WBC 35A (Waco: Word, 1989), pp. 131–132 and R. E. Brown, *Birth of the Messiah*, pp. 475–477.

⁷ *Cf.* P. T. O'Brien, 'Prayer in Luke-Acts', *TynB* 24, 1973, pp. 113–116 and M. M. B. Turner, 'Prayer in the Gospels and Acts', in D. A. Carson (ed.), *Teach us to Pray: Prayer in the Bible and the World* (Exeter: Paternoster; Grand Rapids: Baker, 1990), pp. 59–64.

⁸ R. Banks, *Jesus and the Law in the Synoptic Tradition*, SNTSMS 28 (Cambridge, London, New York and Melbourne: Cambridge University Press, 1975), p. 91, argues that Jesus attended the synagogue because of the opportunities for ministry it provided rather than out of faithfulness to Jewish tradition. Lk. 4:16, however, makes a general statement about his custom of attending the synagogue on the Sabbath day and suggests that the chance to teach in his own home town arose from that practice.

⁹ L. Coenen, *NIDNTT* 1. 291–298, makes an interesting comparison between *synagōgē* and *ekklēsia*, in terms of background and usage.

¹⁰ *Cf.* H. H. Rowley, *Worship in Ancient Israel*, pp. 213–229. G. F. Moore (*Judaism* I, pp. 286–288) argues that the development of the synagogue owes much to the Pharisees in the second century BC.

¹¹ The reading from the Prophets may not have been according to any fixed rule by New Testament times and may have been left to the choice of the leader of the particular synagogue. Anyone could then be invited to expound the Scripture reading, though this was not an invariable part of the service. It is not entirely certain when the recital of select psalms was incorporated into the synagogue meeting, though it would seem natural for some patterning of the temple liturgy to have taken place in this regard while the temple was still standing.

¹² G. F. Moore, *Judaism* I, pp. 289–307.

¹³ H. W. Turner, *From Temple to Meeting House*, p. 101 (my emphasis). H. C. Kee, 'The Transformation of the Synagogue after 70 C. E.', *NTS* 36, 1990, pp. 1–24, argues that there is no evidence to speak of synagogues in Palestine as architecturally distinguishable edifices prior to the year 200.

¹⁴ R. A. Stewart, 'The Synagogue', *EQ* 43, 1971, pp. 40–41, 44–45, shows how

sanctity came to be attributed to the synagogue in rabbinic literature, beginning with the ark and the rolls of Scripture. *Cf.* G. F. Moore, *Judaism* I, p. 436.
[15] For a detailed discussion of synagogue services and their possible influence on Christian liturgical development, *cf.* R. T. Beckwith, 'The Jewish Background of Christian Worship', in C. Jones, G. Wainwright, and E. Yarnold (eds.), *The Study of Liturgy* (London: SPCK, 1978), pp. 39–51, and R. T. Beckwith, *Daily and Weekly Worship: From Jewish to Christian*, Alcuin/GROW Liturgical Study 1 (Bramcote: Grove, [2]1989).
[16] R. Banks, *Jesus and the Law*, p. 107 (my emphasis). Note particularly his conclusions (pp. 237–263). D. J. Moo, 'Jesus and the Authority of the Mosaic Law', *JSNT* 20, 1984, pp. 5–6, rightly observes that, although Jesus appears to be faithful to the written law, it is impossible to infer from this that he wished his followers to observe it equally faithfully: 'Jesus' adherence to the written law could simply reflect an aspect of the old age which was destined to pass away in the new age.'
[17] Ex. 30:19; 40:13. *Cf.* W. L. Lane, *Mark*, pp. 245–246.
[18] R. J. Banks, *Jesus and the Law*, p. 141. Contravention of the Mosaic law at this point is unlikely since Jesus has just argued from the law about the invalidity of Pharisaical traditions.
[19] R. J. Banks, *Jesus and the Law*, pp. 144–145, argues that, as in Rom. 14, Mark's argument may not necessarily have involved a total repudiation of the food-laws so far as Jewish-Christians were concerned. So long as it was recognized that all foods are 'clean' and that food laws are no longer a matter of obligation before God, individuals were free to observe them if they wished. *Cf.* D. J. Moo, 'Jesus and the Mosaic Law', pp. 14–15, 28–29.
[20] *Cf.* R. Martin-Achard, 'Quelques remarques sur la nouvelle alliance chez Jérémie', in C. Brekelmans (ed.), *Questions disputées d' Ancien Testament* (Louvain: Duculot, 1974), pp. 154–157. This article goes on to discuss the uniqueness of Jeremiah's oracle when compared with other prophecies of Israel's future (pp. 158–164).
[21] Many commentators understand Mk. 2:28 as a conclusion by the evangelist, rather than by Jesus himself. This is not required by Mark's wording, however, and is certainly not the best way to read the parallels in Mt. 12:8 and Lk. 6:5. The underlying, and more difficult question is whether Jesus alluded to himself as 'the Son of Man' in describing his earthly activity. Note the excursus: 'The Son of Man as a christological title', in D. A. Carson, 'Matthew', pp. 209–213.
[22] R. J. Banks, *Jesus and the Law*, p. 131. *Cf.* D. A. Carson (ed.), *From Sabbath to Lord's Day*, pp. 58–157. D. J. Moo ('Jesus and the Mosaic Law', p. 30) rightly concludes that 'the change in redemptive "eras" brings with it a change in the locus of authority for the people of God, but it does not bring a liberation from authority as such'.
[23] *Cf.* W. L. Lane, *Mark*, pp. 380–381, and A. Feuillet, 'La coupe et le baptême de la passion (Mc, x, 35–40; *cf.* Mt, xx, 20–23; Lc, xii, 50)', *RB* 74, 1967, pp. 377–382.
[24] *'āšām* can mean 'guilt offering', with or without sacrifice (*cf.* 1 Sa. 6:3–4, 8, 17), or simply 'payment' (*cf.* 2 Ki. 12:16 [MT 17]). *lytron* never translates *'āšām* in the LXX but is not far from equivalent to the latter meaning. *Cf.* R. T. France, *Jesus and the Old Testament* (London: Tyndale, 1971), pp. 119–120.

[25] The link between Is. 43:3–4 and 53:10–12 is helpfully argued by S. Kim, *'The "Son of Man" ' as the Son of God*, WUNT 30 (Tübingen: Mohr, 1983), pp. 52–58.

[26] The concept of salvation in Luke-Acts is clearly outlined by I. H. Marshall, *Luke: Historian and Theologian* (Exeter: Paternoster; Grand Rapids: Zondervan, 1970).

[27] R. T. France, *Jesus and the Old Testament*, p. 115. France rightly opposes those who question whether Jesus used this text to point to his death as vicarious and redemptive.

[28] S. Kim, *'The "Son of Man" ' as the Son of God*, p. 38. I am not convinced by Kim's argument, pp. 43–50, that the saying recorded in Mk. 10:45 was originally spoken in the context of the Last Supper. It is reasonable to conclude, however, that Mk. 10:45 is an anticipation and alternative expression of the eucharistic words of Jesus.

[29] I. H. Marshall, *Last Supper and Lord's Supper* (Exeter: Paternoster, 1980), pp. 57–75, reviews the arguments for and against the conclusion that the meal was a Passover celebration, particularly noting the problem of the chronology of John's Gospel. He concludes that 'Jesus held a Passover meal earlier than the official Jewish date, and that he was able to do so as the result of calendar differences among the Jews' (p. 75). For another assessment of the differences between John and the Synoptics at this point cf. W. L. Lane, *Mark*, p. 498 (especially note 33) and R. T. Beckwith, 'Cautionary Notes on the Use of Calendars and Astronomy to Determine the Chronology of the Passion', J. Vardaman and E. M. Yamauchi (eds.), *Chronos, Kairos, Christos*, FS J. Finegan (Winona Lake: Eisenbrauns, 1989), pp. 198–205.

[30] Cf. J. Jeremias, *Eucharistic Words*, pp. 225–226.

[31] *Ibid*, pp. 252, 256–262.

[32] On the basis of Jesus' death, the apostle Paul exhorted the Corinthians 'to keep an ongoing feast of the celebration of God's forgiveness *by holy living*', G. D. Fee, *The First Epistle to the Corinthians*, NICNT (Grand Rapids: Eerdmans, 1987), pp. 218–219, my emphasis.

[33] J. Jeremias, 'This is My Body…', *ExpT* 83, 1972, p. 203.

[34] The argument that the Aramaic behind *to sōma mou* is *gûpî*, meaning 'my person' or 'myself', is proposed by J. Behm, *TDNT* 3. 736, and a variety of commentators such as C. E. B. Cranfield, *The Gospel According to Saint Mark*, CGNTC (Cambridge, London and New York: Cambridge University Press, 1959), p. 426, and W. L. Lane, *Mark*, p. 506. J. Jeremias, *Eucharistic Words*, pp. 198–201, 221–222, strongly contests this.

[35] I. H. Marshall, *Last Supper and Lord's Supper*, p. 87. Marshall, pp. 86–88, assesses the arguments of Jeremias in the light of significant challenges to his position.

[36] S. Kim, *'The "Son of Man" ' as the Son of God*, pp. 64–65. His whole chapter is designed to establish the authenticity of Jesus' teaching about his death as an atoning and covenant-establishing sacrifice, in the face of various scholarly arguments to the contrary.

[37] W. Eichrodt, *Theology of the Old Testament* I, p. 98. R. Bultmann, *Theology of the New Testament* Vol 1 (ET, New York: Scribner; London: SCM, 1952), p. 121, gives a similar, but more extensive definition of the word 'cult' and concludes

on that basis that *'the meetings and services of the Christian congregation* obviously *cannot be termed originally cultic'* (his emphasis).

[38] For a brief survey of religious meals in the ancient world and their significance see I. H. Marshall, *Last Supper and Lord's Supper*, pp. 18–29.

[39] The literature attempting to trace Jesus' exact words and to determine which of the synoptic forms is most primitive is immense (*cf.* J. Jeremias, *Eucharistic Words*, pp. 96–203 and I. H. Marshall, *Last Supper and Lord's Supper*, pp. 30–56). Lk. 22:19b–20 is not found in some manuscripts of the 'western' textual tradition but is well attested by a wide range of manuscripts. It is likely that the shorter version arose because an ancient editor of the text was puzzled by the mention of two cups in Luke's account and removed the reference to a second cup. *Cf.* B. M. Metzger (ed.), *A Textual Commentary on the Greek New Testament* (London/New York: United Bible Societies, 1971), pp. 173–177. Matthew and Mark may have omitted the command to repeat the rite because the Lord's Supper had already become an established custom in the churches addressed. The original position of the command is 'probably as in Lk., and it was repeated in Paul's formula for the sake of the parallelism', I. H. Marshall, *The Gospel of Luke*, NIGTC (Exeter: Paternoster; Grand Rapids: Eerdmans, 1978), p. 804.

[40] D. Jones, *'Anamnēsis* in the LXX and the interpretation of 1 Cor. 11:25', *JTS* 6, 1955, pp. 183–191, provides a helpful summary and critique of some of the interpretations that have been offered in connection with this term. *Cf.* G. D. Fee, *First Corinthians*, pp. 552–554.

[41] J. Jeremias, 'This is my body...', pp. 196–197; *Eucharistic Words*, pp. 232–236. *Cf.* J. Behm, *TDNT* 3. 728–730.

[42] Writers like E. Brunner, *The Misunderstanding of the Church* (ET, London: Lutterworth, 1952), p. 60, speak of the 'cultic assembly for the common hearing of the word for the prayer of fellowship, and for the celebration of the sacrament'. Others are more rigorous and argue that 'it is doubtful whether the primitive community knows of a cult at all', H. Conzelmann, *An Outline of the Theology of the New Testament* (ET, London: SCM, 1969), p. 46; 'liturgy, places, rites have no role at all' (*Ibid*, p. 258).

[43] C. K. Barrett, *John*, p. 436.

[44] So, for example, J. Jeremias, *Eucharistic Words*, pp. 107–108. He rightly indicates, p. 136, that if Jn. 6:51c, 53–58 is a homily on the eucharistic words of Jesus this could have been intelligible 'only to the initiated'!

[45] *Cf.* J. D. G. Dunn, 'John VI—A Eucharistic Discourse?', *NTS* 17, 1970-1, pp. 329–332. I am greatly indebted to Dunn's article in the argument that follows. D. A. Carson (*John*, pp. 276–280, 294–302) offers a helpful survey of different interpretations of this passage and an explanation of the relevant verses that is similar to my own.

[46] *Cf.* J. D. G. Dunn, 'John VI', p. 331, and J. Jeremias, *Eucharistic Words*, pp. 221–231. C. K. Barrett (*John*, pp. 298–299) rightly notes the emphasis on the reality of the incarnation in the use of this terminology but then makes a jump in his argument by saying this 'unmistakably points to the eucharist'.

[47] C. K. Barrett, *John*, p. 306. Like Dunn, Barrett, p. 304, notes that the words 'the flesh counts for nothing' (v. 63) must relate in some way to the statement in v. 53 about the flesh of the Son of Man, and comments: 'there is no revelation

apart from the Spirit and the Word, and no reception of the revelation apart from the initiative of God himself (6:44)'.

[48] J. D. G. Dunn, 'John VI', p. 335.

[49] S. Kim, *The "Son of Man" ' as the Son of God*, pp. 67–71. M. Hengel, *The Atonement: the Origin of the Doctrine in the New Testament* (ET, London: SCM, 1981), pp. 33–75, argues that the ransom saying and the supper sayings of Jesus lie behind Paul's teaching that Christ 'died for our sins' (1 Cor. 15:3) and that he was 'given up for our sins' (Rom. 4:25).

CHAPTER FIVE

Temple and community in the Acts of the Apostles

> If 'there is no longer any "cultus" in the ancient
> sense', it is equally true, conversely, that all life has
> become 'cultus' in a new sense. Life has no other
> purpose than to be rendered up to God in adoration
> and gratitude.[1]

Contemporary Christianity shows a great deal of interest in what
Acts has to say about the life and growth of the earliest churches.
Books on 'worship in the early church' often devote considerable
attention to passages about early Christian gatherings, to draw
lessons for church life today. Such studies have their place and
this chapter will conclude with some reflections on the relevant
material. It is remarkable, however, that the key terms for
worship examined previously are rarely used by Luke, and that
only once is such terminology applied to the activity of a Christian meeting. As with the gospels, there is a need to ask more
fundamental questions about the theology of worship in this
New Testament book.

An obvious starting-point for this investigation is Luke's presentation of the temple and its role in the messianic era. It will be
important to consider what happens to certain themes associated
with the temple in the Old Testament. When the sermons in
Acts proclaim the risen and glorified Jesus as the source of life
and blessing for Israel and the nations, the implication is that he

is to be the centre of true worship. As the focal point of God's plans for Israel in the End-time, Christ fulfils and replaces the temple and the whole method of approach to God associated with it. The message for Gentiles is not in the end very different: a relationship with the living and true God is to be found by turning from idols to serve the living Lord Jesus. By the Spirit-inspired preaching of the gospel, the ascended Lord draws people from every nation, race and culture to himself. As in the Old Testament, a genuine engagement with God depends on the word of the Lord.

Luke's limited use of traditional terms for worship is similar to that of other New Testament writers. In broad terms, Christian life and ministry are viewed as the way to worship or serve the God of Israel under the new covenant. More specifically, such worship is the expression of faith in Jesus as Lord and Christ. Within this framework of thought, what Acts says about early Christian gatherings is examined.

The earliest disciples and the temple

Continuing associations with the temple

In the first volume of Luke's work, the temple appears as *the place of divine revelation*. The evangelist begins and ends his infancy narrative with an important revelation in the temple (Lk. 1:5–22; 2:41–50) and records that the prophecies of Simeon and Anna about Jesus were also given in the temple courts (2:25–38). The law and the temple were preparatory to Christ and pointed to him. With these narratives, Luke makes the point that the godly in Israel acknowledged Jesus and saw their piety leading inevitably to him. Jesus' final visit to Jerusalem and the temple is then the focus of the lengthy central section of this gospel (9:51 – 19:46). Following his much abbreviated account of the cleansing of the temple (19:45–46), Luke indicates that Jesus adopted the temple court as the place for propagating his own teaching about God and his purposes (19:47–48; *cf.* 21:37–38).

The third gospel also emphasizes that the temple was *'a house of prayer' for Israel* (19:46, *cf.* 1:8–10; 2:27–32, 36–38; 18:10–14) and thus concludes with the disciples returning to Jerusalem after the ascension of Christ, where they 'stayed continually at the temple, praising God' (24:53). While it is true that Luke betrays a predominantly positive view of the temple, it is over-stating the case to argue that the evangelist avoids making the temple the object of God's wrath.[2]

The Acts of the Apostles continues to portray the temple as *a place of revelation*. Most obviously, the disciples met regularly in the temple courts to teach and encourage one another (Acts 2:46; 5:12) and to give public testimony to the gospel about Jesus (3:11–26; 4:2; 5:42). This was not simply for the practical reason that the temple was a place where crowds could be easily addressed, but because the disciples, like their master, wanted to take the word of salvation to the centre of Judaism itself. Later, the apostle Paul received an important vision in the temple. This experience, however, actually led him away from the temple (22:17–21), so that he could preach the resurrected Christ as the centre of true worship for the nations (*e.g.* 17:16–33).

The temple also remained for a while *a place of public prayer* for Christians. As well as meeting 'house to house', where they ate together and praised God as the community of the Messiah (2:46–47), the earliest Christians apparently went up to the temple at the set hours of prayer (3:1), continuing their association with the traditional practices of their religion (*cf.* also 21:20–26; 22:17–21).[3] Since 'the ninth hour' (RSV, 3 p.m.) was the time of the afternoon sacrifice, the most natural way to read Acts 3:1 is to suppose that the disciples participated in the prayers associated with the burnt offering and incense at that time (*cf.* Ex. 29:38–43).[4]

This may at first seem strange, considering the indications in Jesus' teaching that he would somehow replace the temple in the plan and purpose of God. Apart from the fact that the implications of his position must have taken some time to be worked out, however, there are other factors to be considered. As a group of pious Jews, aware of the fulfilment of Israel's hopes in the person and work of the Christ, they perceived that their fundamental task was to bear testimony to Jesus before their fellow Israelites (*cf.* 1:8) and so become the means by which other Jews might be

138

spared in the coming judgment and share in the blessings of the messianic era (*cf.* 3:17–26). They were aware of being distinct within their generation, the beneficiaries of the new covenant (*cf.* 2:38–41).[5] It was logical for them to meet together to express their new-found relationship with God through Christ and to strengthen one another in the role given to them by God. However, if they were to function as the faithful remnant, the Servant community called to bring Israel back to God (*cf.* Is. 49:5–6), they could not immediately disengage themselves from the temple and separate themselves from the traditional practices of their religion:

> The remade Israel does not turn aside from the
> old which still has claims upon her. The relation-
> ship is still open-ended. Though there may be
> little positive hope that Israel as a whole will
> repent, the relationship is not closed and
> Christianity has not turned aside from its
> source.[6]

By preaching in the temple, the Jerusalem Christians related Jesus most closely to Jewish hopes about the End-time. The messianic redemption had been accomplished. Christ had poured out the promised Spirit on the disciples in Jerusalem and made them witnesses to him as the heavenly Lord. In him the blessings of 'the last days' were being realized (2:1–39). Since the early preachers, however, focused on Jesus as the only source of eschatological salvation, and warned of divine judgment against those who rejected this gospel, the temple became *the place where they experienced opposition and arrest* (4:3; 5:25–26, *cf.* 21:27–30). Preaching about the centrality of the exalted Christ in God's plans for Israel was a way of indicating that Jesus fulfils and replaces the temple and the whole structure of worship associated with it. Such a message inevitably led to the exclusion of Christians from the temple and in due course also from the synagogues.[7]

The radical teaching of Stephen
Luke does not record the charge of the false witnesses at Jesus'

trial nor mention any claim to destroy the temple and rebuild it when he presents the mockery of those who witnessed the crucifixion (Lk. 23:35).[8] In his account of the trial of Stephen, however, he notes this accusation:

> This fellow never stops speaking against this holy
> place and against the law. For we have heard him
> say that this Jesus of Nazareth will destroy this place
> and change the customs Moses handed down to us
> (Acts 6:13–14, cf. v. 11).

As in the case of Jesus, the witnesses were apparently called false because they misrepresented what Stephen said. He seems to have taught that Jesus was the one in whom the law and the temple found fulfilment, predicting that judgment was coming upon Jerusalem because of its failure to acknowledge this. The story of Stephen is used by Luke to summarize the rejection of the gospel by Jerusalem as a whole and Stephen's speech explains why this happened: 'Jerusalem preferred to remain with the Temple and to regard that as the final mark of God's favour, rather than let it lead them to Jesus to whom it pointed.'[9]

Stephen responds to his accusers with counter-accusations, based on an interpretation of Israel's history (7:1–53) and set within the framework of an apocalyptic vision of Jesus the Son of Man, who is observed 'standing at the right hand of God' (7:55–56). This vision may be a way of asserting the readiness of the Son of Man to act in judgment against apostate Israel. Alternatively, it may be contrasting Jesus' 'place' in heaven with the temple as a nationally delimited 'holy place' in Jerusalem. Christ's heavenly and universal rule suggested the end of the temple as an expression of God's special relationship with Israel, since God's glory and purposes for the nations are clearly bound up with the glorified Christ.[10] Stephen makes no specific reference to the charge that he was 'against the law', though he accuses Israel of being disobedient to the law and hostile to Moses (7:35–39). The climax of this disobedience has been the rejection of Jesus as 'the Righteous One', sent by God (7:52–53). Most of the speech responds to the charge of being 'against the temple', as Stephen asserts that the temple has been the focal point of Jewish disobedience.

Some scholars have argued that Stephen's speech was an attack on the building of the temple itself. They suggest that, for Stephen, the erection of the temple was a declension from God. 'Better in his eyes is the Meeting-Tent in the desert where God and His folk may ever be on the move, than a material building which attempts to "localize" God – an attempt hopeless from the start, as the very builders realized (1 Ki viii.27).'[11] It would be more accurate, however, to say that the speech is an attack, not upon the temple itself, but 'upon an attitude which assigned permanence and finality to it. It is a discussion of the Jews' attitude to it in the light of their rejection of the Christ.'[12] Stephen is asserting that the promise to Abraham finds its ultimate fulfilment, not in the law given to Moses nor in the temple, but in Jesus to whom everything in the Old Testament points.

Stephen's speech, therefore, has a very important function in the narrative of Acts. It shows that the expulsion of the earliest Christians from Jerusalem and the temple was the result of their preaching of Christ, which raised fundamental questions about the permanence of the institutions of Judaism. Furthermore, it provides a theological introduction to Luke's narrative of the Gentile mission, by reaffirming that the Lord of heaven and earth cannot be tied to a single place (7:48–50, citing Is. 66:1–2) and that Jesus as Son of Man has been exalted to the right hand of God. Devotion to the temple must not halt the advance of the divine plan for the people of God, which focuses on Jesus the glorified Messiah, who is Lord of all (cf. 10:36).

The narrowness of attitude which Stephen opposed comes to the fore again most dramatically with the later arrest of Paul. Even though he was engaged in traditional purification rites at the temple, some of his Jewish opponents from the province of Asia seized the opportunity to accuse him publicly (21:26–30). 'This is the man who teaches all men everywhere against our people and our law and this place', they said. 'And besides, he has brought Greeks into the temple area and defiled this holy place' (21:28). Here the issue was not simply the supposed presence of his Greek friends in the sanctuary but the way he preached to Gentiles (*cf.* 26:20–21). His teaching seemed to undermine Jewish beliefs about the centrality and permanence of the law and the temple in God's purposes.

The Old Testament had spoken about the nations going up 'to the house of the God of Jacob', to learn from him so that they might 'walk in his paths' (Is. 2:3). The theme of the Gentiles making a pilgrimage to Zion is clear in a number of prophecies. But the earliest Christian preachers indicated that the nations would find God in Jesus Christ. This was their testimony as the renewed Israel, as those who acknowledged the fulfilment of God's purposes for Zion in the Messiah and his people. The temple and the law were God's provisions for Israel until the dawning of the messianic era. Cultic regulations and other barriers to fellowship between Jews and Gentiles were now being removed by God himself, so that people from every nation could be united in his service (*e.g.* Acts 10:9–48; 15:1–35).

The coming of the Spirit and the preaching about Christ

Stephen's defence is designed to point Israel away from the temple to the resurrected and glorified Son of Man. Stephen may well have been the most radical exponent of this theme, but his focus on the exalted Lord Jesus is consistent with various other examples of preaching to Jewish audiences in Acts (*e.g.* 2:14–36; 3:12–26; 4:8–12; 13:16–41). Israel must be renewed by responding appropriately to the message about Jesus.

Peter's Pentecost sermon (2:14–40), with its application of the prophecy of Joel, is widely recognized as being programmatic for Acts as a whole. Joel 2:28–32 predicts that, 'before the coming of the great and glorious day of the Lord', God will pour out his Spirit on all flesh, and all will prophesy. Whereas the Spirit especially designated and empowered the prophets and other leaders of the people under the old covenant, God promised that all his people would be possessed by the Spirit in the last days. Joel's prophecy corresponds to some extent with Jeremiah's promise that all God's people would know him and obey him in a new way (Je. 31:31–34). It also parallels to some extent Ezekiel's vision of the Spirit as 'the life-principle of a nation which truly knows the LORD and is inwardly his people' (Ezk. 36:26–27; 37:14; 39:29).[13] The Spirit is the 'organ of communication' between God and his people, guiding them and giving them power to witness to their Lord.[14] The coming of the Spirit is another way of talking about the coming of God to dwell amongst his people, to fulfil the ideal of the temple and to transform their lives by his presence (*cf.* Ezk. 40 – 48). Acts goes on to show how the Spirit-indwelt community came to include believing Gentiles along with the Jewish disciples of Jesus (10:44–48; 11:15–17; 17:32–33).

Peter's sermon proclaims that the witnesses of Jesus' resurrection have received from the exalted Lord the promised Holy Spirit (2:32–33). Consequently, these are 'the last days' (2:16–17), and Jesus is the Lord upon whom everyone must call in order to be saved from the coming judgment of God (2:21, 33–36; *cf.* 22:16). The mode of the Spirit's bestowal on the Day of Pentecost corresponds to the missionary vocation of the disciples: his coming is indicated by the gift of prophetic speech and 'tongues' for the purpose of proclaiming the gospel to people from every nation. Those who repent and call upon Jesus as Lord and Christ, being baptized 'in the name of Jesus Christ', are promised that their sins will be forgiven and that they themselves will receive the gift of the Holy Spirit (2:37–39). In this way they will share in the benefits of the new covenant and participate in the new community of the people of God.

Thus, the Spirit in Acts is the witness to the fact that Jesus lives and is 'the present Lord'.[15] Spirit-inspired preaching about Jesus is the way in which his power and authority are made known and people are enabled to respond to the great saving events of his death, resurrection and ascension. In this way they may engage with the ascended Lord himself. As we shall see, Paul's preaching to Gentiles expresses the same truth in different terms. In the perspective of Acts, the glorified Lord Jesus is the new point of contact between heaven and earth for people of every race without distinction. The focus is not so much on his redemptive work as a fulfilment of the sacrificial system, but on the idea that God's glory and kingly power are supremely expressed in Christ.

This confirms an observation made at the end of chapter

three. Preaching about Christ must be at the heart of a Christian theology of worship. As in the Old Testament, the word of the Lord is central to a genuine encounter with God. Those who are concerned about God-honouring worship will be concerned about the proclamation of the gospel, in the world and in the church, in public teaching and private dialogue. If worship is an engagement with God on the terms that he proposes and in the way that he alone makes possible, preaching Christ is a key to that engagement. Acts points to the proclamation of the heavenly rule of Christ, with all its implications, as the means chosen by God to draw people into relationship with himself, through Christ, in the power of the Holy Spirit. God's great act of redemption in Christ is the basis of a call to enter into and enjoy the blessings of the new covenant. Worship in New Testament terms means responding with one's whole life and being to the divine kingship of Jesus.

The inclusion of the Gentiles

The world of paganism

In the first century of the Christian era, Rome was the capital of a huge empire, comprising many races and religions. From the time of Alexander the Great (356–323 BC) Greek culture and its religious notions and practices had continued to have the most pervasive influence on the Mediterranean world, reaching to Asia Minor, to Palestine and Egypt, to Rome and distant Gaul. No official Greek religion appeared such as was known in Babylonia, in Egypt, in Rome or among the Jews. Many local 'cults' were transported to new sites by missionary efforts or were copied by other communities. New cults were practised alongside older cults, sometimes being fused with one another in the course of time. Polytheism is essentially tolerant of all faiths. Thus, throughout the Roman Empire, religion was essentially the result of the fusion of local traditions and elements common to the wider world of Greek thought and practice.

All the important processes in the world were thought to be

activated by the gods and different gods were regarded as being responsible for particular functions and spheres of life.[16] The object of religion was to secure the goodwill of the gods by faithfully carrying out the prescribed ritual. This was necessary in order to benefit individuals, families, cities and the wider community, or to prevent some disaster from occuring. Three main means were employed to regulate the relationship with the gods: prayers, sacrifices and divination. Sacrifices were intimately connected with prayers because they were viewed as the means by which the gods could be induced to yield to a request. Divination, which was based on the belief that natural phenomena reveal the will of the gods, was practised in the form of astrology or by observation and interpretation of events such as the flight of birds or the timing of a thunderstorm.

Traditional religion came under much criticism with the rise of philosophy in ancient Greece. The moral character of the worshipper was far more important to these thinkers than the perfection of any sacrifice. The only worthwhile prayer was considered to be the prayer for spiritual qualities, particularly virtue. The idea that the gods were dependent on sacrifice for their sustenance or gratification was recognized as absurd, for it treated the gods as inferior to humans! With the spread of belief in fate, divine necessity or chance, some philosophers pointed out that sacrifice was useless: 'a rigidly determined world, whether ruled by gods or not, was incapable of change'.[17] A complete repudiation of material sacrifices, however, was extremely rare. The philosophers mostly exposed the illogicalities of the traditional views of sacrifice and sought to find a way of reconciling their insights with popular religion.[18]

Paul's preaching to the pagans

The account of Paul's ministry in Athens (Acts 17:16–34) gives some indication of the way the Christian message had to be preached to convince the pagan mind. The theme of worship is at the heart of this confrontation, as in the much briefer record of Paul's preaching at Lystra (14:11–18). Luke first notes that, when Paul was waiting for his friends in Athens, 'he was greatly distressed to see that the city was full of idols' (17:16). His reaction was twofold. As was his custom, he turned first to the synagogue and reasoned with the Jews and God-fearing Greeks. Doubtless he preached Jesus as the Christ and showed how the Scriptures had been fulfilled in his death and resurrection (*cf.* 13:16–41; 17:2–4). However, he also reasoned in the market-place daily with 'those who happened to be there' (17:17). Paul may well have employed some of the argument detailed later in the chapter, but those who heard him were convinced that his message was essentially about 'Jesus and the resurrection' (v. 18). In other words, Paul was not simply engaged in apologetics or pre-evangelism. He apparently saw that the preaching of Jesus and the resurrection was the key to persuading those who were given over to idolatry.

For all that, some of his listeners categorized him as yet another preacher of 'foreign gods' or strange powers (*xenōn daimoniōn*, v. 18).[19] Such novel teaching had to be examined by the experts in the court of the Areopagus, an ancient institution exercising jurisdiction in religion and morals in Athens (vv. 19–20). Paul's defence carefully weaves the themes of ignorance and worship together. He notes the extent of their religious feeling, as indicated by the many objects of their devotion (*sebasmata*), but insists that the altar dedicated 'to an unknown god' is a pointer to their ignorance of the true God (vv. 22–23). When the text of the following verses is closely examined, it is clear that he puts forward a number of Old Testament perspectives about the character and purpose of God, the foolishness of idolatry, and human responsibility in relation to God, without actually quoting scripture (vv. 24–29).[20] The true God cannot be accommodated in human sanctuaries and have his needs met by those who would serve him (*therapeuetai*, v. 25),[21] since he is the creator of all things.

> The God who made the world and everything in it is the Lord of heaven and earth and does not live in temples built by hands. And he is not served by human hands, as if he needed anything, because he himself gives all men life and breath and everything else (Acts 17:24–25).

Each part of this carefully worded statement attacks an

important presupposition of paganism. Furthermore, God's ordering of nature and history is designed to provoke men and women to 'seek him and perhaps reach out for him and find him' (vv. 26–27). The characteristic response of humanity has been the lie of idolatry, even though it is totally illogical and has often been acknowledged as such by pagan poets and philosophers (vv. 28–29). Such 'ignorance' of God is actually culpable. In the framework of teaching about the judgment of God against all false worship, Paul then introduces again the theme of Jesus and the resurrection (vv. 30–31).

The apostle's conclusion is that Gentiles can seek after God and find him by turning in repentance from their idolatry and believing in the resurrected Jesus. By implication, this is the way for them to offer acceptable worship to 'the living and true God' (*cf.* 1 Thes. 1:9–10).[22] Such preaching about the resurrection from the dead and the need to acknowledge the divine kingship of Jesus inevitably led the early Christians into direct conflict with the pluralism and relativism of the Greco-Roman world.

Homage and service under the new covenant

Homage to the ascended Lord

Considering the importance of *proskynein* in the LXX, it is surprising that this term is rarely employed in the New Testament outside the Gospels of Matthew and John and the book of the Revelation. Luke's only use in relation to Jesus is in the context of the ascension narrative.[23] When Jesus was taken up into heaven, the disciples 'worshipped him' and then returned to Jerusalem with great joy, where they stayed continually at the temple, praising God (Lk. 24:52–53). Perhaps Luke reserved the term for this climactic moment to indicate that this was at last the real recognition of Christ by the disciples.[24] This verse highlights what may be called the paradox of early Christian worship. Adoration was offered to the glorified Jesus while praise continued to be offered to the God of their ancestors in the traditional context of the Jerusalem temple!

As the earliest disciples proclaimed the exalted Christ and called upon their fellow Israelites to acknowledge him as the giver of the Spirit (Acts 2:33), 'the author of life' (3:15), and their only saviour in the coming judgment (4:12), they were, in effect, summoning them to worship Jesus, as they themselves had done. Yet Luke did not go on to employ *proskynein* in Acts to describe either initial acts of homage and devotion to Christ or the content and purpose of regular Christian gatherings. He restricted the term to a quite technical usage, applying it to those engaged on a pilgrimage to honour God in the traditional temple services (Acts 8:27; 24:11, *cf.* Jn. 12:20) or to the practice of idolatry (Acts 7:43, adapting Am. 5:26). Such terminology was presumably not applied to Christian meetings in Acts or the epistles because of its particular association with the rites of paganism or with the Jewish cult centred at Jerusalem.

The confession of Jesus Christ as Son of God, Lord and Saviour, was at the very heart of the earliest Christian preaching (*e.g.* Acts 2:36; 5:42; 9:22; 10:36; 1 Thes. 1:9–10; Col. 1:28; 2:6–7). Such confession was also the essential response to that preaching required from those who joined the apostolic group and were baptized 'in the name of Jesus Christ' (*e.g.* Acts 2:38; Rom. 10:9–13; Heb. 3:1; 4:14). Its centrality to the Christian life is further suggested by various indications in the Pauline letters of primitive credal statements (*e.g.* Rom. 1:3–4; 10:9–10; 1 Cor. 8:5–6), and possibly some hymn fragments (*e.g.* Col. 1:15–20; Phil. 2:5–11), celebrating 'the elevation of Jesus to a position of transcendent status and a uniquely close connection with God'.[25] Some of these remnants of early church tradition may take us back to Palestinian congregations and to Christians whose native language was Aramaic, as with the untranslated Aramaic prayer *Maranatha* ('Our Lord [or, O Lord] come!', 1 Cor. 16:22).

Prayer to Jesus as Lord was offered by Stephen (Acts 7:59–60), in a way that is striking when compared and contrasted with the prayers of Jesus to the Father (Lk. 23:34, 46). Ananias also prayed to Jesus as Lord (9:10–17, where v. 17 shows that the 'Lord' addressed was Jesus) and designated the followers of Jesus as those who call on his name (9:14; *cf.* 22:16). Again, it is most likely that Jesus is the Lord addressed in prayer by the disciples in 1:24.[26] Paul is represented as calling upon him as Lord on the Damascus road (9:5; 22:10; 26:15–18) and in a subsequent vision in the temple (22:17–21). In this connection it is interesting to note that Paul habitually associated the name of the Lord Jesus Christ with that of God the Father in his prayers (*e.g.* Rom. 1:7; 1 Cor. 1:3; 1 Thes. 3:11–13; and 2 Thes. 2:16–17, addressed first to 'our Lord Jesus Christ himself').[27] Christians could also be defined by Paul as those who 'call on the name of our Lord Jesus Christ' (1 Cor. 1:2; *cf.* Rom. 10:9–13), adapting an Old Testament expression to indicate that Jesus Christ was the one in whom they put their trust for salvation and to whom they prayed (*e.g.* Gn. 12:8; Pss. 50:15; 105:1; Je. 10:25; Joel 2:32).

As Jesus Christ was acknowledged to be the unique agent of God's saving purposes and the Son of God at his right hand, he became an object of devotional attention in a way that was characteristically reserved for God alone in Jewish tradition. This did not begin at a later stage, under the influence of pagan thinking, but amongst the first circle of Palestinian Jewish Christians. It was an extraordinary development within the Jewish monotheistic tradition, which did not destroy the fundamental notion of belief in one God. In short, it was 'an unprecedented reshaping of monotheistic piety to include a second object of devotion alongside God'.[28] Such devotion to Christ was not restricted to prayer or praise, but involved a pattern of daily obedience to the exalted Lord, which distinguished Christians from every other contemporary religious group.

Serving the Lord

In the 'Song of Zechariah' we are told that the whole purpose of the messianic redemption is to enable God's people to worship or serve him (*latreuein autō*, Lk. 1:74). As in the book of Exodus, God has come to save his people in a mighty way, to fulfil the terms of the covenant he made with Abraham. This time he has used the Messiah as a 'horn of salvation', to set his people free from fear of oppression by their enemies, so that they might serve him. The salvation on view is experienced by means of the forgiveness of sins (v. 77), recalling the promise of Jeremiah 31:34. The service that this makes possible is nothing less than a lifestyle of 'holiness and righteousness before him all our days' (v. 75). Although such language is not much used in Luke–Acts, this passage clearly establishes a theological framework in which to understand the work of Christ and the life of the early church. When the messianic salvation is proclaimed, those who respond to the gospel will be empowered to serve God as he desires.

Luke has the Jews at Corinth charge Paul with persuading the people to worship or fear God (*sebesthai ton theon*) 'in ways contrary to the law' (Acts 18:13), referring to the whole way in which Paul taught that the Gentiles could be related to God. Similarly, he has Paul describing his Christian life and ministry in the broadest possible terms as a way of worshipping or serving the God of Israel: 'I worship (*latreuō*) the God of our fathers, as a follower of the Way, which (the Jews) call a sect' (24:14; *cf.* 27:23). The context suggests that Paul had found the way to serve God that fulfilled the Law and the Prophets. The novelty of Christianity, however, was such that the first believers saw the need to differentiate themselves from their fellow Jews. Even though some regarded them as merely 'a sect' (*hairesis*) of Judaism, Christians preferred to designate themselves as 'those of the Way' (9:1; 19:9, 23; 22:4; 24:14, 22).[29] Their 'worship' was a way of life with Jesus at its centre. Thus, Paul describes his ministry of preaching and teaching about the Lord Jesus at Ephesus as a way of 'serving the Lord' (20:19, using the verb *douleuein*).

Since such traditional worship terms were used with a narrowly cultic reference in other contexts (*e.g.* 7:7, 42), it is clear that they were being adapted to express something quite different in Christianity. The notion of worship was certainly not restricted by Luke to what the early Christians did when they met together.

There is only one context in Acts where the language of worship is specifically applied to the activity of a Christian gathering. In Acts 13:2 the prophets and teachers of Antioch are said to be 'worshipping' or, more literally, 'serving' the Lord (*leitourgountōn ... tō kyriō*) and fasting, when the Holy Spirit calls for the sending forth of Barnabas and Saul on their first missionary journey. The verb *leitourgein* and related words were regularly employed in the LXX in a technical sense, to describe the priestly service of the God of Israel (*e.g.* 2 Ch. 11:14, Joel 2:17, Ezk. 45:4, *cf.* Lk. 1:23; Heb. 10:11). As noted previously, this terminology was not used to describe the worship or service of the Israelite nation as a whole but only the ministry of priests to God, as accredited representatives of the nation, and of Levites to priests. Later Jewish literature indicates some movement towards a general figurative application of these words.[30] The terminology is certainly being used in a transformed sense by Luke.

The meeting on view in Acts 13:2–3 could have involved the whole church, but it is also possible that it was 'a small prayer fellowship of leading men'.[31] Many commentators take verse 2 as a reference to prayer,[32] since verse 3 speaks about prayer and fasting. If this is correct, Luke will be highlighting corporate prayer as the 'cultic' activity which replaces the sacrificial approach to God which was at the heart of Judaism. It is possible, however, that Luke means that 'these prophets and teachers were carrying out *their appointed ministry* in the church'.[33] In other words, the ministry of prophecy and teaching, which was exercised by those especially gifted for the benefit of other believers in the congregation, was a specific way of serving or worshipping God under the new covenant. If the service of God involved a certain lifestyle and ministry in everyday contexts, it also had a definite expression when Christians gathered together. The Pauline letters show even more clearly that ministry to one another can be regarded as a form of worship to God.

Although Acts 13:2 suggests that the terminology of worship may be applied to what Christians do when they meet together, it is important to remember that Luke sets this activity within the broader framework of Christian life and ministry. In the early chapters of Acts he also has much to say about the gathering of believers that goes beyond our traditionally narrow understanding of what worship is. Contemporary churches have much to learn from this material, without pursuing a slavish imitation of the first Christian communities.

The character and function of early Christian gatherings

Acts 2:42 provides a brief summary of the activity of the first group of Christians in Jerusalem, where we are told that 'They devoted themselves to the apostles' teaching and to the fellowship, to the breaking of bread and to prayer.' Some commentators regard the four elements specified in this verse as a primitive liturgical sequence, implying that their meetings regularly involved instruction, [table] fellowship, then the Lord's Supper and prayers.[34] Acts 2:44–47, however, appears to be an expansion on this initial summary and some of the things mentioned there clearly took place at different times and in different places. Luke is giving a description of the ministry of these disciples to one another in a variety of contexts, not simply telling us what happened when they gathered for what we might call 'church'. Here is a brief portrayal of their community life as a whole.

In 4:32 – 5:16 many of the same details are presented in a different order and in an expanded form. The main purpose of this passage is to show the holiness of the Christian fellowship and to demonstrate that 'God is near to, and jealously guards the new community, which is his own possession'.[35] These two summary passages in the early chapters of Acts suggest that Luke was presenting something of an 'apology' for the church to his readers.[36] The new community was not a breakaway movement from Judaism, nor merely one of several sects within Judaism, but the true people of God, the renewed Israel where his Spirit was powerfully at work. Elsewhere, Luke only touches on aspects of what believers did when they met together, or emphasizes historical events to which the activities of a gathering were something of a backdrop (*e.g.* 13:2; 20:7–11).

The centrality of teaching

Luke uses a strong verb in 2:42, 46 (*proskarterountes*, 'devoting themselves to')[37] to stress that the earliest disciples were preoccupied with and persevered in the activities he lists. Their first preoccupation was with the apostolic teaching. Meeting together in the temple courts (2:46) appears to have been for the express purpose of hearing the apostolic preaching (cf. 3:11–26; 5:21), though doubtless there were also opportunities for teaching in the home context. We may surmise that these earliest converts desired to be encouraged in their faith but also to identify with the public preaching of the gospel to their fellow Israelites as an act of testimony to its truthfulness. Apostolic instruction continued to be at the centre of church life later in Gentile contexts (e.g. 11:25–26; 18:11; 19:9–10; 20:7–12, 20–21, 28–32; 28:30–31).

The apostolic teaching was authoritative 'because it was the teaching of the Lord communicated through the apostles in the power of the Spirit'.[38] For later generations of believers the New Testament Scriptures form the written deposit of the apostolic teaching in its many dimensions. The centrality of apostolic teaching to the life of the early Christian communities is consistent with a point made earlier in this chapter: the word of the Lord is at the heart of a genuine engagement with God. It is the means by which God himself communicates with his people and maintains them in a right relationship with himself.

Teaching and preaching the apostolic word in the Christian congregation today may therefore be regarded as both a human and a divine activity. It is a ministry of encouragement and challenge which we can have to one another but it is also God's way of confronting us. It is an essential aspect of what may be termed 'congregational worship' because it is itself an act of worship or service designed to glorify God. At the same time, its aim should be to provoke acceptable worship in the form of prayer, praise and obedience, in church and in the context of everyday life. More will be said about this theme in later chapters, in connection with the letters of Paul and the teaching of Hebrews.

The expression of Christian fellowship

The word 'fellowship' in common parlance means 'friendship' or 'companionship'. But it would be inadequate to consider Christian fellowship merely in such terms. The *koinōn-* words in Greek normally mean 'to share with someone in something' above and beyond the relationship itself, or 'to give someone a share in something'.[39] The terminology is used in a number of New Testament contexts to refer to the joint participation of believers in Christ (*e.g.* 1 Cor. 1:9) or the Holy Spirit (*e.g.* 2 Cor. 13:14) or their share in the demands and blessings of the gospel (*e.g.* Phil. 1:5). Common participation in Christ necessarily leads to a mutual fellowship amongst members of the Christian community (*e.g.* 1 Jn. 1:3).

At first glance, *tē koinōnia* in the absolute sense (literally, 'the sharing') in Acts 2:42 refers to the sharing of material blessings described in verses 44–45.[40] There we are told that 'all the believers were together and had everything in common (*koina*). Selling their possessions and goods, they gave to anyone as he had need' (2:44). Yet this sharing was clearly a practical expression of the new relationship experienced together through a common faith in Christ (*cf.* vv. 38–41). This is affirmed in a later passage, where a similar statement about sharing their possessions is prefaced by the words, 'All the believers were one in heart and mind' (4:32–37). Luke highlights their unity in several contexts by the use of the word *homothymadon* ('together', 1:14; 2:46; 4:24; 5:12). That relationship brought a certain sense of responsibility to one another. The sharing of goods came to include the distribution of food to the needy in their midst (*cf.* Acts 6:1–2) and was certainly not restricted to formal gatherings of the believers. It may be best, therefore, to give *koinōnia* its widest interpretation in 2:42, including within its scope 'contributions, table fellowship, and the general friendship and unity which characterized the community'.[41]

It is important to note that this sharing of property and possessions was voluntary and occasional. The needs of that first community of disciples in Jerusalem were related to the physical and social environment in which they found themselves. Their progressive isolation from unbelieving Israel must have made the economic situation of many very precarious. Here was no primitive form of 'communism', but a generous response to particular problems in their midst (2:45; 4:34–35). The examples given in 4:37; 5:4 show that people did not dispose of their whole estate but only certain portions of it. Believers continued to maintain their own homes and used them for the benefit of others in the church (*e.g.* 12:12). There was no rule about the common ownership of property such as was found among the men of the council of the Qumran Community.[42]

It could be argued that a fundamental reason for meeting together as Christians is to give practical expression to the fellowship that we have in Christ. This may take place as we share in prayer, singing or confession, or in the giving and receiving of various ministries in the congregation. The apostle Paul talks about the Lord's Supper as an expression of our common participation or fellowship 'in the blood of Christ' and 'in the body of Christ' (1 Cor. 10:16–17, using the word *koinōnia*). Acts, however, suggests that genuine Christian fellowship will also need to be expressed in other ways and in other contexts. In the Old Testament, a generous treatment of the poor and needy in the land is an expression of true worship. God declares that he will have no regard for sacrifices and religious festivals apart from such a commitment (*e.g.* Dt. 26:12–13; Is. 58:6–7; Am. 5:11–24). It is not surprising, then, to find New Testament writers expressing the sentiment that generosity and self-sacrificing care for others is the outworking of a genuine relationship with God in Christ (*e.g.* Heb. 13:16; Jas. 1:27; 1 Jn. 3:17–18). There is an obligation to do good to all people, but 'especially to those who belong to the family of believers' (Gal. 6:10).

The sharing of material blessings in the congregational meeting by means of a regular Sunday 'collection' is hardly enough! Money may be given for the support of Christian leaders or for the benefit of those outside the church, but the participants are not necessarily taught by such a process to discern and meet the practical needs of others in the local congregation. Teaching on this important biblical theme, together with specific exhortation, will be necessary to provoke believers to care for one another in everyday-life situations, and to express some form of genuine community appropriate to the particular group.

Eating together

'The breaking of (the) bread' (*tē klasei tou artou*) in Acts 2:42 most obviously refers to the common meals shared by the earliest disciples in their homes (v. 46). They met 'by households' (*kat' oikon*) and they met 'daily' (*kath' hēmeran*), perhaps particularly because of the physical needs of many in their community. Some commentators argue that the expression in verse 42 is a technical term for the Lord's Supper and that this was already separated from the ordinary meals of the Jerusalem Christians in some way.[43] However, 'to break bread' in other contexts describes an ordinary meal in terms of the Jewish custom of initiating the meal by breaking a loaf and distributing bread to all present (e.g. Lk. 24:30, 35; Acts 27:35). To 'break bread' was to eat together. The adoption of this term as a title for the Lord's Supper is not formally attested until the second century AD (cf. Didache 14:1; Ignatius, Eph. 20:2). When Luke mentions in Acts 2:46 that they were 'breaking bread in their homes', he goes straight on to say that (literally) 'they were partaking of food with glad and sincere hearts'. The language implies that they were eating food to sustain physical life. What is the ground for giving the expression a different meaning in verse 42?

It might be argued that the reference to the meeting of the Christians in Troas 'on the first day of the week' in order to break bread (klasai arton) is a pointer to a formal Sunday gathering for the purposes of the Lord's Supper (20:7).[44] Paul's discussion with them, however, occupied their attention until after midnight and again after the meal, suggesting that it was a very unstructured and informal meeting. When Luke mentions that Paul finally broke bread (perhaps on behalf of everyone present), he adds 'and when he had eaten, he engaged in much further conversation until dawn' (v. 11, lit.). It is really quite artificial to suggest that the meal by which Paul satisfied himself after such a long time was somehow distinct from 'the breaking of bread'. Since Christian meetings were largely held in the context of private homes, it is natural that they expressed their fellowship in terms of eating together.

In my judgment, therefore, 'the breaking of bread' in Acts cannot be taken to refer to a liturgical celebration distinct from the everyday meals that believers shared together. Such meals were doubtless 'full of religious content because of the recollection of the table fellowship which Jesus had with his followers during his earthly ministry'.[45] The reality of Christian fellowship was expressed from the earliest times, as Jesus intended it, in the ordinary activity of eating together. Furthermore, these meals were presumably given a special character by the fact that they were sometimes associated with teaching, or prayer, or praise.

Perhaps the grace at the beginning or end of the meal focused particularly on the person and work of the Lord Jesus, reminding the believers of the basis of their fellowship in him. In this way, a meal could be given the same sort of significance that Paul wished to ascribe to the community suppers at Corinth (1 Cor. 10:16-17; 11:17-34). Indeed, it is reasonable to suggest that

> to break bread and share a cup together would be to recall not only the unseen presence of the Lord and many meals formerly shared with him, but also the New Covenant which he had inaugurated at that particular meal in the upper room, in the context of his sacrificial self-surrender at Passover-time, in which they found themselves bonded into God's people.[46]

I am not trying to drive a wedge between the fellowship meals in Acts and the teaching of Jesus at the Last Supper or the teaching of Paul about the Lord's Supper at Corinth.[47] The point has been to stress that eating together in Acts was an activity of profound spiritual significance. It was a way of expressing the special relationship which believers had with one another in Christ and the special responsibility to one another involved in that relationship. These meals may well have been informal expressions of what was later more structured and organized. Discussion of the Pauline material in chapter seven will demonstrate the similarities and differences in the Corinthian situation.

Since the celebration of the Lord's Supper in contemporary churches is now almost always separated from a communal meal, it is important to consider what has been lost by this development. How can we modify the way in which we have the Lord's Supper to give greater expression to the fact that we meet as the body of Christ? If the structures of our church life make it impossible to celebrate the Lord's Supper in the context of a real meal, are there other ways to encourage God's people to eat together and minister to one another in the relaxed atmosphere of table-fellowship?

Prayer and praise

The use of the definite article and the plural in the expression 'the prayers' (*tais proseuchais*, 2:42) suggests that the reference is to specific prayers rather than to prayer in general (despite NIV, 'to prayer'). In the context, this most obviously points to their continuing participation in the set times of prayer at the temple (3:1; *cf.* 2:46). Their eating together in households, however, involved 'praising God' (2:47) and must also have involved prayer in the strict sense of petition. Christians in Acts are certainly portrayed in a great variety of contexts at prayer. After the ascension, the disciples 'all joined together constantly in prayer' (1:14). From then on we are told of corporate prayer for guidance (1:24), a meeting to give thanks for deliverance from persecution and to pray for effectiveness in gospel ministry (4:24–30), leaders' meetings to pray for those beginning a new ministry (6:6; 13:3; 14:23), a church meeting to pray for the release of Peter from prison (12:5, 12), and numerous other examples of individual or corporate prayer.

> Luke–Acts as a whole, therefore, constitutes a powerful encouragement and prophetic call to the church to be a church of prayer: not just to pray for its own perseverance as the people of God under pressure in this age, and for salvation at the end... but for continual faithfulness in witness to the gospel now, and for fresh inbreakings of God's grace and power now, such as point to the mercy, glory and power of the ascended Lord until he comes.[48]

The challenge to many contemporary churches is to give more place to such prayer in their public meetings, to share the vision of the early Christians for the progress of the gospel and the glory of God, and to encourage congregational members to meet for prayer in a range of contexts outside the formal gathering of the church.

Conclusion

The temple in Acts continues to function as a centre of revelation and prayer for the early Christians, until their preaching about Jesus leads to expulsion. The doctrine of the new temple is not enunciated in Luke's work, though it is clear from the apostolic preaching that Christ fulfills the ideal of the new temple. The resurrected Christ pours out the divine Spirit on the disciples in Jerusalem and through their testimony becomes the means by which the blessings of the End-time are offered to the nations. 'The author of Acts is concerned simply to show how the temple of Jerusalem played its predicted role as the venue of the eschatological fulfilment and then gave way to the new salvation which is not confined to a particular topographical location.'[49]

The traditional terminology of worship is not much used with reference to Christians in Luke–Acts. Where it is, a theological framework may be established in which to understand the work of Christ and the life of the early church. Calling upon Jesus as Saviour and Lord, as an initial response to the gospel and as a lifestyle of dependence in prayer, is at the heart of what it means to be a Christian. The exalted Lord Jesus is the object of devotion in the early churches. From another perspective, Christian life and ministry should be viewed as a way of serving God. Christ is the one who makes possible the forgiveness of sins and the outpouring of the Spirit predicted by the prophets, so that God's people are liberated to serve him in a new way. Such worship finds particular expression when Christians gather to minister to one another in word or deed, to pray, and to sound forth God's praises in teaching or singing, but it is not to be restricted in our thinking to these activities.

Fundamentally, the earliest Christians met to express their relationship together to the Lord and their responsibilities in that relationship. While Acts suggests some parallels between Christian meetings and the activities of the synagogue, it must be stressed that Luke presents the community life of the earliest Christians in terms that set it apart from Pharisaical Judaism, with its focus on the study and application of the law. Only a very general correspondence between certain features of the synagogue and Christian gatherings may be discerned from Luke's evidence.[50] Again, although parallels might be drawn with the Qumran community, there is nothing of the monastic lifestyle, with its focus on ritual and moral regulations, in Luke's presentation of early Christianity. Rather, there is an awareness of being the community of the End-time, loosed from the strictures of Judaism, focusing on Jesus and the prophetic Scriptures, having its own distinctive forms of prayer and praise, relating to one another and serving one another in everyday contexts such as the household.

It would be simplistic to argue that what was done in the earliest churches is automatically a norm for us today. In particular, the informality of the household gatherings portrayed in Acts was clearly a function of their size and the undeveloped state of the church. Other cultural and historical factors contributed to the development of different patterns of assembly and ministry in different places, as time went by. However, there must be a sense in which Luke is commending the example of the Jerusalem church, about which he has so much to say, to other churches in his generation. This chapter has isolated certain principles that are worth examining again and applying to the contemporary scene, where there is much confusion about the meaning of worship and the purpose of the Christian gathering.

Formality and informality are not theological categories. Yet sometimes people imply that formality in church services is somehow more conducive to acceptable worship than informality. Others argue that informality is preferable because it allows for greater expression of biblical teaching about the congregation as the body of Christ. Formality may be the expression of a very narrow and inadequate view of worship and informality may be an excuse for lack of preparation or any serious attempt to engage collectively with God. Apart from the size of the gathering, the question of formality or informality will often be decided in practical terms by the personalities of those in charge and by the particular traditions of the group in question. There are certainly theological considerations, however, that must challenge and inform our thinking on this issue. Some of these have already been identified in Acts but will be developed and expounded further in subsequent chapters.

Notes

[1] C. F. D. Moule, *Worship in the New Testament*, Ecumenical Studies in Worship No. 9 (London: Lutterworth, 1961), p. 84, responding to an assertion by E. Schweizer.

[2] *Cf.* F. D. Weinert, 'The Meaning of the Temple in Luke–Acts', *BTB* 11, 1981, p. 87. He artificially isolates the temple from what Jesus says about the fate of Jerusalem in Luke's Gospel. In reality, Luke does not 'spatially or theologically distinguish the temple from the city (Jerusalem)' (C. H. Giblin, *The Destruction of Jerusalem*, pp. 58–59). On the other hand, it is clear that Mark and Luke have different emphases in their presentation of the same teaching of Jesus. Thus, Jesus' eschatological teaching is given in the temple (Lk. 21) rather than over and against it (Mk. 13).

[3] This is the most satisfactory understanding of the plural *tais proseuchais* ('the prayers') in 2:42. On the probable continuance and ultimate adaptation of the great festivals of Judaism by the earliest disciples see C. F. D. Moule, *Worship in the New Testament*, pp. 15–17.

[4] Josephus (*Antiquities* 14. 4. 3) indicates that public sacrifices were offered in the temple 'twice daily, in the early morning and about the ninth hour'. It is specious to argue that the early Christians used the temple only for prayer and not for sacrifice, considering the close connection between the two aspects of this daily ritual at the temple. If they had wanted to make a complete break with the Jewish sacrificial system they would have had to absent themselves from the afternoon sacrifice completely.

[5] Although the new covenant is not mentioned by name in Luke's second volume and Je. 31:31–34 is not cited, Lk. 22:20 suggests that we should look for indications of the fulfilment of that prophecy in Acts. The language of Acts 2:38 is particularly suggestive in this regard, with its offer of the forgiveness of sins. The promise of the Holy Spirit relates to Joel 2:28–32, which parallels in sense the prophecy of Je. 31:34 that 'they will all know me, from the least of them to the greatest'.

[6] E. R. Franklin, *Christ the Lord: A Study in the Purpose and Theology of Luke–Acts* (London: SPCK, 1975), p. 78.

[7] 'The fact of Jesus brings meaning to the Temple, but it also emphasizes its inability to make the Abrahamic covenant a reality unless it leads to him' (E. R. Franklin, *Christ the Lord*, p. 102). Note Franklin's helpful exposition of Peter's speech in Acts 3, showing how extensively Jesus is portrayed as the one in whom the covenant promises are confirmed for Israel.

[8] The evangelist may have wished to emphasize the responsibility of the political leaders for Jesus' death or to avoid any suggestion that Jesus himself wished to destroy the temple. R. J. McKelvey (*The New Temple*, pp. 86–87) suggests that Luke delayed recording this charge until Acts 6 because he wished to make the point that the judgment on Jerusalem and its temple 'is suspended till the gospel, duly fulfilled in the gift of the Spirit, has been offered and rejected, i.e. till the first stage of the dominical commission ("you shall be my witnesses *in Jerusalem*") has been executed'.

[9] E. R. Franklin, *Christ the Lord*, pp. 102–103.

[10] *Cf.* C. H. Giblin, *The Destruction of Jerusalem*, p. 110 n. 14. For an alternative view of the significance of Stephen's vision see C. K. Barrett, 'Stephen and the

Son of man', in W. Eltester and F. H. Kettler (eds.), *Apophoreta* (Berlin: Topelmann, 1964), pp. 32–38.

[11] R. A. Cole, *The New Temple*, p. 40. M. Simon, 'Saint Stephen and the Jerusalem Temple', *JEH* 11, 1951, p. 127, argues that 'the building of the Temple by Solomon seems to stand on the same plane as the making of the golden calf'. For Simon this means that Stephen's stance on the temple is different from Luke's, *cf.* M. Simon, *St Stephen and the Hellenists in the Primitive Church* (London: Longmans, 1958), pp. 24–26.

[12] E. R. Franklin, *Christ the Lord*, p. 105. Reference to the temple as (a house) 'made with hands' (7:48, *cheiropoiētois*, *cf.* Mk. 14:58) comes close to Stephen's description of the idol that was made in the wilderness (7:41). Franklin rightly notes, however, that 'the question here is not one of worship, and so of idolatrous activity, but rather of a man-made institution which, by seeking to express some claim upon God, limits the divine freedom and so impairs the divine transcendence'.

[13] G. W. H. Lampe, 'The Holy Spirit in the Writings of St. Luke', in D. E. Nineham (ed.), *Studies in the Gospels: Essays in Memory of R. H. Lightfoot* (Oxford: Blackwell, 1957), p. 162. Lampe gives further references to show how the bestowal of the Spirit was a primary characteristic of the age of final redemption in Jewish expectation.

[14] *Cf.* M. M. B. Turner, 'Spiritual Gifts: Then and Now', *Vox Evangelica* 15, 1985, pp. 7–64, especially pp. 14–15, on 'the Spirit of prophecy' in Acts.

[15] E. R. Franklin, *Christ the Lord*, p. 46. Franklin points out that the power of Jesus is active through his 'name' (*e.g.* 3:6, 16; 4:10) and that 'his name provides a direct and immediate bond between him and the community'. He draws a parallel with the function of 'the name of God' in the Old Testament.

[16] *Cf.* R. M. Ogilvie, *The Romans and their Gods*, p. 10. He points out that there was no dogma in Roman religion: 'a Roman was free to think what he liked about the gods; what mattered was what religious action he performed' (p. 2). The only sects which had anything approximating to a creed in the Christian sense were the mystery cults which came to Rome mainly from the East.

[17] F. M. Young, *Sacrificial Ideas*, p. 19. Young's whole treatment of the philosophical criticisms of sacrifice (pp. 15–34) is very helpful. *Sacrifice and the Death of Christ* (London: SPCK, 1975) is a popular version of her more technical study.

[18] For political reasons, to maintain social stability, they were prepared to practise the traditional rites and even to endorse sacrifice to the genius of the Emperor, which became a test of loyalty to the Roman Empire. When Christians refused to sacrifice in this way they came into conflict not only with the political authorities but also with those philosophers who were keen to support the system.

[19] For a brief analysis of the Stoic and Epicurean philosophies and their reaction to Paul's message see F. F. Bruce, *The Book of the Acts, NICNT* (Rev. ed., Grand Rapids: Eerdmans, 1988), pp. 330–331. When Paul spoke about 'Jesus and the resurrection' it is possible that they understood him to be speaking about 'the personified and divinized powers of "healing" and "restoration" '.

[20] So argues F. F. Bruce (*Book of the Acts*, pp. 334–335), while defending the authenticity of this speech and discussing its relation to the theology of Rom. 1

– 3. The essential content of the speech is biblical, 'but the presentation is Hellenistic' (p. 341).

[21] In chapter two I point out that in Greek literature the *therapeuein* word-group regularly conveys the notion of cultivating the favour of the gods by sacrifice. Consequently, it is rarely used in a religious sense in the LXX and is only used in that way in Acts 17:25 in the New Testament.

[22] On the preaching of the resurrected Christ as the centre of true worship for the nations, *cf.* R. F. O'Toole, 'Paul at Athens and Luke's Notion of Worship', *RB* 89, 1982, pp. 185–197. However, his insistence that this speech is a 'Lukan literary work' needs to be weighed in the light of the arguments by F. F. Bruce, *Book of the Acts*, pp. 334–342.

[23] Note, however, the significant response of Simon to Jesus in the narrative of Lk. 5:1–11. After the miraculous catch of fish he 'fell down at Jesus' knees' (*prosepesen tois gonasin Iēsou*, v. 8), acknowledging himself to be a sinner in the presence of this extraordinary manifestation of the power and presence of God. However, in the progression of Luke's narrative this is not yet a confession of the divinity of Christ. Luke regularly records that people 'fell down' before Jesus as a gesture of respect, associated with supplication or gratitude, using *piptein* (5:12; 8:41; 17:16) or *prospiptein* (5:8; 8:28, 47).

[24] So J. A. Fitzmyer, *Luke X-XXIV*, p. 1590. Even though this text is missing from some ancient manuscripts, Fitzmyer rightly argues for it to be regarded as original.

[25] L. W. Hurtado, *One God, One Lord: Early Christian Devotion and Ancient Jewish Monotheism* (London: SCM; Minneapolis: Fortress, 1988), p. 95. *Cf.* R. P. Martin, 'Some Reflections on New Testament Hymns', in H. H. Rowdon (ed.), *Christ the Lord: Studies in Christology Presented to Donald Guthrie* (Leicester: IVP, 1982), pp. 37–49, R. T. France, 'The Worship of Jesus: a Neglected Factor in Christological Debate?', in *ibid*, pp. 17–36, and M. Hengel, *Between Jesus and Paul* (Philadelphia: Fortress; London: SCM, 1983), pp. 78–96.

[26] 'In view of the fact that in 1:2 the same verb is used of Jesus choosing the apostles, it is more probable that he is the one addressed here' (I. H. Marshall, *Acts*, TNTC [Leicester: IVP; Grand Rapids: Eerdmans, 1980], p. 66). *Cf.* F. F. Bruce, *Book of the Acts*, p. 47.

[27] *Cf.* G. P. Wiles, *Paul's Intercessory Prayers*, SNTSMS 24 (Cambridge, London, New York and Melbourne: Cambridge University Press, 1978), p. 55 n. 3, on the linking of God and Christ in prayer language. Paul's pleading with 'the Lord' three times to take away his 'thorn in the flesh' (2 Cor. 12:8–10), was probably also a prayer to Christ, since the apostle goes on to equate the answer ('my power is made perfect in weakness', v. 9) with his experience of 'the power of Christ'. So R. P. Martin, *2 Corinthians*, WBC 40 (Waco: Word, 1986), p. 417, and L. W. Hurtado, *One God, One Lord*, pp. 104–105.

[28] L. Hurtado, *One God, One Lord*, p. 100. Against those who propose that the worship of Christ was a late development, resulting from the impact of Greco-Roman thinking on Christianity, see especially Hurtado, pp. 93–100. He argues persuasively that such devotion was a direct outgrowth from, and indeed a variety of, Jewish traditions.

[29] I. H. Marshall (*Acts*, pp. 168–169) suggests that behind this term lies the concept of 'the way of the Lord/God' (18:25–26) as the 'way of salvation'

(16:17), and notes parallels in the literature of the Qumran Sect and other religious groups. *Cf.* G. Ebel, *NIDNTT* 3. 935–943.

[30] H. Strathmann, *TDNT* 4. 221. *Cf.* Wisdom 18:21 and Dn. 7:10 in particular and note the application of the more general Hebrew word for 'service' (*ᵃbōḏâ*) to prayer by the Rabbis (*Ibid*, p. 225).

[31] H. Strathmann, *TDNT* 4. 227. *Cf.* E. Schweizer, *Church Order in the New Testament*, SBT 32 (ET, London: SCM, 1961), pp. 73, 172.

[32] So E. Haenchen, *The Acts of the Apostles* (ET, Oxford: Blackwell; Philadelphia: Westminster, 1971), pp. 395–396, Bo Reicke, 'Some Reflections on Worship in the New Testament', in A. J. B. Higgins (ed.), *New Testament Essays – Studies in Memory of T. W. Manson* (Manchester: Manchester University Press, 1959), p. 195, and I. H. Marshall, *Acts*, p. 215.

[33] F. F. Bruce, *Book of the Acts*, p. 245 (my emphasis). *Cf.* 1 Clement 44:3 and Didache 15:1.

[34] So J. Jeremias, *Eucharistic Words*, pp. 118–122, followed by I. H. Marshall, *Luke: Historian and Theologian*, pp. 204–206, and *Acts*, p. 83. E. Haenchen (*Acts*, p. 191) argues strongly against this position, asserting that 'the activities paired with *kai* represent detached and self-contained units'. C. F. D. Moule (*Worship in the New Testament*, pp. 18–19) argues positively for the view that vv. 44–47 expand on v. 42.

[35] *Cf.* D. P. Seccombe, *Possessions and the Poor in Luke–Acts*, SNTU Serie B, Band 6 (Linz: A. Fuchs, 1982), p. 213. Earlier in the same chapter Seccombe outlines the parallels between Acts 2:42–47 and 4:32 – 5:16.

[36] *Ibid.*, pp. 215–218. See note 41 below for the relevance of this apologetic to Hellenistic readers.

[37] J. Jeremias (*Eucharistic Words*, pp. 118–119) fancifully follows a rare usage of the related noun to denote regular visits to the synagogue. He argues that this verb in Acts means 'to attend worship regularly'. However, the verb normally means 'to occupy oneself diligently with something', 'to pay persistent attention to', 'to hold fast to something' or 'continually to be in' (W. Grundmann, *TDNT* 3. 618).

[38] F. F. Bruce, *Book of the Acts*, p. 73.

[39] *Cf.* F. Hauck, *TDNT* 3. 804–809.

[40] So C. F. D. Moule, *Worship in the New Testament*, pp. 18–19. He suggests that this is more appropriate in the flow of the argument than alternative interpretations, such as 'the fellowship of the Holy Spirit' or 'the fellowship of the (sacramental) bread and wine'. F. Hauck (*TDNT* 3. 809) summarily dismisses the suggestion that it can signify 'the community of goods'.

[41] D. P. Seccombe, *Possessions and the Poor*, p. 204. Seccombe argues from the use of *koinōnia* in Hellenistic literature that Luke's description of the common life, meals and material sharing of the Jerusalem church was designed 'to commend Christianity, or perhaps the church itself, to people for whom *koinōnia* was a supreme virtue' (pp. 200–209).

[42] According to 1QS 6, the discipline for someone admitted at Qumran into the 'council of the community' was as follows: 'his property and earnings shall be handed over to the Bursar of the Congregation who shall register it to his account and shall not spend it for the Congregation'. After successfully completing the two-year probationary period, 'his property shall be merged',

translation of G. Vermes, *The Dead Sea Scrolls in English* (Harmondsworth and New York: Penguin, 1962, p. 82). Vermes (p. 30) rather superficially compares this with Acts 2:44–45; 4:32 – 5:2.

43 J. Jeremias (*Eucharistic Words*, pp. 120–121) takes 'the fellowship' of Acts 2:42 to refer to the fellowship meal (called the Agape) and 'the breaking of bread' to refer to 'the Eucharist' which had become separated from the meal proper. However, as noted above, this is an illegitimate narrowing of the meaning of *koinōnia* in the context. I. H. Marshall (*Last Supper and Lord's Supper*, p. 127) rightly proposes that here and in 1 Cor. 11:17–34 'the Lord's Supper proper took place in the context of a fuller meal held by the congregation'.

44 *Cf.* I. H. Marshall, *Acts*, p. 325; W. Foerster, *TDNT* 3. 1096.

45 J. Behm, *TDNT* 3. 730. He argues that Acts 2:42, 46 'has nothing to do with the liturgical celebration of the Lord's Supper' (p. 731), but says that the meal in 20:11 'within the context of the Pauline mission' must be the cultic meal described by Paul as the Lord's Supper in 1 Cor. 11:20. It is not likely, however, that Luke would use the same expression in two different ways like this.

46 C. F. D. Moule, *Worship in the New Testament*, p. 21. Moule rightly argues that 'it is not in the words "the breaking of the loaf", but in their context that one must look if one is to detect any further significance in what the Christians did together at their meals' (p. 20).

47 C. F. D. Moule (*Worship in the New Testament*, pp. 21–26) ably challenges the distinction made by some scholars between a primitive Palestinian fellowship-meal and a sacramental, Hellenistic 'Eucharist'.

48 *Cf.* M. M. B. Turner, 'Prayer in the Gospels and Acts', in D. A. Carson (ed.), *Teach us to Pray: Prayer in the Bible and the World* (Grand Rapids: Baker; Exeter: Paternoster, 1990), p. 75.

49 R. J. McKelvey, *The New Temple*, p. 84. Against R. A. Cole (*The New Temple*, pp. 48–49), McKelvey (pp. 89–90) does not think that David's fallen and rebuilt 'tent' (*skēnē*) in the quotation from Am. 9:11 in Acts 15:15–18 can be taken to mean that the resurrected Christ is the new temple.

50 For the possible influence of synagogue services on Christian liturgical development, see chapter four note 15, p. 132.

CHAPTER SIX

Paul and the service of the gospel

No longer is religion to be a sector of life as was the
case with the elusive and empty divinity cults.
Christianity is a total consecration involving
belonging, obedience, brotherly love, in short, total
service and adoration of the living and true God.[1]

Anyone seeking to discover Paul's teaching about worship might
turn first to passages dealing with congregational meetings and
various aspects of ministry within the body of Christ. The apostle, however, nowhere directly and specifically describes such
activities as 'worship'.

Worship terminology common to Judaism and Hellenism is
certainly found throughout his writings, employed in a transformed and renewed sense. Although such terms regularly occur,
nowhere does he present a developed theology of worship under
the new covenant like that of Hebrews. He comes closest to this
in Romans, with passages from other letters revealing some of
the same assumptions. Indeed, his almost incidental use of
transformed worship terminology on some occasions suggests
that the readers must have been familiar with such teaching
from his original instruction to them.

The aim of this chapter is to uncover the substructure of
worship theology in Paul's writings. The following chapter
focuses on his teaching about the gathering of the church. The

death of Jesus as the means of reconciliation with God and life in the eschatological era is the basis of the worship theology he expounds. The preaching of the gospel in the power of the Holy Spirit brings Jews and Gentiles to serve God together, consecrated to him in the totality of their lives. Paul's use of cultic terminology signals the end of traditional cultic thinking, for there is now nothing holy in the cultic sense 'except the community of the holy people and their self-abandonment in the service of the Lord to whom the world and all its dominions belong'.[2]

Worship as the consecrated lifestyle of the converted

In one of his earliest writings, Paul describes the conversion of the Thessalonians in these striking terms: 'you turned to God from idols to serve the living and true God, and to wait for his Son from heaven, whom he raised from the dead – Jesus, who rescues us from the coming wrath' (1 Thes. 1:9–10). The pattern of preaching implied here contrasts Christianity with all the cults of paganism and presents Jesus as the key to a relationship with the true God. The verb *epistrephein*, which simply means 'to turn around' or 'to return', is used in a technical sense, to signify the total reorientation of life involved in abandoning idolatry for the worship of the living God (*cf.* Acts 14:15; 15:19; 26:18, 20).[3]

It was pointed out in the discussion of worship terminology in chapter two that the verb *douleuein*, which is used in 1 Thessalonians 1:9 to designate this new relationship with God, was regularly applied in secular contexts to the obligations of a slave (*doulos*) to his master. Since it conveyed the notion of total dependence and of obedience without any right of personal choice, it was generally not regarded as an appropriate expression of service to the gods in Greek religion. The Greek translators of the Old Testament, however, showed no hesitation in using this word to describe the bond-service due to the God of Israel (almost always translating the Hebrew *'āḇaḏ*). In fact, *douleuein* is the most common term for the cultic service of God in the LXX, 'not in the sense of an isolated act, but in that of total commitment to the Godhead'.[4] For God was regarded as the majestic king, who had delivered Israel from bondage in Egypt (*e.g.* Ex. 13:3, 14; 20:2), thereby laying claim to their exclusive devotion and obedience.

As Paul moved through the Greco-Roman world, he had to confront the claims of various religious 'cults' (*e.g.* Acts 14:11–18; 17:22–31; 19:24–27) and to guide his converts about how to live in an environment dominated by pagan ideals and practices (*e.g.* 1 Cor. 8:7–13; 10:14–22). Sometimes he appears to have used their terminology in a polemical way to highlight the distinctiveness of Christianity, but it is going too far to suggest that he presents Christianity as a new cult.[5] Conversion from idols was the necessary preliminary to a life of service to the living and true God. The motivation for this radical reorientation was the preaching about Jesus as God's Son, raised from death, soon to return from heaven, who even now is rescuing believers from the coming judgment (1 Thes. 1:10; *cf.* 4:14; 5:9–10). As outlined in the rest of 1 Thessalonians, serving God meant doing his will (4:3; 5:18), living so as to please him in all things (4:1; *cf.* 2:4). It meant avoiding sexual immorality and pursuing brotherly love, working out the practical implications of that consecration to God which is the consequence of true conversion and thus of the Spirit's presence and power (4:3–12).

In other words, Christianity was to be distinguished from the various cults which flourished in Thessalonica, not by any rituals or secret practices but by the consecrated lifestyle of its adherents.[6] Believing that the day of the Lord would come 'like a thief in the night' (5:2), they were to be alert and self-controlled, encouraging one another with the promises and challenges of the apostolic teaching which they had received (4:13 – 5:15). Within the context of this concern for godly living there was to be mutual ministry amongst the believers, as an expression of their service to God. They were exhorted to be joyful, to pray continually, to give thanks in all circumstances, and not to despise the prophetic ministry that the Spirit might grant to some in their midst (5:16–22).

Acceptable worship and the sacrifice of Christ

The well-known exhortation to present your bodies as 'a living sacrifice, holy and pleasing to God, which is your understanding worship' (Rom. 12:1, my translation) is by no means the first indication of Paul's theology of worship in his letter to the Romans. The theme emerges at a number of key points in the document. Foundational to the apostle's theology of worship is the teaching about mankind's refusal to glorify and serve God acceptably (1:18 – 3:20).

False religion and the wrath of God

Speaking first in quite general terms, Paul asserts that 'the wrath of God is being revealed from heaven against all the godlessness and wickedness' of those who 'suppress the truth by their wickedness' (Rom. 1:18). As the argument proceeds, it becomes clear that what is suppressed is specifically 'the truth about God' (1:25, RSV): the truth that there is one creator and lord of the universe and that human beings are accountable to him. Failure to acknowledge God appropriately has led to the chaotic situation where false religions and distorted human relationships are characteristic of human experience (1:21–32). The essence of sin is the holding back of a true knowledge of God and its implications, and therefore a failure to worship him acceptably.

Paul's claim that 'what may be known about God is plain to them, because God has made it plain to them' (1:19) is used as a basis for blame.[7] Humanity's failure to respond appropriately to what may be known about God in and through his creation is culpable, 'without any excuse' (1:20, lit.):

> For although they knew God, they neither glorified
> him as God nor gave thanks to him, but their
> thinking became futile and their foolish hearts were
> darkened. Although they claimed to be wise, they
> became fools and exchanged the glory of the immortal
> God for images made to look like mortal man and
> birds and animals and reptiles (Rom. 1:21–23).

169

Paul here reflects the Old Testament perspective that the knowledge of God should lead to appropriate worship and obedience.[8] Idolatry is an obvious indication of the rejection of a right relationship with the Creator. Giving glory to God in biblical thought means responding appropriately to God's own self-revelation, acknowledging his holiness, majesty and power (e.g. Ps. 29:1–2; Lk. 17:18; Rom. 4:20; Rev. 4:9; 11:13) and not giving the praise that is exclusively due to God to any other (e.g. Is. 42:8; Acts 12:23).[9] It means declaring, but also reflecting in lifestyle, something of the glory or revealed character of God. Consequently, the apostle elsewhere highlights the need to 'glorify God with your body' (1 Cor. 6:20) and writes of the need to do everything 'for the glory of God' (1 Cor. 10:31). 'The whole point of creation is that God should have a reflection in which he reflects himself and in which the image of God as the Creator is revealed, so that through it God is attested, confirmed and proclaimed.'[10]

Glorifying God means not exchanging 'the glory of the immortal God' for the lie of idolatry (Rom. 1:21–23). The language here echoes statements made about Israel in Psalm 106 (LXX 105):20, with reference to the making of the golden calf at the time of the exodus, and in Jeremiah 2:11, with reference to their forsaking the LORD for other gods at a later time. This suggests that Paul's accusation in Romans 1 is directed against the ungodly in Israel and not simply against the pagan world. In line with Jewish tradition, Paul implies that Israel's fall into idolatry, after God had confronted them with his glory at Sinai, was the equivalent in their history to Adam's fall after creation.[11] In the light of God's special revelation of himself to Israel, such rebellion was all the more reprehensible (cf. Rom. 2:17–29). Associated with the failure to acknowledge and glorify God is a futility of thinking and a darkening of 'their foolish hearts'. Humanity is fundamentally impaired at the level of understanding and judgment because of the rejection of the true knowledge of God. It is significant, therefore, that Paul later links the renewing of the mind with the notion of right worship being restored through the work of Christ (12:1–2).

Positively, Paul states that the glorification of God involves the element of thanksgiving (1:21): 'they ought to have recognized their indebtedness to his goodness and generosity, to have recognized him as the source of all the good things they enjoyed, and so to have been grateful to him for his benefits'.[12] Paul then implies that there is another appropriate response to God's self-revelation in creation and redemptive history, for he condemns all who have 'exchanged the truth of God for a lie, and worshipped and served created things rather than the Creator – who is forever praised. Amen' (1:25). In other words, there is a reverential fear and devotion which is due to God alone.

The verb *esebasthēsan* ('worshipped' or 'reverenced') is part of a whole word group used very commonly in the Greek world to denote responses of awe and respect before important people, gods, or overwhelming situations.[13] By New Testament times, this word and the more common verb *sebomai* could encompass a reverential attitude to the gods as well as the cultic activity which gave expression to that reverence. When Paul uses the combination *esebasthēsan kai elatreusan*, it is likely that he intends the second, more specific verb to give more precision to the first verb, so that the sense is 'revered and served cultically'.[14] The esteem and reverence paid to created things, which has always found expression in false religion, particularly in acts of cultic service (*latreiai*), should have been directed to the living and true God.

The sacrificial significance of Christ's death

The opening chapters of Romans illustrate how both Jews and Gentiles have failed in their own distinctive ways to reverence and serve God acceptably. Refusal to glorify God as God has its consequence in every form of wickedness, abuse, hypocrisy and injustice in human relationships. God's abandonment of men and women to the consequences of their rebellion against him is an expression of his wrath, anticipating the final revelation of his wrath on the day of judgment (Rom. 1:18, 24, 26, 28; 2:5). Yet Paul's exposition of the work of Christ and its consequences (3:21 – 11:36) shows how God has acted to transform this disastrous situation. Now it is possible for all to engage with God in a new way, on the basis of Christ's sacrifice, offering the worship that is pleasing to him.

The apostle first explains how believers are justified freely by

God's grace 'through the redemption that came by Christ Jesus' (3:24). The word *apolytrōsis* ('redemption') recalls Israel's deliverance from slavery in Egypt, to be set free to serve God as a distinct and holy people (*cf*. Lk. 1:68–75). However, since such terminology was regularly used in Greek literature in contexts where the payment of a ransom was in view, Paul could also be suggesting that the deliverance through Jesus was at a price. The flow of the argument in Romans 3:24–25 suggests that the 'cost' of redemption is the death of Christ, seen as the gift of divine grace, and the 'price' of it is 'the sacrificial offering made to God'.[15]

God provided Christ as the ultimate sacrifice, 'a sacrifice of atonement by means of his blood, to be received through faith'.[16] Some commentators have argued that the word *hilastērion* here portrays Christ as the anti-type of the 'mercy seat' or 'place of atonement' which covered the ark in the holy of holies (*e.g.* Ex. 25:17–22; Lv. 16:14, 15–16). It is more appropriate, however, to view Christ as the 'means of atonement' or 'sacrifice of atonement', rather than as the 'place of atonement'.[17] The expression 'by means of his blood' points to the atoning significance of his death. The wrath of God is averted by Jesus' death, though, paradoxically, as in Old Testament teaching about the sacrificial system, it is God who provides the means of atonement. The sprinkling of sacrificial blood was a crucial part of the annual Day of Atonement sin offering (Lv. 16) and Paul would seem to be indicating that Jesus has fulfilled and replaced that central rite of Old Testament religion (*cf*. Heb. 9:11–14), rendering the whole sacrificial system no longer necessary.[18]

The sacrificial and atoning significance of Christ's self offering is also brought out in Ephesians 5:2, where Jesus is said to have given himself up 'for us' (*hyper hēmōn*), 'as an offering and sacrifice, whose fragrance is pleasing to God' (lit.: *prosphoran kai thysian tō theō eis osmēn euōdias*).[19] This collection of technical terms from the Old Testament suggests again that all the sacrifices of Judaism find their fulfilment in the self-offering of Christ.[20] Yet, in this context, Christ's sacrifice is also set forth as an example and a motivation for believers, to impel those who benefit from his redemptive work to 'walk in love' as he did (*cf*. 2 Cor. 5:14–15; Col. 2:6–7).

In Romans 5:8–9 Christ's blood or death is again highlighted as the means by which sinners are justified and saved from the wrath of God. It is the eschatological sacrifice, which secures for believers all the blessings of the new covenant and the kingdom of God. In 5:19, however, it is through his obedience that 'the many will be made righteous'. As Adam headed the line of disobedience and sin, Jesus heads the line of humanity which lives under the sign of obedience. The atoning value of his obedience, which culminates in his death, lies in the fact that he surrenders himself completely to the Father as the representative of sinful humanity. Thus, it is implied by Paul's argument that we may only relate to God on the basis of Christ's perfect 'worship', which is his self-offering. Jesus' death was a once-for-all sin offering, providing the atonement towards which the propitiatory rites of the old covenant were ultimately pointing. This teaching is expounded more obviously in Hebrews 10:5–22 (*cf.* also Heb. 5:7–10).

Romans 6:1–10 makes it clear that baptism into Christ means baptism into his death, in order to live with him and for him (*cf.* 2 Cor. 5:15). Christians enter into fellowship with Christ in his total self-surrender to the will of the Father in order to find acceptance with the Father through his atoning work on their behalf. The moral implication of this is to live out the new obedience which baptism into Christ's death entails (Rom. 6:11–23; *cf.* 12:1–2). Christian obedience is made possible by the self-giving obedience of Jesus Christ. If Jesus' death is the unique and never-to-be-repeated sin offering of the new covenant, faith expressed in obedience is the 'holocaust' or 'burnt offering' which Christians can offer to God because of that sin-offering. 'Dying with Christ, being crucified with him in baptism, stamps the whole earthly life of the Christian, sanctified by his Spirit, with the cultic character of his death on the cross.'[21]

The worship that Christ makes possible

The phrase 'through faith' in Romans 3:25 indicates how the saving benefits of Christ's unique and unrepeatable sacrifice are to be appropriated. In the chapters that follow, the apostle goes on to describe the nature of that faith and its consequences in terms of obedience and sanctification (*cf.* especially 6:11–23).

Justification by faith opens up the possibility of serving God in a new way, in the power of the Holy Spirit. Such a relationship with God is available for Jews and Gentiles alike, since anyone who calls upon Christ as Lord may be saved (*cf.* 10:9–13). In Romans 12:1 Paul begins to draw out the practical implications of the preceding theological exposition, suggesting a radically new understanding of worship in terms of a right response to the gospel:

> Therefore, I urge you, brothers, in view of God's mercies, to offer your bodies as a living sacrifice, holy and pleasing to God, which is your understanding worship (Rom. 12:1, my translation).

The uniqueness of Paul's approach to this subject is indicated by the way he introduces it. He implores his readers 'by means of the mercies of God' (lit.: *dia tōn oiktirmōn tou theou*). It is as if all God's merciful deeds, expounded so far in the letter, make their own appeal in Paul's exhortation.[22] God's mercies, supremely expressed in the saving work of Christ, the gift of his Spirit, his perseverance with faithless Israel and his gracious offer of salvation to the Gentiles, call forth the response of grateful obedience, with all the implications outlined in the following chapters. In addressing them as 'brothers', he makes it clear that his entreaty is for those who know themselves to be the recipients of those mercies and who are now united in the community of Christ. This call to worship is thus similar to the foundational statements of passages like Exodus 19:4–6; 20:1–3; Deuteronomy 10:14–22, where the redemptive initiative of God establishes and dictates the sort of engagement with the LORD that is required of Israel.

The apostle wrote at a time when aspirations for a more spiritual worship abounded in various milieus in both Judaism and Hellenism. The expression *logikē latreia* (which I have rendered 'understanding worship') recalls various criticisms of sacrifice then being made in the Greco-Roman world. The adjective *logikos* was a favourite term of the Greek philosophers, especially the Stoics, for whom it meant 'belonging to the sphere of the *logos* or reason' and hence 'spiritual' in the sense of 'suprasensual'.[23]

Since rationality is what distinguishes human beings from animals and relates them to the gods, traditional sacrifices were repudiated by some writers and various forms of 'rational sacrifice' (*logikē thysia*) were advocated instead. In some texts this refers to attitudes of mind and purity of life, but in texts influenced by mysticism some form of religious ecstasy or even silence is regarded as the proper worship. The Hermetic tracts, probably dating from the third century AD in their present form, appear to use *logikos* quite specifically with reference to sacrifices on a rational plane, offered by the rational part of the soul.[24]

The LXX does not employ *logikos*, though the Old Testament prophets clearly indicated that God was honoured, not merely by ritual observance, but by a genuine spiritual and moral engagement with him (*e.g.* Is. 1:10–16; 29:13; Mi. 6:6–8). God's essential requirement was repentance, faith and obedience, especially expressed in the concern to establish righteousness and holiness in the community of his people. The sacrificial system was designed to promote such a response and not to be a cover-up for sin. In late Judaism, while the need for cultic observance continued to be stressed, deeds of love, and activities such as fasting, prayer and the study of the law were often regarded as being as pleasing to God as temple offerings.[25]

If the term 'spiritualization' is to be applied to developments in Judaism, this should not be confused with what such terminology meant in Hellenism. In some Jewish writings, such as the Epistle of Aristeas and the works of Philo, Hellenistic and Jewish ideas about a truly spiritual worship were certainly blended. Whereas, however, in Hellenism generally there was a movement towards interiorizing worship, culminating in teaching about the importance of silence before an impersonal and ineffable divinity, in Judaism the movement was towards a development of the ethical implications of ritual worship. The way for New Testament teaching was to some extent forged by Jewish thinkers placing the doing of God's will at the heart of what they said about sacrifice, rather than by Hellenism. Nevertheless, what is distinctive for Paul is not the moralization and spiritualization of the notion of sacrifice, but the fact that Christian worship involves the presentation of ourselves to God on the basis of the single, atoning sacrifice of the death of Jesus, in the power of the Holy Spirit.

It seems highly likely that the apostle chose to use the expression *logikē latreia* precisely because of

> the spiritualizing tradition and nuances which it represented – its polemic context of spiritual-moral sacrifice against bloody animal sacrifice, its implications of life according to the logos, its mystic nuance of silent prayer. Paul would thus be taking up, in quotation marks as it were, a religious slogan common in certain circles at the time. In so doing he completely transforms the saying, while opposing it to those conceptions of spiritual worship so much in vogue at the time. Certainly no more the bloody animal sacrifices of the past, but not either the pure interiority of the Mystic. The Christian's spiritual worship involves an extreme of realism – the bodily offering of himself.[26]

If Paul's expression is translated 'spiritual worship', there is a danger of accenting the inwardness of Christian worship and not taking sufficient account of the fact that we are to yield our bodies to God's service. On the other hand, the translation 'rational worship' may only suggest a contrast between the offering of rational beings and the sacrifice of irrational animals. The mind is certainly central to Paul's perspective here, but the focus is not simply on rationality. The service he calls for is the obedience of faith expressed by those whose minds are being transformed and renewed by God, so that they may no longer be conformed in lifestyle to the values, attitudes and behaviour of 'this age' (Rom. 12:2; *cf.* Col. 3:9–10; Eph. 4:22–24). Consequently, it may be best to read 'understanding worship', and to recognize from the context that this means 'the worship which is consonant with the truth of the gospel',[27] or the service rendered by those who truly understand the gospel and its implications.

Responding to Paul's exhortation

The phrase used to express the sacrificial action of Christians is 'to present your bodies as a living sacrifice'. Although it never appears in the LXX, *paristanai* ('to present') is a standard Hellenistic word for the offering of a sacrifice.[28] The aorist tense is employed to indicate the decisiveness required in presenting ourselves to God for his service. Rightly understood, evangelism will involve a challenge to the unconverted to respond to God's grace in this way. Yet the fact that Paul addresses those already committed to Christ in this letter suggests that the command should be taken in a summary way, as defining the response that is always to be regarded as the essence of Christian worship.[29] The initial presentation of ourselves to God in Christ, made at conversion/baptism, needs to be renewed on a regular basis.

The sacrifice that pleases God is our 'bodies', meaning ourselves as a totality, not just skin and bones (*cf.* 6:13, 16, 'offer yourselves', *paristanein heautous*)! Christ's obedience makes possible a new obedience for the people of God. The apostle is not simply considering some form of inner consecration here, but the consecration of ourselves as a whole, able to express our obedience to God in concrete relationships within this world (*cf.* 1 Cor. 6:20). As those who have been brought from death to life by means of Jesus' death and resurrection (*cf.* Rom. 6:4–11), we belong to God as a 'living sacrifice' (*thysian zōsan, cf.* 6:12–14). As those called to be saints (*cf.* 1:7, *klētois hagiois*), we are to live out that consecrated relationship in terms of practical holiness (*hagian*, 12:1) and so prove to be acceptable or pleasing to God (*euareston tō theō*). Thus, Paul has transposed the notion of sacrifice across a double line – 'from cultic ritual to everyday life, from a previous epoch characterized by daily offering of animals to one characterized by a whole-person commitment lived out in daily existence'.[30]

We are sanctified or consecrated to God because Jesus Christ died and rose for us, and because the Spirit enables us to believe the gospel and yield ourselves to God (*cf.* 1 Cor. 1:30; 2 Thes. 2:13; 1 Pet. 1:2). Consequently, the sacrifice we offer is already holy. We are holy, like the Israelites redeemed from Egypt, because God has graciously brought us to himself. However, that holiness needs to be expressed in our bodily life (1 Cor. 6:19–20; 2 Cor. 7:1), by living out the call to a holy life (1 Thes. 4:1–12). Under the new covenant 'we no longer have material offerings distinct from the giver but rather the personal offering of the body, of earthly life, inseparable from the existence of the one who offers. It is at this point that the holy merges with the ethical with which it may so easily be equated.'[31] The life that is truly acceptable to God is the life consecrated to him through self-abandonment to the saving work of Jesus Christ. It is the life that seeks to serve him in the context of everyday relationships and responsibilities, in the power of his Holy Spirit.[32]

The first two verses of Romans 12 place the concluding chapters of the letter under the umbrella of worship. That theme emerges again explicitly in 14:18 ('anyone who serves [*douleuōn*] Christ in this way is pleasing [*euarestos*] to God and approved by men') and the notion of an offering acceptable to God continues in the section dealing with Paul's particular ministry which begins in 15:14. From Romans 12 – 15 it is clear that acceptable worship involves effective ministry to one another within the body of Christ, maintaining love and forgiveness towards those outside the Christian community, expressing right relationships with ruling authorities, living expectantly in the light of Christ's imminent return, and demonstrating love especially towards those with different opinions within the congregation of Christ's people.

If the sphere of Christian worship is the world and every relationship in which Christians find themselves, what is the particular application of Romans 12:1–2 to the congregational meeting or 'church service'? The following verses suggest immediately that the exercise of gifts and ministries in the congregation is an expression of our service to God: we worship God by prophesying, serving, teaching, encouraging, contributing to the needs of others, exercising leadership and showing mercy to others in the fellowship of God's people (12:3–8). These activities may continue outside the formal meeting of the church but they are an essential part of such meetings in the perspective of several New Testament passages. While all ministry must be understood as a response to God's grace, and not in any sense a cultivation of his favour, ministry to others is an important aspect of our self-giving to God. The next chapter will explore this theme in greater detail.

If God is to be glorified by such service, Romans 12:1–2 suggests that Christians need to be continually reminded of 'the mercies of God'. Our focus must be on his gracious initiative, in order to maintain saving faith in Jesus Christ and what he has done, and to elicit appropriate expressions of that faith. Once again, the centrality of gospel proclamation to the meeting of Christ's people must be affirmed. Ministries of the word of God need to be exercised in the congregation to enable us to engage with God and serve him appropriately.[33] If Christians are not to be conformed to the pattern of this world but are to be transformed by the renewing of their minds, a gospel-based ministry of teaching and exhortation is essential.

Gospel ministry as a specific expression of Christian worship

At the beginning and end of Romans, Paul employs the language of worship to describe his apostolic ministry (1:9; 15:16). Although the first reference could perhaps be mistaken for an aside, the second is clearly integral to the argument of chapter 15. These passages together show that Paul's considered view of his apostolate was that it was the means by which he was especially called to worship or serve God under the new covenant.

In his introductory thanksgiving (1:8–17), the apostle names God as witness when affirming how constantly he remembers the Roman Christians in his prayers. God is described as 'the one whom I serve in my spirit in the gospel of his Son' (lit.). As noted previously, *latreuō* ('I serve') in the LXX regularly refers to the service of Israel's God or service offered to the gods of the nations. While the verb *leitourgein* and related terms were reserved for the priestly ministry in Israel, the *latreuein* word-group was used to describe the cultic service of the people as a whole. There are contexts where this verb is used to convey the idea of fidelity and devotion to God as lord and master in the broadest possible terms (*e.g.* Dt. 10:12–13; Jos. 24:14–24). The terminology was mostly, however, with the specific sense of honouring God by ritual observance (*e.g.* Ex. 3:12; 2 Sa. 15:8).

The words 'in my spirit' (*en pneumati mou*) in Romans 1:9 primarily refer to Paul's spirit, rather than the Holy Spirit, yet it is surely right to assume that he means his spirit renewed and inspired by the Spirit of God (*cf.* Phil. 3:3). In this way he differentiates Christian service from other forms of worship as a service flowing from and motivated by a renewed spirit and one in which the whole person is engaged. The expression 'in the gospel' (*en tō euangeliō*) suggests that he specifically had in view his apostolic ministry.[34] Paul's apostolic ministry was a particular expression of the worship that all Christians are to offer to God (Rom. 12:1). His proclamation of the gospel was a religious act comparable with the praise offered in conjunction with the sacrificial ritual of the tabernacle or temple. Intercessory prayer was an aspect of Paul's service to God, but it is clear from what follows in the context that gospel preaching was the focus and goal of all his activity (*cf.* 1:11–15).[35]

At the conclusion of the letter, Paul again describes his gospel work using transformed worship terminology. As 'a minister (*leitourgos*) of Christ Jesus to the Gentiles', he is the one designated by God to bestow blessing on the Gentiles with the gospel (Rom. 15:16). The word *leitourgos* need not imply a sacral function.[36] However, what follows suggests that he is engaged on Christ's behalf in discharging a 'priestly' ministry in the 'cult' of the gospel (*hierourgounta to euangelion*).[37] There is no question of Paul acting as a mediator between his converts and God. This sacral terminology is used metaphorically to portray the ministry of preaching by which he enables the Gentiles to offer themselves to God as an acceptable sacrifice, 'sanctified by the Holy Spirit'. Many commentators take the expression *hē prosphora tōn ethnōn* to mean 'the offering which consists of the Gentiles', implying that Paul offers the Gentiles to God like a priest. It would, however, be 'much more in accord with the rest of St. Paul's liturgical expressions to take "the offering of the Gentiles" as the offering made by the Gentiles'.[38] The language here recalls Romans 12:1 and suggests that gospel preaching is necessary to bring about that obedience of faith through Jesus Christ

(15:18; *cf.* 1:5; 16:19), which is the 'understanding worship' of the eschatological era. This is clearly a response his converts themselves must make. Paul's ministry makes it possible for the Gentiles to 'glorify God for his mercy' (15:9).

The expression 'consecrated by the Holy Spirit' (NEB, *hēgiasmenē en pneumati hagiō*) in Romans 15:16 stands in apposition to 'acceptable' (*euprosdektos*) and indicates that the work of the Spirit in drawing the Gentiles into relationship with God through Jesus is what makes them acceptable to God. Paul goes on to reinforce the idea that the acceptability of the Gentiles' self-offering to God is directly related to his preaching, by asserting that the Spirit is at work through his ministry, in what he says and does (vv. 17–19). The Spirit, who is actively present in both preacher and listener, is a necessary agent of the worship of the new era inaugurated by Christ. Another way of expressing the same truth is to say that Christ himself has been at work through the ministry of Paul, drawing the Gentiles into relationship with himself. Although the primary reference is to Paul's evangelistic preaching, by which individuals are brought to Christ and churches are established, it is clear that the apostle sees his ongoing ministry to believers, even the writing of this letter, as a means of enabling Christians to live the consecrated life that is pleasing to God.

Paul's 'priestly' ministry was radically different because it was conducted out in the world, rather than in some sacred place, and the offering it made possible breached 'the fundamental cultic distinction between Jew and Gentile'.[39] The breaking down of the distinction between sacred and profane was part of the breaking down of the division between those two groups within humanity. The gospel demanded that the cultic barriers prescribed in the Old Testament be left behind. Paul's own role as apostle to the Gentiles was foundational to this new life in the Spirit, with evangelism and teaching about the implications of the Christian message being his God-given 'liturgy'. His ministry was the divinely appointed means of uniting Jews and Gentiles in the praise and service of God, thus fulfilling the prophetic promises regarding the End-time (*cf.* 15:5–12). Since preaching was not regarded as a ritual activity in Paul's world, he clearly gives that ministry a novel significance when he describes it as the means by which he worships or serves God.

Paul's ministry was in many respects unique and he clearly used transformed cultic terminology to highlight this fact. Nevertheless, it seems legitimate to argue by way of extension that such terminology can be applied, at least in some measure, to those who share in the apostolic task today. Missionary preaching and the establishment of churches in the truths of the gospel can be described as fulfilling a God-given 'liturgy' or service to the churches. At the same time, these vital activities can be regarded as specific and particular expressions of Christian 'worship' or service to God. Any gospel ministry can be described as 'priestly' in the sense that it enables people to present themselves as a 'living sacrifice' to God through Jesus Christ. It must be recognized, however, that there is always a danger that the metaphorical and spiritual dimension to Paul's thought may be obscured by describing Christian ministry in such terms.

This soon happened, as church history progressed.

> What began in Christianity as a metaphorical and spiritual conception was by the age of Constantine ready to be taken literally again. The extension of sacrificial language had come to encompass *the ministry as a special priesthood* (Cyprian), *the table as an altar* and *buildings as temples* (Eusebius). Sacrifice was increasingly *materialized* and traditional content was put into the words. Sacrifice became again not only praise and thanksgiving but also *propitiatory* (Origen and Cyprian). A blending and transformation of conceptions – pagan, philosophical, Jewish and Christian – created a new complex of ideas. We not only use words, but words use us.[40]

Sacrifice, faith and the Spirit

It is not possible to examine the use of worship terminology in all of the letters attributed to Paul. The next chapter will focus particularly on what may be learned from 1 Corinthians and Ephesians. This chapter concludes with some observations from the letter to the Philippians.

The 'sacrificial service' of Christian faith

The apostle uses transformed sacrificial terminology to describe his own ministry to the Philippians and the way their faith expressed itself in ministry to him:

> But even if I am being poured out like a drink offering (*spendomai*) on the sacrifice and service coming from your faith (*tē thysia kai leitourgia tes pisteōs hymōn*), I am glad and rejoice with all of you. So you too should be glad and rejoice with me (Phil. 2:17–18).

Since both *thysia* ('sacrifice') and *leitourgia* ('service') stand under the same article in the Greek it is possible that Paul means 'the sacrificial service of your faith'. The words *tēs pisteōs hymōn* ('of your faith') may imply that faith itself is the sacrificial offering on view (RSV, 'the sacrificial offering of your faith'). The broader context of the argument in Philippians, however, suggests rather that the reference is to faith as the basis or motivation for their sacrificial ministry (NIV, 'the sacrifice and service coming from your faith'). Similar terminology in 2:30 and 4:18 indicates that Paul is talking about the care they have shown to him, engendered by their faith.

As noted in chapter two, the noun *leitourgia* ('service, ministry') was used in the LXX almost exclusively for the service of priests and Levites in the temple. In the New Testament, however, apart from two references to such ritual activity (Lk. 1:23; Heb. 9:21) and one to the high-priestly work of Christ (Heb. 8:6), *leitourgia* is used in a non-cultic way to describe the service rendered to meet the needs of others. In 2 Corinthians 9:12 it refers to the collection for the poor in Jerusalem (*cf.* Rom. 15:27 *leitourgēsai*), and in Philippians 2:30 to the ministry of Epaphroditus to Paul, on behalf of the Philippians. Epaphroditus is styled as 'a minister' (*leitourgos*) in 2:25, since he brought the material gifts of the Philippians to Paul (4:18) and risked his life to complete in person what was lacking in their 'ministry' to him (2:30, *hymōn...tēs pros me leitourgias*). The ordinary secular sense of rendering a service to someone is the most obvious meaning of the terminology here. Yet the wider context suggests that God is honoured and served by means of such service to others.

One of Paul's aims in writing to the Philippians was to express his gratitude for the gifts received from them. He calls attention to the spiritual significance of their ministry to him in 4:18 by the use of cultic terminology: the gifts are described as 'a sweet fragrance, a sacrifice acceptable and pleasing to God'.[41] The expression *osmē euōdias* (lit., 'a sweet fragrance') is part of the technical language of sacrifice in the Old Testament, being applied to burnt offerings (Ex. 29:18, 25; Lv. 1:9), cereal offerings (Lv. 2:2, 12) and peace offerings (Lv. 3:5).[42] Such language implied that God delighted in the sacrifices of his people, when they were offered as he directed. Paul, however, applies this terminology to a monetary gift. Sacrificial giving for gospel ministry is thus shown to be an expression of the worship pleasing to God under the new covenant.

In short, the 'sacrifice and service coming from your faith' mentioned in 2:17 refers to the ministry rendered by the Philippians to the apostle. It would include their prayers and their sending of Epaphroditus with material support for Paul in his missionary activity. As Paul wrote, he particularly had in mind their care for him in the context of his imprisonment. *Leitourgia* was not added to *thysia* to suggest that the Philippians performed a priestly act, but to indicate that their sacrifice was expressed in active service.[43]

Gospel ministry and the ultimate sacrifice

The other image that is used in Philippians 2:17 is that of Paul himself being offered as a 'libation' (RSV, *spendomai*, 2:17). In the Greek world, the verb *spendō* was used to denote the pouring out of 'a portion of drink on the ground or on a cultic site as an offering to the gods'.[44] In the LXX, such terminology was applied to drink offerings or libations of oil that were poured out over or beside a burnt offering with its accompanying cereal offering (*e.g.* Nu. 15:3–10; Lv. 23:13, 18). So Paul is indicating that he has a sacrifice to offer in connection with the sacrificial service coming from the faith of the Philippians.

It is most likely that Paul is alluding to the possibility of martyrdom with the use of such imagery.[45] By this means he indicates that he is prepared to go to the limit for the sake of the gospel.[46] The only other occurrence of *spendomai* in the New Testament is 2 Timothy 4:6 (lit., 'for I am already being poured out and the time of my departure has come'), where the context rather than the word itself suggests imminent martyrdom. Here, there is a note of certainty, but in Philippians 2:17, martyrdom is considered in a more hypothetical fashion.

With the employment of this well-known cultic imagery in such an unusual fashion, the apostle suggests that his own death might be the drink offering to be added to the Philippians' sacrificial service. If the Old Testament imagery is to be pressed, the sacrifice of his life would be the libation to complete their offering to God. Such is his commitment to them in the fellowship of the gospel, that he is prepared to be 'poured out', not for the glory of martyrdom, but as a modest 'drink offering', added to the primary offering of their faith. He is willing for such a death to be reckoned to their credit and not to his and calls upon them to rejoice with him at such a prospect.

Worship inspired by the Spirit

In Philippians 3 there is a rapid change of tone and mood in the argument, as Paul seeks to warn his readers about the dangers of false teaching in their midst. His emotions run high when he refers to his opponents as 'those dogs, those men who do evil, those mutilators of the flesh' (3:2) and then uses a variety of rhetorical effects to contrast their error with the truth. Much scholarly debate has taken place about the identity of these false teachers, with some commentators suggesting that there may have been two, or even three different groups of people under attack in this chapter![47] For our purposes, it is sufficient to note that the argument at the beginning of the chapter points to the Jewish aspects of their propaganda. They apparently insisted that men should be circumcised before they could worship God acceptably. In so doing, they indicated that their confidence was in rituals and human achievements, rather than in Jesus and the gospel of salvation by God's grace alone.

The derogatory term 'mutilation' (*katatomē*) is applied to these agitators in Philippians 3:2. 'Circumcision' (*peritomē*) is the term that might have been expected, since it was the name regularly given in the New Testament to Jews (*e.g.* Rom. 3:30; 4:9; Gal. 2:7–9) or Jewish Christians (*e.g.* Gal. 2:12; Col. 4:11; Acts 10:45; 11:2), drawing attention to that physical sign of Israel's covenant relationship with God. In fact, Paul applies this important expression to himself and to his readers in verse 3 (using the emphatic form *hēmeis gar esmen hē peritomē*, 'for we are the circumcision'). This indicates that Jewish and Gentile Christians now constitute the new community of the people of God. The remaining clauses of the verse then set forth what it means for Christians to be 'the circumcision' of the new age: 'we who are the circumcision, we who worship by the Spirit of God, who glory in Christ Jesus, and who put no confidence in the flesh.'

When the apostle claims that the special mark of Christians is that they 'worship by the Spirit of God' (*hoi pneumati theou latreuontes*) he is not simply contrasting Israel's external rites with true spiritual worship. Just as the title 'the circumcision' applies now in a transformed way to Christians and not to Israel, so 'the service of God' belongs exclusively to Christians as the community possessed and led by the Spirit of God.[48] The 'service' on view will involve more than prayer and praise, since the Spirit is given to inspire and empower a new lifestyle in Paul's teaching (*e.g.* Rom. 8:4, 9–11, 14).

The following expressions indicate in a positive and negative fashion the sort of engagement with God that this entails. To 'glory in Christ Jesus' and 'put no confidence in the flesh' is to follow the example of Paul in verses 4–11 – rejecting circumcision, Jewish descent, and obedience to the law as the basis of a relationship with God, turning from self-confidence to trust in Christ and what he has achieved for believers by means of his death and resurrection. It is the work of the Holy Spirit to enable such a response to the gospel and to motivate Christians to a life shaped by the gospel realities.

In other words, Philippians 3 emphasizes that the service of God in the gospel era is initiated and maintained by the Spirit of

God. It is a service rendered on the basis of the preaching of the gospel, motivated by, and informed by the saving work of Jesus Christ. How the Spirit operates when Christians gather together remains to be investigated. The focus here is not on the exercise of the Spirit's gifts nor on the inwardness of the Christian's response to God. What stands out from this context is the idea that worship by the Spirit is essentially trust in Christ crucified and the saving implications of his death.

Conclusion

The perspective offered by Paul's use of certain traditional worship terms, is that expressions of faith in the saving work of Jesus Christ and ministries that encourage such faith are specifically the worship acceptable and pleasing to God in the gospel era. There is a new kind of service to God made possible through the preaching of the gospel. This is so because Jesus' death provides the ultimate sacrifice of atonement, fulfilling and replacing the Old Testament sacrificial system. Evangelism can be viewed as the task of challenging people to yield themselves to God, calling upon them to respond in grateful obedience to all his mercies in Christ. The Spirit is given to enable trust in the promises of the gospel and to bring men and women from every race into a sanctified relationship with God and with one another, in the community of the new covenant. Such is the means chosen by God to deal with our failure to acknowledge and serve him appropriately. An engagement with God through Christ is now the only way to offer the worship that is due to him.

The presentation of ourselves 'as a living sacrifice, holy and pleasing to God', means serving him in a whole range of relationships and responsibilities. When Christians become preoccupied with the notion of offering God acceptable worship in a congregational context and thus with the minutiae of church services, they need to be reminded that Paul's focus was on the service of everyday life. In the sixties and seventies of this century, we were urged to see that the real life of the church was in the world. But the 'religionless Christianity' that evolved was far removed from Paul's priorities and perspectives. As the century draws to a close, there is generally more interest in congregational life and ministry but a dangerous tendency towards introversion in many churches. Indeed, congregational worship in some contexts can be like 'a narcotic trip into another world to escape the ethical responsibilities of living a Christian life in this world'.[49]

The preaching of the gospel is designed to bring about a consecrated lifestyle that will enable believers to glorify God, by word and deed, wherever and whenever they can. This view of worship highlights the importance of the family, the workplace and leisure activities as the sphere in which to work out the implications of a genuine relationship with God.

Yet, within this broader framework, Paul focuses on gospel proclamation and support for gospel ministry as the worship which is acceptable and pleasing to God. 'The service of the gospel' is not simply the relationship with God made possible through the preaching of the message of salvation. The Spirit motivates and equips believers for ministry to one another in the congregation and for service in the world. Obedience to apostolic teaching and apostolic ministry to nurture Christian faith and obedience are different aspects of the worship by which Christians are to honour God and express the reality of their relationship with him through Jesus Christ.[50] This means that evangelism and the strengthening of believers emerge again as a priority for those concerned to offer to God 'acceptable worship'.

Notes

[1] R. Corriveau, *The Liturgy of Life: A Study of the Ethical Thought of St. Paul in his Letters to the Early Christian Communities*, Studia 25 (Bruxelles and Paris: Desclée de Brouwer; Montreal: Les Editions Bellarmin, 1970), p. 35.

[2] E. Käsemann, 'Worship and Everyday Life. A Note on Romans 12', *New Testament Questions of Today* (ET, London: SCM, 1969), p. 192.

[3] *Epistrephein* is used in the LXX to translate the Hebrew verb *šûb*, when the notion of Israel returning to the God of the covenant is in view (*e.g.* 1 Sa. 7:3; Is. 6:10; 44:22; Je. 3:22). It is not surprising, therefore, to discover that this term is also used in the New Testament when the gospel is being preached to Jews (*e.g.* Acts 3:19; 20:21; 26:20; 2 Cor. 3:16). *Cf.* G. Bertram, *TDNT* 7. 722–729.

[4] K. H. Rengstorf, *TDNT* 2. 267. *E.g.* Jdg. 2:7; 10:16; 1 Sa. 7:3–4; 12:20; 2 Ch.

30:8; Pss. 2:11; 100 [LXX 99]:2; Is. 56:6; 65:13–15; Je. 2:20; Mal. 3:17–18. Many times in the LXX *douleuein* is used with reference to the service of other gods.

5 *Cf.* R. J. Banks, *Paul's Idea of Community: The Early House Churches in their Historical Setting* (Sydney: Anzea; Exeter: Paternoster; Greenwood: Attic, 1979), pp. 25–27, 37–38, and M. Harding, 'Church and Gentile Cults at Corinth', *Grace Theological Journal* 10.2, 1989, pp. 203–223.

6 *Cf.* K. P. Donfried, 'The Cults of Thessalonica and the Thessalonian Correspondence', *NTS* 31, 1985, pp. 336–356, especially pp. 341–342. Note the use of consecration / sanctification terminology in 1 Thes. 4:3, 4, 7; 5:23; 2 Thes. 2:13; 3:13. Although such terms were employed in the LXX in connection with the cult, consecration was never purely a ritualistic matter in the OT but concerned one's way of life (*cf.* H. Seebass, *NIDNTT* 2. 223–228).

7 'God's knowability is not merely a characteristic or "spin off" of creation but was willed and effected by God', J. D. G. Dunn, *Romans 1 – 8*, WBC 38A (Waco: Word, 1988), p. 57.

8 *E.g.* Jdg. 2:10–13; 1 Sa. 2:12; Ps. 79:6; Je. 22:16; Ho. 4:1–6; 8:2–3. The knowledge of God in the Old Testament involves an acknowledgment of him in one's thinking and behaviour and is almost equivalent to the fear of God (*e.g.* Ho. 4:1; 6:6; Is. 11:2, 9; Pr. 1:7; 9:10). *Cf.* R. Bultmann, *TDNT* 1. 696–701.

9 In biblical Greek, the verb 'to glory' (*doxazein*) fundamentally means 'to value', 'to honour', 'to extol' or 'to praise'. It can be used with reference to the honouring of certain people (*e.g.* 2 Sa. 10:3; Sirach 7:31; Mt. 6:2; *cf.* Rom. 11:13) or the honouring of God (*e.g.* Ex. 15:1–2, 6, 11, 21; Mt. 5:16; 9:8; Lk. 2:20; 5:25; Rom. 15:6, 9). There is a particular significance attached to the notion of glorifying God in the Old Testament because of the idea that God's glory (*doxa*) is his manifest presence.

10 K. Barth, *Church Dogmatics* II/1, trans. G. W. Bromiley and T. F. Torrance (Edinburgh: T. & T. Clark, 1957), p. 673. Barth's discussion (pp. 666–677) of the connection between the revelation of the glory of God and God's glorification by his creatures is very helpful. 'To give honour to God means that in our existence, words and actions we are made comformable to God's existence; that we accept our life as determined by God's co-existence, and therefore reject any arbitrary self-determination' (p. 674).

11 *Cf.* J. D. G. Dunn, *Romans 1 – 8*, pp. 60–61.

12 C. E. B. Cranfield, *A Critical and Exegetical Commentary on the Epistle to the Romans* ICC Vol.I (Edinburgh: T. & T. Clark, 1975), p. 117. Cranfield rightly argues that the words *ē ēycharistēsan* single out thanksgiving for special mention as a particular element in the glorification which is owed to God.

13 *Esebasthēsan* is a form of *sebazomai*, which is found in the New Testament only in Rom. 1:25 and rarely elsewhere. This verb was used in Greek literature as a substitute for the more common word *sebomai* in certain tenses.

14 C. E. B. Cranfield (*Romans* I, p. 124) and other commentators rather too readily dismiss the notion that *esebasthēsan* may still in NT times denote the attitude of reverence. *Cf.* W. Foerster, *TDNT* 7. 173 and my discussion of this terminology on pp. 70–72.

15 I. H. Marshall, 'The Development of the Concept of Redemption in the New Testament', in R. J. Banks (ed.), *Reconciliation and Hope*, FS L. L. Morris (Exeter: Paternoster, 1974), p. 163. Marshall highlights the paradox that

redemption terminology can be used to express a 'cost' borne by God and an offering made or 'price' paid to God.

[16] RSV and NEB rightly indicate that *en tō autou haimati* is to be connected with *hilastērion*, showing that it was by means of his blood / death that Christ was a sacrifice of atonement, rather than with *dia pisteōs* ('through faith in his blood', as in AV and NIV). *Cf.* Cranfield, *Romans* I, pp. 210–211.

[17] *Cf.* C. E. B. Cranfield, *Romans* I, pp. 214–218, for a helpful discussion of the issues. He suggests that the absence of the definite article before *hilastērion* in Rom. 3:25 is an argument against identifying Christ as the anti-type of the mercy seat. Furthermore, 'the mercy-seat would surely be more appropriately regarded as a type of the Cross' (p. 215).

[18] It is possible that Paul's language here also reflects the description of the death of the Maccabean martyrs in 4 Macc. 17:22. However, if Jesus' death is viewed in any sense as that of a martyr, it is expounded as a uniquely redemptive event that secures forgiveness and deliverance from every power that keeps people from serving God.

[19] Translation of M. Barth, *Ephesians 4 – 6*, AB 34A (Garden City, NY: Doubleday, 1974), pp. 557–560. Even though *thysia* regularly denoted animal sacrifices and *prosphora* other types of offerings, it is possible that *prosphoran kai thysian* is a hendiadys ('sacrificial offering'), with the second term defining more specifically the meaning of the first.

[20] R. Corriveau, *The Liturgy of Life*, p. 198. Note the use of the expression *eis osmēn euōdias* in connection with the burnt offerings in Gn. 8:20–21; Ex. 29:18, 25; Lv. 1:9, 13, 17, *etc.*

[21] R. Corriveau, *The Liturgy of Life*, p. 177. 'It is this primordial union between Christ and the Christian, between Christian living and Christ's death and resurrection, which gives to the Christian and his life the essential quality of worship' (p. 185).

[22] Note the way Paul similarly uses *dia* with the genitive to imply that the character of God is actually the basis and means of his appeal in Rom. 15:30 ('by our Lord Jesus Christ and by the love of the Spirit', *cf.* 1 Cor. 1:10) and 2 Cor. 10:1 ('by the meekness and gentleness of Christ'). *Cf.* Rom. 12:3 ('by the grace given to me').

[23] G. Kittel, *TDNT* 4. 142. Note the helpful analysis of relevant texts from various religious and philosophical traditions by E. Ferguson, 'Spiritual Sacrifice in Early Christianity and its Environment', in W. Haase (ed.), *Aufstieg und Niedergang der Römischen Welt*, II 23:2 (Berlin, New York: de Gruyter, 1979), pp. 1152–1189. *Cf.* P. Seidensticker, *Lebendiges Opfer (Rom 12,1). Ein Beitrag zur Theologie des Apostels Paulus*, Neutestamentliche Abhandlungen (Münster: Aschendorff, 1954), pp. 17–28.

[24] *Cf. Corpus Hermeticum* I *(Poimandres)*, 31. In XIII, 18–19, *logikos* seems to be connected with the idea that the worship of the reborn person really proceeds from the indwelling divine Logos.

[25] *Cf.* E. Ferguson, 'Spiritual Sacrifice', pp. 1156–1162.

[26] R. Corriveau, *The Liturgy of Life*, p. 179. He observes that Philo could speak of the *nous*, the *dianoia* or *aretē* as sacrifices but could never speak of the body as a sacrifice, since this whole idea was foreign to his Hellenistic framework of thought. Again, Paul goes beyond anything in the Qumran tradition, where the

concern for spiritual sacrifices is set within the context of a highly elaborated concern for ritual purity in the present and the hope for restoration of ritual sacrifice at a renewed temple in Jerusalem.

[27] Cranfield, *Romans* II, p. 605. C. F. Evans, 'Rom 12:1–2: The True Worship', in L. de Lorenzi (ed.), *Dimensions de la vie chrétienne* (Rome: Abbaye de S. Paul, 1979), pp. 20–22, argues for the rendering 'rational'.

[28] *Cf.* B. Reicke and G. Bertram, *TDNT* 5. 837–841.

[29] If the expression 'your understanding worship' (*tēn logikēn latreian hymōn*) is taken in apposition to 'bodies', the reference is specifically to our bodies as victims in the cult of the new covenant. However, if the phrase is taken in apposition to all that proceeds, a more dynamic and appropriate meaning is given to *latreia*: the presentation of ourselves to God in Christ is the essence of Christian worship.

[30] J. D. G. Dunn, *Romans 9 – 16*, WBC 38B (Waco: Word, 1988), p. 710. Dunn rightly observes that the subsequent dominance of *thysia* in reference to the Eucharist or Lord's Supper in the writings of the Church Fathers represents 'something of a regression from Paul's eschatological perspective'.

[31] R. Corriveau, *The Liturgy of Life*, p. 171. Compare his comments on 2 Cor. 7:1.

[32] For the sacrifice or life acceptable to God, note other contexts where the adjective *euarestos* is used (2 Cor. 5:9; Eph. 5:10; Phil. 4:18; Col. 3:20; Heb. 13:21). Similarly note the use of the adverb (Heb. 12:28) and the related verb (Heb. 11:5–6; 13:16).

[33] *Cf.* D. W. Torrance, 'The Word of God in Worship', *The Scottish Bulletin of Evangelical Theology* 1, 1983, pp. 11–16. This is a helpful article in many respects, though the writer's view of Scripture and its use in preaching seems to be too narrowly Christological.

[34] Paul can use *euangelion* to refer to the proclamation of the gospel rather than to its content (*cf.* Rom. 1:1; 15:16; 1 Cor. 4:15; 2 Cor. 2:12; 8:18; Gal. 2:7). *Cf.* P. T. O'Brien, *Introductory Thanksgivings in the Letters of Paul*, NovTSup 49 (Leiden: Brill, 1977), pp. 213–214.

[35] Since *latreuein* can be used specifically for the ministry of prayer (*e.g.* Lk. 2:37; Acts 26:7) some commentators interpret the phrase *latreuō en tō pneumati mou* to mean that praying is 'the inward side of his apostolic service contrasted with the outward side consisting of his preaching, etc' (C. E. B. Cranfield, *Romans* I, p. 77). However, such a distinction between the inward and outward side of Paul's service seems artificial. The portrayal of Paul's apostolic ministry in terms of transformed cultic language has been extensively investigated by A.-M. Denis, 'La fonction apostolique et la liturgie nouvelle en esprit', *RSPT* 42, 1958, pp. 401–436, 617–656.

[36] *Cf.* Rom. 13:6, where the civic authorities are God's benefactors (*leitourgoi theou*). The word *leitourgos* is used 14 times in the LXX, in most cases with the ordinary secular sense of a 'servant'. However, in Is. 61:6; Ne. 10:40 and Sirach 7:30, the context indicates that ministering priests are specifically meant.

[37] Although the verb *hierourgein* does not occur in the LXX, it is used by Josephus and Philo with reference to the offering of the firstfruits, spiritual burnt offerings and the sacrifice of investiture. By derivation it means 'to perform the work of a priest', but it is also used in Jewish and non-Jewish texts

in the broadest sense 'to present or offer sacrifices', without specifying whether or not a priest is responsible for the action. *Cf.* G. Schrenk *TDNT* 3. 251–252.

[38] J. Murphy-O'Connor, *Paul on Preaching* (London: Sheed & Ward, 1963), p. 288, following A.-M. Denis, 'La fonction apostolique', pp. 405–406. So also R. Corriveau, *The Liturgy of Life*, p. 152, and D. W. B. Robinson, 'The Priesthood of Paul in the Gospel of Hope', in R. J. Banks (ed.), *Reconciliation and Hope*, FS L. L. Morris (Exeter: Paternoster, 1974), pp. 231–245, especially pp. 231–232.

[39] J. D. G. Dunn, *Romans 9 – 16*, pp. 860–861. He rightly observes, 'The more clearly cultic is the imagery, the more striking Paul's transformation of it by application to his missionary work.'

[40] E. Ferguson, 'Spiritual Sacrifice', p. 1189 (my emphasis), concluding a very helpful study of the use of such terminology in early Christianity and its environment.

[41] The word for sacrifice in 2:17 (*thysia*) is applied in the New Testament to the sacrificial death of Christ (Eph. 5:2; Heb. 9:26; 10:12; *cf.* 9:23) and to various practical expressions of faith by Christians, based on and motivated by the saving work of Jesus (Phil. 2:17; 4:18; *cf.* Rom. 12:1; Heb. 13:15–16).

[42] *Cf.* also Gn. 8:21; Nu. 15:2, 10; 28:2, 24, 27; Dn. 3:37 (LXX) and the metaphorical or spiritualized use of Sirach 24:15; 39:13–14; Jubilees 2:22 and other intertestamental literature. Note S. Daniel, *Recherches sur la vocabulaire du culte dans la Septante*, Études et Commentaire (Paris: Klincksieck, 1966), pp. 175–197.

[43] *Cf.* P. T. O'Brien, *Commentary on Philippians*, NIGTC (Grand Rapids: Eerdmans, 1991), pp. 308–310. Contrast H. Strathmann, *TDNT* 4. 227.

[44] O. Michel, *TDNT* 7. 528. *Cf.* A.-M. Denis, 'La fonction apostolique', pp. 631–634.

[45] *Cf.* J. B. Lightfoot, *St Paul's Epistle to the Philippians* (London/Cambridge: Macmillan, 1869), pp. 116–117, and F. F. Bruce, *Philippians*, GNC (San Francisco: Harper & Row, 1983), pp. 63–64. Bruce rightly argues that the reference is to a willing yielding of Paul's life to God, not specifically to the outpouring of blood, as in some pagan cults (*cf.* Ps. 16:4).

[46] This 'libation' is not the extreme case of the labours Paul mentioned in the previous verse, because the Greek suggests a progression of thought in v. 17 to the possibility of something additional and climactic for Paul. The hypothetical nature of the argument in v. 17 means that it does not conflict with the confidence previously expressed by Paul about his immediate future (1:24–26). Contrast A.-M. Dennis, 'La fonction apostolique', pp. 630–650, followed by R. Corriveau, *The Liturgy of Life*, pp. 124–136 and G. F. Hawthorne, *Philippians*, WBC 43 (Waco: Word, 1983), pp. 105–106.

[47] *Cf.* R. P. Martin, *Philippians*, NCB (London: Oliphants; Grand Rapids: Eerdmans, 1976), pp. 22–34.

[48] *Cf.* D. E. Garland, 'The Composition and Unity of Philippians', *NovT* 27, 1985, pp. 169–170. Contrast what is said about Israel in Rom. 9:4 ('theirs is the worship', *hē latreia*).

[49] W. H. Willimon, *The Service of God: Christian Work and Worship* (Nashville: Abingdon, 1983), p. 41.

[50] It is particularly clear from Rom. 1:5; 16:26 that the goal of Paul's ministry,

as expressed in non-cultic terms, was to bring about and encourage 'the obedience of faith'. This I take to mean 'an obedience motivated by and dependent upon faith', *cf.* G. N. Davies, *Faith and Obedience in Romans, JSNTS* 39 (Sheffield: *JSOT,* 1990), pp. 28–30.

CHAPTER SEVEN

Serving God in the assembly of his people

> There are varieties of gifts, but the same Spirit; and
> there are varieties of service, but the same Lord; and
> there are varieties of activities, but it is the same God
> who activates all of them in everyone. To each is
> given the manifestation of the Spirit for the common
> good (1 Cor. 12:4–7, NRSV).

While it is true that every sphere of life provides the Christian
with the opportunity to glorify and serve God, it would be a
mistake to think that worship in the Pauline letters is simply
synonymous with ethics.[1] For one thing, as I have observed, the
terminology of worship is used quite specifically with reference
to gospel preaching and the ministries that support gospel work.
There is a declaratory side to glorifying God and a sacrificial
service in the cause of the gospel that needs to be highlighted as a
vital part of the Christian's 'understanding worship'. This may
find expression in the congregational gathering or in the context
of everyday life.

If it is the logic of Paul's teaching that sacred times and sacred
places are superseded, it is still valid to ask whether he views
what Christians do when they gather together as in any way
different from the service they are to offer God in everyday life.
We talk about a 'church service' but what do we consider to be
at the heart of such an event? What is the purpose of Christian

assembly in Paul's theology? In what sense do we gather to worship God? Are there other, more appropriate New Testament terms that could be used to highlight the nature and significance of the meeting of God's people? This chapter concentrates on passages dealing with congregational ministry and seeks to relate them to Paul's teaching about the nature and purpose of the church.

Meeting God when the church gathers

Paul's single application of the common worship term *proskynein* is in 1 Corinthians 14:24–25, where he mentions the possibility of an unbelieving 'outsider' entering a church gathering when 'all prophesy' (RSV). Such a person may be convicted of sin because 'the secrets of his heart' may be disclosed. Falling on his face (*pesōn epi prosōpon*), he may 'worship God' (*proskynēsei tō theō*) and acknowledge his presence among them. The gesture itself is not so important but what it represents is crucial. The worship described here is an act of submission or unconditional surrender to God, similar to the spontaneous response of people in the Old Testament when confronted by God (*e.g.* Gn. 24:26–27; Ex. 4:31; 34:8). Such language suggests the conversion of the unbeliever, thus fulfilling prophecies like Isaiah 45:14, describing the coming of the nations to pay homage to Israel's God. Although the conversion of an unbeliever in the course of a church service is much to be desired, however, evangelism is not the primary purpose of the gathering, according to 1 Corinthians 14.

The apostle does not use *proskynein* in connection with the regular gathering of God's people for prayer, praise and mutual encouragement, but it is logical that such activities should be characterized as worship.[2] A genuine relationship with God will involve ongoing expressions of submission to his character and will, in the form of personal and corporate acts of obedience, faith, hope and love. Prayer and praise should characterize Christian living in every context (*e.g.* 1 Thes. 5:16–18; Col. 3:17) and must, therefore, be at the heart of any corporate engagement with God. However, it is misleading to think of church services

195

simply as occasions for worship in the sense of prayer and praise. Paul's teaching requires us to recognize also the central importance of the concept of edification for the meeting of God's people.

At a more general level, 1 Corinthians 14:24–25 suggests that God presences himself in a distinctive way in the Christian meeting through his word and the operation of his Spirit. Since it is prophecy and not evangelistic preaching that brings the unbeliever to his knees in this context, it will be helpful to consider what that particular ministry involved before discussing other ways by which God might make his presence known amongst his people.

Prophecy in the congregation

The prophecy flourishing in Corinth and in other congregational contexts in New Testament times (*cf.* 1 Thes. 5:19–22; Rom. 12:6; 1 Pet. 4:11) cannot simply be equated with the prophecy of Old Testament figures like Isaiah and Jeremiah. The apostles appear to be the true heirs of that prophetic mantle, since they claim absolute divine authority for their words and call upon believers to acknowledge that authority (*e.g.* 1 Cor. 14:37–38; Gal. 1:11–12; *cf.* 2 Pet. 3:2, 16).[3] By contrast, the prophetic ministry given to certain members of the Corinthian church required assessment and evaluation, which implied the possibility of challenging and even rejecting such contributions (1 Cor. 14:29; *cf.* 1 Thes. 5:21–22). This suggests that their prophecy did not carry the weight of being actual 'words from the LORD' in the Old Testament prophetic sense, yet it was distinguishable from other human words in that it was the result of a revelation (*apokalypsis*, 14:30), a prompting of the Spirit of God.[4] The apostles functioned as foundational prophets, transmitting the revelation which was applicable to all the churches, providing the touchstone for assessing all other ministries, and subsequently forming the basis of New Testament Scripture. The revelation given to the Corinthian prophets was of a different character.

Their ministry was for the 'strengthening, encouragement and comfort' (*oikodomēn kai paraklēsin kai paramythian*) of the local church (14:3). Yet, other verbal ministries, including singing, tongues with an interpretation, and teaching, were also meant to have this effect (14:26). What made prophecy distinctive was the fact that it was based on spontaneous, God-given 'revelation'. Without a revelation or insight from God there could be no prophecy. With such insight, the prophet could speak to the specific needs of the moment when the congregation gathered, needs which otherwise may only have been known to God (cf. 14:25; Rom. 8:26–27).[5] Although prophecy may have involved insight into the meaning and application of scriptural texts or gospel themes – Paul certainly expected people to learn or be instructed by it (14:31) – this does not mean that prophecy was simply identical with what we call preaching.

Christians continue to debate whether the gift of prophecy manifested at Corinth is really available to the churches today. The charismatic movement has made this a vital issue in many places. Whatever conclusion we reach, 1 Corinthians 14 surely speaks to us of the value and importance of spontaneous, verbal ministries of exhortation, comfort or admonition by congregational members (cf. 1 Thes. 4:18; 5:11, 14; Eph. 4:15). Such mutual ministry is often confined to the home group, or to times of personal interaction after church services. Why is it not also encouraged in the public gathering of the whole church? Many Christian traditions rightly emphasize the need for regular and systematic exposition of Scripture and the teaching of 'sound doctrine' by those gifted and appointed for this task (cf. 1 Tim. 4:6, 11, 13; 5:17; 2 Tim. 2:1–2, 14–15; 4:1–5; Tit. 1:9).[6] If the balance of New Testament teaching is to be preserved, however, there should be some space for the informal contributions of members.

The word of Christ among his people

Paul actually expects Christ to be encountered as his people share with one another a whole range of verbal ministries in the congregational gathering. For example, as they 'sing psalms, hymns and spiritual songs', with gratitude in their hearts to God, they will fulfil the apostolic injunction, 'Let the word of Christ dwell among you richly' (Col. 3:16; cf. Eph. 5:19–20).[7] As the gospel or 'the word of Christ' is proclaimed and applied in the congregation, so Christ himself makes his character and presence known and impresses his will on his people. Clearly, any gospel-based ministry of encouragement or admonition will be a means by which Christ engages with his people. This will happen when the Scriptures are formally expounded and taught or when believers informally exhort one another to live out their obedience to the gospel.[8] The Spirit, who unites believers in a common relationship with God through faith in Christ, gifts and inspires them to be the means by which he continues to confront them with his truth (1 Cor. 12:4–13).

Such texts suggest that, when Christians meet together to minister to one another, there is a corporate, spiritual engagement with God, in the Holy Spirit, through his words. In this connection, it has been rightly observed that, in the Bible as a whole,

> words play a peculiarly important role (in contrast to
> primitive worship where the action is dominant and
> the word seems to have little role at all), first because
> faith comes by hearing – the word must be
> proclaimed – and secondly because response in words
> is the specifically human way by which man makes
> known to himself and to others that he has received
> the word.[9]

One model for the Christian congregation is Israel gathered at Mt Sinai to receive the word of the Lord (Ex. 19 – 24), or assembled in Jerusalem to hear the book of the law read by Ezra and interpreted by the Levites (Ne. 8 – 9). Yet the profound difference in the New Testament view of the Lord's assembly is that he comes to his people wherever they are gathered in his name and he encounters them through the ministry which he enables them to have to one another, as an outworking of the promises of the new covenant. We meet with God when we meet with one another.

Further insight into the nature and purpose of the Christian gathering can be gained from considering Paul's teaching about the church. The key notions of the church as 'the temple of the Holy Spirit', God's 'building' and 'the body of Christ' will receive particular attention in the following pages and the implications for a theology of the gathering will be explored.

Thanksgiving, prayer and praise

Thanksgiving, prayer and praise play a very significant role in Paul's letters, as he regularly reports his own personal practice, incorporates wish-prayers or expressions of praise at appropriate points in his argument, and urges his readers to honour God by following his example. Strictly speaking, prayer involves petition for one's own needs or intercession on behalf of others. Thanksgiving for Paul means especially expressing gratitude to God for his work in the lives of others (*e.g.* 1 Cor. 1:4–9; Phil. 1:3–5). When he uses the language of praise, his focus is on the divine blessings in which he has also shared (*e.g.* 2 Cor. 1:3–11; Eph. 1:3–14). These elements of Jewish worship, transformed in terms of gospel perspectives, were clearly central to the apostle's view of the Christian life.[10] By implication, we can learn what should characterize these activities in the Christian assembly.

There is a close connection between thanksgiving and prayer in Paul's correspondence. Although he is constantly thankful for past blessings and every sign of God's power presently at work in the lives of his converts, 'he will permit no satisfaction with them, but constantly in every letter exhorts and urges the churches to move forward in their Christian life'.[11] As he gives thanks for particular churches, he becomes more and more aware of their need for maturity or perseverance in faith, hope and love, especially as his thoughts turn to their ultimate encounter with God on the day of Christ's return (*e.g.* 2 Thes. 1:11–12; Phil. 1:9–11; Col. 1:9–14). The praise introductions to his letters (*e.g.* 2 Cor. 1:3–11; Eph. 1:3–14), and the benedictions, doxologies and outbursts of praise which occur at significant points in his argument (*e.g.* Rom. 1:25; 11:36; Eph. 3:20–21), are an invitation to glorify God for who he is and what he has done for his people as a whole.

An important source of words and motifs in Paul's prayers was the early Christian preaching. Words such as 'gospel', 'the word of God', 'grace' and 'faith' appear again and again. In one way or another, his thanksgivings for the work of God in the lives of those addressed are 'causally linked to the gospel or its right reception'.[12] Terms applied to the gospel in thanksgiving are sometimes then applied with a slight change of meaning to believers, when he tells them how he prays for them (*e.g.* Col. 1:6, 10). Growth to maturity takes place as Christians pray for one another in the way that the apostle suggests, asking God to supply all the resources they need through the operation of his word and his Spirit in their lives (*e.g.* Eph. 3:14–19; Col. 1:9–14).

In addition to various general exhortations to pray and give thanks (*e.g.* Rom. 12:12, 14; Eph. 6:18; Phil. 4:4–7; 1 Thes. 5:16–18), Paul also appealed quite specifically for his fellow believers to share in the struggle of his apostolic ministry by uniting in prayer for him (*e.g.* Rom. 15:30–32; Eph. 6:19–20; Col. 4:2–4; 2 Thes. 3:1–3). This prayer was to involve more than vague generalities. It was to be a genuine calling upon God to open 'doors' for the gospel and enable his servant to preach without hindrance.

The gospel message elicits a trust that enables us to approach the Father in the name of Jesus with confident requests for ourselves and others. Such prayer is an expression of the privileged status of the children of God in the present, which carries with it the hope of sharing the glory of God (*cf.* Rom. 8:15–17). Petitionary prayer is thus an important means of persevering in faith and obedience in the midst of all kinds of testing.

The church as the temple of the Holy Spirit

The sanctity of the local congregation

In the opening chapters of 1 Corinthians, the apostle deals with a problem of strained relationships in that congregation. Difficulties arose from different evaluations of the ministries of their leaders. Describing the way God works through his human agents to achieve his purposes for the church, Paul employs an agricultural metaphor: 'I planted the seed, Apollos watered it, but God made it grow' (3:6–8). The idea that the Corinthians are the 'field' which God is cultivating through his servants then gives way to the notion that they are God's 'building' (*oikodomē*, 3:9). With this metaphor goes the perspective that Jesus Christ is the 'foundation' and Paul the 'skilled master of works' (*architektōn*, 3:10),[13] who has laid the foundation through his evangelistic ministry (*cf.* Rom. 15:20). The warning which follows is about the way to build a structure on that foundation that will survive the test of God's judgment (3:10–15). In effect, Paul is challenging them to go on applying to their corporate life and relationships nothing more nor less than the gospel truths and the traditions which they received from him.

With the words 'Do you not know that you are God's temple and that God's Spirit dwells in you?' (3:16, RSV) the apostle introduces into his argument another important metaphor for the church.[14] The building that God is erecting on the foundation of Paul's preaching about Jesus is a community of people indwelt by the Holy Spirit (*cf.* 2 Cor. 6:16; Eph. 2:21–22). There may be vestiges in the epistles of the belief that Christ himself is the new cultic centre and dwelling-place of God (*e.g.* Col. 2:9–10; Eph. 2:20–22; and 1 Pet. 2:4–8). But by and large the writers present the view that Christians in union with Christ fulfil the temple ideal. The individual's body is said to be 'a temple of the Holy Spirit' in 1 Corinthians 6:19–20,[15] but the temple is the local congregation in 3:16–17. As the Spirit creates one body (1 Cor. 12:13), so he has formed one 'temple' at Corinth.

The expression *naos tou theou* marks out the Corinthian church as the divine sanctuary where God's Spirit dwells.[16] The imagery reflects the Old Testament idea that God was specially present in the midst of his people (*e.g.* Ex. 29:44–46; 33:14–16; Ps. 114:2). Prophecies about the restoration of Israel after the Babylonian exile included the promise of the gift of God's Spirit, as the means by which he would dwell in or among his people and bless them in a new way (*e.g.* Joel 2:28–32; Is. 44:3–5; Ezk. 36:27–28; 37:14). The hope of a new temple, which was another way of speaking about the ultimate renewal of God's people, finds expression in the reality of the Christian congregation!

Thus, the New Testament teaches that God's dwelling on earth is no special building or sanctuary within a building: it is the people of God themselves. We are the temple of the Lord. This important perspective is obscured when church buildings are treated as 'holy places', when furniture and other objects are regarded as sacred, and when architecture and ceremonies suggest that God is somehow more present in one part of the building than another. Paul would have us transfer ideas of reverence and sanctity to the congregation that meets there! It is a terrible travesty of New Testament teaching when church members are more concerned about bricks and mortar than they are about the life and health of the congregation. The people of God continue to be the Spirit-filled community when they disperse and go about their daily affairs, but their identity as 'the temple of the Lord' finds particular expression when they gather together in Jesus' name, to experience his presence and power in their midst.

The point of the metaphor here is that the Corinthian congregation must be wary of defiling and destroying that dwelling-place of God by divisiveness and quarrelling (*cf.* 1:10–17; 3:1–5, 18–23). 'If anyone destroys God's temple, God will destroy him; for God's temple is sacred, and you are that temple' (3:17). Believers must zealously guard the unity created by the Spirit, for 'to cause disunity in the church is to desecrate the temple of God and desecration of a holy place leads to its destruction'.[17] God's special presence amongst his people is to be acknowledged, not by ritual or ceremony, but by the preservation of the integrity and vitality of the congregation. This takes place as the members do whatever they can to strengthen and maintain its life. As we shall see, this is what Paul means by edification.

If the danger to the church is internal in 1 Corinthians 3, it is external when Paul applies the imagery of the temple again in 2 Corinthians 6:14 – 7:1. After a series of antitheses warning his readers against compromise with heathen society, he asserts:

> For we are the temple of the living God. As God has
> said: 'I will live with them and walk among them,
> and I will be their God, and they will be my people.'

> 'Therefore come out from them
>   and be separate,
>   says the Lord.
> Touch no unclean thing,
>   and I will receive you.'
> 'I will be a Father to you
>   and you will be my sons and
>   daughters,
>   says the Lord Almighty.'
>   (2 Cor. 6:16–18)

The cultic regulations of the Mosaic law, which were intended to secure the holiness of God's people by isolating them from contact with the heathen, have been abolished in Christ (*cf.* Mk. 7:14–19; Acts 10:9–15; Eph. 2:14–16). Yet the separation in belief and lifestyle which those regulations sought to achieve is still required of Christians. They are not free to engage in relationships with unbelievers that compromise their holy fellowship with the living God (2 Cor. 6:14–16).[18]

Leviticus 26:12 is combined with Ezekiel 37:27 in this passage to make the point that the new temple expectations of the Old Testament are fulfilled in the church. Even more so than the tabernacle of old, the Christian congregation is God's 'dwelling', and should therefore be 'set apart for its sacred purpose'.[19] The separation motif is continued in 2 Corinthians 6:17 with a quote from Isaiah 52:11 ('Therefore come out from them and be separate, says the Lord. Touch no unclean thing, and I will receive you'). Once again, a text which originally had a cultic meaning, being directed to the priests and Levites at the time of the Babylonian exile, finds an ethical application in the flow of Paul's argument. To this is attached the promise of God to be the Father of those who obey his call to holiness (*cf.* Ezk. 20:34, 41).

The passage concludes as it began, with a challenge to live a holy and separated life: 'Since we have these promises, dear friends, let us purify ourselves from everything that contaminates body and spirit, perfecting holiness out of reverence for God' (2 Cor. 7:1). Paul uses transformed cultic language to indicate that a sanctified lifestyle is the 'worship' appropriate to the new temple. Reverence for God is to be expressed by living differently from those around us. Paul does not mean that Christians are to withdraw from effective contact with unbelievers (*cf.* 1 Cor. 5:9–10). The challenge is to avoid any compromise with paganism (*cf.* 2 Cor. 6:16, 'idols'). Wherever we go and whatever we do, we need to remember that we belong to the community called to reflect God's character and purposes in the world and to the world.

I would conclude, then, that one of the reasons for gathering together as God's 'holy temple' is to recall his promises and to encourage one another to live out in everyday life that holiness which is his gift to us in Jesus Christ (*cf.* 1 Cor. 1:30).

A heavenly entity

The church that is described as God's temple in Ephesians 2:19–
22 is a heavenly, rather than a local, assembly. Earlier in the
chapter, the readers are numbered among those whom God has,
even now, 'raised...up with Christ and seated...with him in the
heavenly realms in Christ Jesus' (2:6; *cf.* Col. 3:1–4; Heb. 12:22–
24). Christian believers have experienced God's power and salvation 'in the heavenly realms...in Christ' (1:3) and are already
assembled with him there.[20] This gathering includes Gentiles,
who were previously excluded from citizenship in Israel and
were 'foreigners to the covenants of the promise, without hope
and without God in the world' (2:11). They have now been
brought near to God 'through the blood of Christ' (2:13) and
have been given access to the Father by the saving work of Christ
and the subsequent operation of the Holy Spirit (2:18; *cf.* Rom.
5:2). Christ is portrayed in verses 14–18 as 'the bringer of cosmic
peace, the reconciler of heaven and earth as the two parts of the
divided universe',[21] for he destroyed the barrier between Jew and
Gentile by his death and made it possible for both to be recon-
ciled to God on the same basis, 'through the cross'.

Gentile believers are now (literally) 'fellow-citizens with the
saints and members of God's household', forming a spiritual
edifice (2:19–20), which is growing into a holy temple in the
Lord (2:21). Jews and Gentiles have an equal place in this new
community, being 'built together' (*synoikodomeisthe*) into 'a dwelling-place of God in the Spirit' (2:22, RSV). The notion of growth
is not specifically linked to that of the temple in the Corinthian
texts. There the temple appears to be consecrated once and for
all by the presence of the living God (2 Cor. 6:16) or the Spirit
(1 Cor. 3:17; 6:19). The figures of the building (*oikodomē*) and the
temple (*naos*), however, are fused in Ephesians 2:19–22 and the
distinct contribution of each image to the total picture must be
carefully considered. 'Viewed as the building the church is still
under construction; viewed as the temple, however, it is an
inhabited dwelling.'[22]

Although, in 1 Corinthians 3:11, Christ alone is the foundation
of God's building activity, in Ephesians 2:20 the apostles and
prophets are the foundation and Christ is the 'cornerstone' or

'keystone'.[23] The Messiah is the one in whom the whole building is joined together and grows (2:21; *cf.* 4:16). Of course, the apostles and prophets are inseparable from the 'preached' Christ. They function as the foundation of the edifice because they are 'official bearers of the revelation of Christ'.[24] The Messiah erects this temple of 'living stones' (*cf.* 1 Pet. 2:4–5) so that God may dwell for ever in the midst of his people and manifest his glory.

What is the implication of all this for the local congregation? Every Christian gathering may be regarded as an earthly expression of the heavenly church.[25] Even now the members of the Messiah's community find the reality of God in their midst, in their holy fellowship. But this is only an anticipation of the ultimate reality, the fellowship of the heavenly city or 'the new Jerusalem', which will one day come down 'out of heaven from God' (Rev. 21:1–4). In that city the ideal of the temple is fulfilled and God's people live in his presence for ever, experiencing the blessings of 'a new heaven and a new earth' (Rev. 21:22 – 22:5). In the new creation, the Old Testament hope of the nations being united in the worship of God is realized (*cf.* Is. 56:6–7; Rev. 7). That too should be anticipated in the gathering of God's people on earth. The task of the church is to keep on looking 'up' or 'forward', rather than merely looking inward at itself or even outward at the world and its needs (*cf.* Col. 3:1–4). We ought to be able to adapt the words of the psalmist and say 'Our feet are standing in your gates, O Jerusalem' (Ps. 122:2).

The metaphor of the temple is used in Ephesians 2 primarily for doctrinal instruction, though the teaching of this passage forms an important background for the exhortations that follow in 4:1–16. There it becomes clear that the spiritual cult of the new temple consists in living a life worthy of our calling, particularly being eager to 'keep the unity of the Spirit through the bond of peace' (v. 3), 'speaking the truth in love' among the people of Christ, so that 'we will in all things grow up into him who is the Head, that is, Christ' (v. 15).

Edification and the gathering of the church

Paul regularly uses the terminology of upbuilding or edification, rather than the language of worship, to indicate the purpose and function of Christian gatherings (*e.g.* 1 Cor. 14:3, 4, 5, 12, 17, 26; 1 Thes. 5:11; Eph. 4:11–16). 'Building' terminology is closely connected with the idea of the church as the temple of God, but it can also be applied without any specifically cultic allusions to the work of God in establishing believing communities (*e.g.* 1 Cor. 3:9–10; Rom. 15:20). Indeed, the concept of the church as the body of Christ sometimes flows together with that of the house or the dwelling of God, so that the language of construction is linked to that of a living organism (*e.g.* Eph. 4:12, 16).

Founding, maintaining and advancing the church

The verb *oikodomein* is used outside the New Testament quite literally for the building of houses, temples and other structures, and figuratively for the establishment of individuals or nations in some situation or way of life.[26] In the LXX it regularly translates the Hebrew *bānâ* in contexts where either a literal or a figurative activity of building may be in view (*cf.* 2 Sa. 7:11–13, where both senses are found). Similarly in the New Testament both senses of 'building' are found in the usage of this verb. The substantive *oikodomē* is common in Koine Greek but not in earlier stages in the development of the language. It can refer to the act of building (*e.g.* 2 Cor. 10:8) or to the construction which is the result of building (*e.g.* Mt. 24:1).

In contemporary English, to say that something was 'edifying' usually means that it was personally helpful or encouraging. It is easy to misinterpret Paul and to think of edification individualistically, meaning the spiritual advancement of individuals within the church. This term, however, regularly has a corporate reference in the apostle's teaching. As with many other biblical concepts, there is a redemptive-historical framework to be understood before we can discover what the New Testament is saying. Paul's notion has its point of departure primarily in the prophetic literature of the Old Testament, where the restoration of Israel after the judgment of exile is promised in terms of God building a people for himself (*e.g.* Je. 24:6; 31:4; 33:7). To 'plant' and to 'build' go together: the opposite is to 'tear down' and 'uproot' (Je. 1:10; 24:6). God does this work by putting his words in the mouths of his prophets (Je. 1:9–10). Furthermore, he promises that if Israel's enemies learn the ways of his people and swear by his name they shall be 'built up' or 'established' among his people (Je. 12:14–17).

The influence of Jesus' teaching on early Christian thinking in this regard must also be considered. The gospels record his use of Psalm 118:22–23 as a pointed climax to his parable about the vineyard and its tenants ('The stone the builders rejected has become the capstone; the Lord has done this, and it is marvellous in our eyes'; *cf.* Mt. 21:42–44; Mk. 12:10–11; Lk. 20:17–18). Jesus implies that his own rejection by the leaders of Israel will be the means by which God establishes his eschatological purposes for Israel and the nations (*cf.* Eph. 2:19–22; 1 Pet. 2:4–8). On a different tack, Matthew 16:18 ('you are Peter, and on this rock I will build [*oikodomēsō*] my church, and the gates of Hades will not overcome it') expresses the notion that the Messiah is the one who must build or establish the renewed community of the people of God, rather than being himself 'the stone' chosen by God.[27]

From Ephesians 4:7–11 we learn that the Messiah builds his church through the people he provides as apostles, prophets, evangelists and pastor-teachers. Priority is given in this context to word ministries (*cf.* 2:20–22), which are 'to prepare God's people for works of service, so that the body of Christ may be built up' (4:12).[28] Just as Jeremiah was told that the message given to him by God would be the means of re-establishing Israel (Je. 1:9–10; 24:6), so also the church is built through the preaching of the gospel. Growth by increase in size would certainly be implied by mention of the gifts of apostles and evangelists in Ephesians 4:11. Introduction of the body metaphor, however, allows also for the idea of the development of the church as an organism from within, by means of its own God-given life (especially vv. 15–16).

From Romans 15:20 it is clear that *oikodomein* primarily refers to Paul's work of evangelism and church planting. However, the use of *oikodomē* in passages like 2 Corinthians 10:8; 12:19; 13:10, suggests that edification involves also a process of teaching and encouragement beyond the initial task of evangelism. It involves 'founding, maintaining and advancing the congregation',[29] as God's eschatological 'building'.

The church as the body of Christ

The concept of edification blends with that of the church as the body of Christ in Ephesians 4:12–16. In Paul's earlier letters the expression 'the body of Christ' is applied to a local congregation. Thus, the Corinthians are told 'you are the body of Christ, and each one of you is a part of it' (1 Cor. 12:27; cf. 10:16–17). As a congregation they are not *a* body of Christ but *the* body of Christ at Corinth. The metaphor is used here particularly to stress the relationships and responsibilities of the members of Christ to one another. Yet the same passage suggests that the concept of the body of Christ may be understood more widely to include all those baptized into Christ (12:13).[30]

As the concept is developed in Colossians 1:18, 24; 2:19; Ephesians 1:22–23; 2:16; 4:15–16, the relationship of the church to Christ as its living and exalted 'head' is explored. Although the relationship of believers to one another is kept in view, the focus is on the dependence of the body on Christ, and on his control over them. In such contexts it is clear that the reference is to all who are united to Christ by faith. Paul does not spell out the connection between this wider concept of the body of Christ and the local church. Christians are still 'the body of Christ' when they are not meeting, but their special relationship to one another and to the Lord finds practical expression when they gather together in his name.[31]

Much can be made of the body image to stress the importance of meeting together for fellowship and mutual ministry. We come to give and to receive, and thus to take our part in the edification of the church, which is the continuing work of God with his people (cf. Rom. 14:19–20). But congregational meetings should demonstrate both the truths conveyed by the body image. Christians are mutually dependent on one another and they are collectively dependent on Jesus Christ for life and power. We meet together to benefit from the relationships and ministries we can share with one another. Yet, in drawing on the resources which Christ himself provides through other believers for the growth and development of his body, we are being strengthened in our relationship with him. The important concept of interacting with one another is not to be divorced from the notion that we come together to engage with God.

According to Ephesians 4:13, the building up of the body of Christ is to take place 'until we all come to meet the unifying faith and knowledge of the Son of God, the Perfect Man, the perfection of the Messiah who is the standard of manhood'.[32] The point of this verse is not to urge us to grow individually, so that each becomes a 'perfect man', nor even to suggest that the church must grow corporately into the likeness of Christ. The ministries given by the ascended Christ to his church (4:11) are designed for the important present activities mentioned in 4:12 'until' (*mechri*) the people of God meet their Lord and share in his glory (4:13). Perfection is not an ideal to be attained but a reality to be met in Christ. Put another way, we may say that the purpose of Christian ministry, and therefore the purpose of the Christian gathering, is to prepare the saints to meet their Lord. All ministry should have this eschatological focus and perspective (*cf*. Col. 1:28–29).

The argument in Ephesians 4:14–16 leads back from the glimpse at eschatological fulfilment to the daily needs of 'the migrating church'.[33] Christians often find themselves 'tossed back and forth by the waves, and blown here and there by every wind of teaching and by the cunning and craftiness of men in their deceitful scheming' (v. 14). Only by being led away from error and established in the truth can the body be sustained and reach the goal Christ has set for it (v. 13). In this context, 'speaking the truth' (*alētheuontes*, v. 15) must mean more than speaking honestly to one another: believers are to speak or to confess orthodox doctrine, but always 'in love'.[34] The growth of the church 'toward him who is the head' takes place by confessing and practising the truth that Christ has revealed. As the church has 'received' and 'learned' Christ, so it should 'continue to live in him, rooted and built up in him, strengthened in the faith', as taught by the apostles (Col. 2:6–7; *cf*. Eph. 4:20–24). In this connection it is interesting to compare 1 Thessalonians 5:11, where the challenge to 'build each other up' means encouraging one another with the sort of teaching imparted by Paul in the preceding paragraphs (4:13 – 5:10). 'Encourage each other with these words', he says (4:18).

The final emphasis of Ephesians 4:14–16 is on the need for members of the body of Christ to be 'rightly related to one another, each making its own contribution, according to the measure of its gifts and function, to the upbuilding of the whole in love'.[35] Edification occurs when Christians minister to one another in word and deed, seeking to express and encourage a Christ-centred faith, hope and love. Pastor-teachers ought to encourage and facilitate such mutual ministry. Clearly this ought to take place when the congregation meets together, but also as individuals have the opportunity to minister to one another in everyday-life situations (cf. Rom. 14:19–21; 1 Cor. 8:1, 10; 10:23). It must be stressed again, however, that Paul's primary focus in Ephesians 4 is not on the need for individuals to grow to maturity, but for individuals to learn to contribute to the life and development of the believing community as a whole.

The expression *eis oikodomēn heautou en agapē* (lit. 'for its own upbuilding in love', Eph. 4:16) clearly affirms this corporate focus. Yet it is important to note that growth comes from Christ (*ex hou*, v. 16) to enable the whole church to grow up into Christ (*eis auton*, v. 15). The body only upbuilds itself in love because Christ is at work joining and holding it together, providing sustenance to it 'through every contact, according to the needs of each single part'.[36] In speaking thus of growth from the head towards the head, Paul goes beyond the physiological notions of his contemporaries to express novel spiritual truths. In the language of Ephesians 2:20–22, although the church has been 'built (by God) upon the foundation of the apostles and prophets', it is far from being a completed house of God. So also the use of the body image in Ephesians 4 conveys something of this eschatological tension:

> In one sense the body of Christ is already complete:
> it is a true body, not simply part of one. In another
> sense that body is said to grow to perfection, a
> process that will be completed only on the final day.
> The body metaphor reflects the 'already – not yet'

tension of the two ages. It is both complete and yet it grows. It is a heavenly entity and yet it is an earthly reality. And it is both present and future with a consummation occurring at the parousia.[37]

Ministry when the church gathers

The terminology of edification occurs more frequently in 1 Corinthians 14 than in any other chapter of the New Testament (vv. 3, 4, 5, 12, 17, 26) and is clearly significant in the development of Paul's argument there about the relative value of prophecy over against tongues. As noted in connection with the Acts of the Apostles, we cannot simply assume that what the early Christians did when they met together is automatically prescriptive for later generations of believers. A number of important theological principles emerge in 1 Corinthians 14, however, that have ongoing relevance.

Although the apostle's main point is to encourage the readers to minister effectively to one another as the body of Christ, his concern is that even the unbelieving stranger should be able to understand what is said, be convinced by it and be converted (vv. 22–25). There is no warrant from this text for saying that every Christian meeting should be designed fundamentally to appeal to unbelievers.[38] On the other hand, as the church is edified intensively – being strengthened, consolidated, and preserved as the community of God's people – it may also be edified extensively – being enlarged by the conversion of those who may be visiting or invited by Christian friends.

The gathering in 1 Corinthians 14 is nothing less than 'the whole church', coming together 'at the same place' (v. 23, *epi to auto*). The first issue in the chapter is intelligibility. Being 'inspired' is not enough: when Christians gather together words should convey meaningful truth. The one who speaks in a tongue 'speaks not to men but to God; for no one understands him, but he utters mysteries in the Spirit' (v. 2, RSV). On the other hand, he who prophesies speaks to people 'for their upbuilding and encouragement and consolation' (vv. 2–3, RSV). Only speech that can be understood by others has the potential for building up or edifying the congregation. Consequently, the apostle urges the person who speaks in a tongue to 'pray that he may interpret what he says' (v. 13). If there is no-one to interpret, the tongues-speaker should 'keep quiet in the church and speak to himself and God' (v. 28). Paul may not be saying that prophecy is the greatest of the gifts on some absolute scale, but only that it is more important than tongues on the scale of reference adopted.[39]

The tongues-speaker 'edifies himself' (v. 4), but the person who prophesies 'edifies the church'. Paul does not rebuke the tongues-speaker for self-edification as such, but indicates that this falls short of the primary goal of Christian assembly (cf. vv. 16–17).[40] Individuals intent on edifying themselves may 'seal themselves off from others and concentrate exclusively on their personal experiences'.[41] Paul's principle here challenges the common assumption that church services should simply be designed to facilitate a private communion with God, either by spiritual exercises or ritual. He envisages that believers will come together for the benefit of one another, drawing on the resources of Christ for spiritual growth by the giving and receiving of Spirit-inspired ministries.

To pursue what is beneficial for the church is to fulfil the opening injunction of 1 Corinthians 14 ('Make love your aim', RSV) and to apply the teaching of the previous chapter. In effect, the argument here, as in Ephesians 4, is that speaking the truth in love is the means by which edification takes place. This emphasis is continued in verses 6–19, where the focus is on bringing to the congregation 'some revelation or knowledge or prophecy or teaching' (v. 6, RSV). Public praying and singing must also be intelligible and consistent with apostolic teaching, so that others may be able to say the 'Amen' and be edified (vv. 16–17). Even though contributions may be rightly motivated they may not be beneficial to others. Certain subjective expressions of faith can even be a source of embarrassment in a public context. Here is an important criterion for assessing the helpfulness of testimonies, hymns, choruses, and various other elements that might go to make up a congregational meeting today.

It is interesting to note that Paul speaks again of the individual being edified in verse 17. Although he is concerned that the Corinthians should abound in spiritual gifts 'for the building up of the church' (v. 12, lit.), it is clear that such edification cannot take place unless individuals are instructed (v. 19) and encouraged (v. 31). Those who lead church services will rightly desire that each person present be moved to faith and repentance by what is said and done. The quality of an individual Christian's engagement with God will then be reflected in his or her concern to enhance the life of the church as a community.

The very act of ministering the truth to one another should be an exercise of love: only when a church is functioning in this way can it be said that it is being edified. For this reason, Paul concentrates in verses 26–40 on the manner in which gifts are to be exercised in the congregation. This section begins with the challenge 'let all things be done for edification' (v. 26, RSV) and concludes with the injunction 'let all things be done decently and in order' (v. 40, RSV). Order and not disorder will be a sign of the Spirit's presence and control, since 'God is not a God of disorder but of peace' (v. 33).

This does not mean that a predictable and rigidly controlled order of service will necessarily be more honouring to God. Paul simply means that one person may speak at a time and only a certain number may reasonably contribute on each occasion. Encouraging others to exercise their gifts is an aspect of edification. Indeed, the majority, including those wishing to contribute, should listen in silence and 'weigh what is said' (v. 29, RSV). Listening with discernment is also part of the task of edifying the congregation, even though it appears to be such a passive role! God is not honoured by a free-for-all, in which people seek to contribute at any cost, regardless of the effect on others. The aim of these and other controls is 'that all may learn and all be encouraged' (v. 31, RSV).

Concluding remarks on edification

The apostle regularly, but not exclusively, employs the terminology of edification to oppose individualism, either in the ethical sphere or in the sphere of congregational ministry. Edification is first and foremost the work of Christ, 'fashioning the whole life of the Church in its members in faith, hope and love'.[42] As Christians utilize Christ's gifts, made available through the Spirit, they participate in this divine activity and further God's purpose for his people collectively. Although the edification of the church is a principle that should govern the thinking and behaviour of Christians in all circumstances, Paul normally employs this notion with reference to the activities of Christian assembly. When Christians gather together to minister to one another the truth of God in love, the church is manifested, maintained and advanced in God's way.

The apostle's teaching calls into question the validity and helpfulness of much contemporary thinking and practice in relation to church services. Mention has been made of the inappropriateness of designing our gatherings primarily to facilitate private communion with God. This can happen in Catholic, evangelical and charismatic traditions alike. Paul would urge us to meet in dependency on one another as the vehicles of God's grace and to view the well-being and strengthening of the whole church as the primary aim of the gathering. There ought to be a real engagement with other believers in the context of mutual ministry, shared prayer and praise, not simply a friendly chat over a cup of coffee after church!

Again, 1 Corinthians 14 challenges the tendency of many Christian traditions to undervalue spontaneity and variety of input in the congregational gathering. Paul expected that members of the congregation would come with some contribution prepared for the occasion or that individuals might be prompted by the Spirit to offer prayer or praise or some other ministry on the spot. Ephesians 4 certainly indicates the importance of pastor-teachers in the equipment of God's people for their work of building up the body of Christ, and the pastoral epistles highlight the teaching role of those identified as leaders in the congregation. However, as noted previously, there should be some public opportunity for spontaneous and informal ministries as well as for the ordered and prepared.

It is sometimes said that the size of our gatherings or the physical context makes it impossible to put such New Testament teaching into practice. People who argue this way show little imagination or willingness to reassess their traditions, even though others in the contemporary scene have found helpful solutions to these problems. It may be a matter of finding appropriate spots in the regular pattern of Sunday services where contributions can be made. It may be a matter of re-arranging the furniture or encouraging people to gather together differently so that those who contribute can be more easily seen and heard.

Of course, it is equally possible to lose the vertical dimension and consider the congregational meeting as little more than an occasion for human fellowship. The balance of Paul's teaching suggests that we view mutual ministry as the context in which to engage with God. Edification and worship are different sides of the same coin.

The Lord's Supper at Corinth

Although the terminology of edification is not used in Paul's discussion of 'the Lord's Supper' at Corinth, the issue of edifying the church is undoubtedly prominent. Much discussion has taken place about the relationship between the gathering in 1 Corinthians 11 'to eat' (*eis to phagein*, v. 33) and the gathering in 1 Corinthians 14 for the exercise of gifts and ministries. It is true that 'nothing in 11:17–34 envisages anything apart from a meal, and nothing in chap. 14 envisages a communal or sacramental eating'.[43] Paul moves quite naturally, however, from discussing public praying and prophesying by women in 11:2–16, to the abuses associated with the Lord's Supper (11:17–34, 'when you come together as a church', 11:18), and then again to the proper exercise of gifts and ministries in 1 Corinthians 12 – 14 ('when the whole church gathers', 14:23, lit.). There is no compelling reason to deny that Paul is speaking progressively about different parts or aspects of the same meetings in these chapters.

The first reference to their communal meal is in the context of urging the Corinthians not to attend pagan feasts (1 Cor. 10:14–22). The unique relationship shared by Christians with their Lord, and expressed by eating together in his name, makes any association with demon-worshippers at idolatrous feasts an impossibility. Those who participate in pagan sacrifices are 'partners with demons' (*koinōnoi tōn daimoniōn*, 1 Cor. 10:20, RSV). By implication, those who 'drink the cup of the Lord' and 'partake of the table of the Lord' (10:21) are partners with Christ and express their fellowship with him in the common meal.[44]

The third cup at the Passover, for which God was 'blessed' or 'thanked', was called 'the cup of blessing'.[45] It was this cup that Jesus interpreted as 'the new covenant in my blood' at the conclusion of the Last Supper (*cf.* 1 Cor. 11:25). When Paul mentions 'the cup of blessing which we bless' (1 Cor. 10:16, RSV), he implies that this technical Jewish expression was used by the Corinthian Christians in connection with their fellowship meals, suggesting a formal link with the Last Supper. With a form of thanksgiving for the work of Jesus, their drinking together was a means of demonstrating a 'common participation' (*koinōnia*) in 'the blood of Christ' – namely 'in the benefits of Christ's passion'.[46] The idea of sharing in the benefits of the covenant established by Christ in his death meant that they did not consider their table to be an altar where sacrifice was taking place, but 'a fellowship meal where in the presence of the Spirit they were by faith looking back to the singular sacrifice that had been made and were thus realizing again its benefits in their lives'.[47]

'The bread that we break' (1 Cor. 10:16) also recalls the language of the Jewish meal (*cf.* Acts 2:46; 20:7, 11; 27:35). Eating together, with a focus on Christ's death and its implications for congregational life, is a means of expressing 'a common participation in the body of Christ'. To eat the 'one loaf' (10:17) is to share with others in 'that company which, through its union with Christ, has by anticipation entered upon the new age which lies beyond the resurrection'.[48] A Christian congregation is not an ordinary association like a club, where people simply meet because of common interests or ideals: it is a gathering that arises out of sharing together in the benefits of Christ's saving work. If the exercise of gifts and ministries was associated with such common meals, that would further express what it meant to be the Messiah's community.

Mention of the cup before the bread in 1 Corinthians 10:16 is unusual. Paul's purpose is probably to put the focus on the vertical dimension first (the relationship of believers with their Lord), before turning to the implications for relationships amongst believers. His encouragement to the Corinthians to recognize their unity in the body of Christ as they ate from one loaf (1 Cor. 10:17) prepares for the extended argument of 11:17–34 about divisions in their meetings. These divisions appear to have had a social dimension – the 'haves' devouring their own supper at the meal and failing to share with the 'have nots' (11:21)[49] – as well as a theological dimension – not treating one another as fellow members of Christ. By humiliating those who had nothing, those with plenty to eat and drink were 'despising the church of God' (11:22, lit.).

Their behaviour indicated to the apostle that their gathering together as the church was for the worse rather than the better, and that it was not, in fact, 'the Lord's Supper' that they were eating (11:20)! The noun *deipnon* ('supper') was used in the Hellenistic world for the main meal of the day, usually eaten toward evening or at night. The adjective *kyriakon* ordinarily meant 'belonging to the Lord' but may have been understood in this context to mean 'in honour of the Lord'.[50] As long as individuals were preoccupied with consuming their own private meals (*to idion deipnon*, 11:21) when the church gathered, they could not possibly be holding a meal in honour of the Lord Jesus.

Their coming together 'to eat' (11:33) was for the purpose of sharing a real meal and not for a token or symbolic feast. However, the technical expressions 'the cup of blessing which we bless' and 'the bread that we break' (10:16), in association with Paul's reminder about the tradition concerning the Last Supper (11:23–25), imply that their common meals were to have a special character. In Jewish fashion, they presumably began their supper with a thanksgiving in connection with the breaking of bread and concluded with a thanksgiving over the shared cup.[51] Jesus' teaching and example at the Last Supper should have transformed these Jewish customs for them into expressions of new covenant theology. In reality, the tradition about the Last Supper was not being observed (11:23; *cf.* v. 2), because they were not reflecting the true meaning of that meal in their life together. There is no ground for saying that some kind of sacramental meal was held separately from their regular 'dinner in honour of the Lord'.

In 11:26 Paul asserts that eating the bread and drinking the cup is a means of proclaiming the Lord's death until he comes.

Christ's sacrifice had made it possible for them to share together in the life of the age to come. By their disregard for one another they were negating the very point of that death – 'to create a new people for his name, in which the old distinctions based on human fallenness no longer obtain'.[52] The paragraph that follows (11:27–32) warns them of the dire consequences of continuing to eat and drink 'without discerning the body' (11:29, RSV), that is, without recognizing the significance of their partnership in the body of Christ. The Corinthians were to receive or welcome one another as fellow believers at 'the Lord's table' and to satisfy their personal needs at home if necessary (vv. 33–34).[53]

The Lord's Supper, which has so often throughout church history been understood as a means of deepening the personal communion of believers with their Lord, is clearly meant to focus the eyes of the participants on one another as well as on God. We do not simply meet to have fellowship with God but to minister to one another as we express our common participation in Christ as our Saviour and Lord. Any distinction between 'love feast' and 'Eucharist', or 'fellowship meal' and 'Holy Communion', is artificial from a New Testament point of view.

Readers should consider again some of the comments made in chapter five about the fellowship meals in the Acts of the Apostles. The church supper described in 1 Corinthians may have been more formal and structured than the daily experiences of table-fellowship mentioned in Acts. But Paul is concerned that the same sort of commitment to one another as the body of Christ should be expressed. It is the 'horizontal' significance of the Lord's Supper that is so often played down in contemporary practice. Many churches need to reassess the way in which they celebrate the Supper, to recover something of this essential dimension. According to Paul, those who disregard their responsibility to welcome and care for fellow believers in this context cannot be worshipping or serving God acceptably!

Conclusion: Worship in church and in the world

Paul's application of transformed worship terminology to the work of Christ, the preaching of the gospel, and the new life-orientation of believers, testifies to the understanding of a new kind of worship.

> The New Testament knows no holy persons who
> substitutionally perform the service of God for the
> whole people of God, nor holy places and seasons or
> holy acts, which create a distance between the cultus
> and the life of every day and every place. All
> members of the church have access to God (Rom.
> 5:2) and a share in the Holy Spirit; all of life is
> service to God; there is no 'profane' area.[54]

This revolutionary use of the terminology of worship with reference to a Christ-centred, gospel-serving, life-orientation is obscured by the common practice of restricting any talk of worship to what is done in church. Furthermore, people who emphasize that they are 'going to church to worship God' tend to disregard what the New Testament says about the purpose of the Christian assembly. If Christians are meant to worship God in every sphere of life, it cannot be worship as such that brings them to church. 'Corporate worship' may express more accurately what is involved, but Paul's emphasis is on coming together to participate in the edification of the church.[55]

To put the focus on edification is not to suggest that the church service is the one area of the Christian life where we do not worship God! The evidence assessed so far suggests that the exercise of gifts in any context may be regarded as an expression of worship, if the ministries are genuinely for the benefit of others and for the glory of God.[56] While all ministry must be understood as a response to God's grace, and not in any sense a cultivation of his favour, ministry to others is an aspect of our service or self-giving to God. Moreover, edification is really God's work in our midst.

At the heart of Christian gatherings there should be a concern to proclaim and apply the truths of the gospel, to keep the focus on God's gracious initiative, to stimulate and maintain saving faith and to elicit appropriate expressions of that faith in the assembly and in everyday life. Prayer and praise are clearly worship when they are faith responses to the gospel. Even prayer and praise, however, must be conducted in church in a way that will edify the congregation. They cannot be purely private, God-directed activities when others are present.

It may be best to speak of congregational worship as a particular expression of the total life-response that is the worship of the new covenant. Inasmuch as we meet to encounter Christ in one another, for the giving and receiving of ministries and for response to such ministries, we meet to worship or engage with God. 'However much the "liturgy" must be seen as a spiritual worship of God embracing the whole of life (Rom. 12:1, 2), this does not alter the fact that the indwelling in and communion of Christ with the church have their point of concentration and special realization in its unity as assembled congregation.'[57]

Church meetings should not be regarded simply as a means to an end – a preparation for worship and witness in everyday life – but as 'the focus-point of that whole wider worship which is the continually repeated self-surrender of the Christian in obedience of life'.[58] The church is at the centre of God's redemptive purposes for the universe (cf. Eph. 3:10–11), the earthly and temporal anticipation of the fellowship of the new creation, where God will be served without compromise or hindrance (Rev. 7:15; 22:3). Ministry exercised in love amongst the people of God is a sign of the Spirit's transforming power already at work in those who believe. Ministry exercised for the building up of the body of Christ is a significant way of worshipping and glorifying God.

Those who regularly measure the value of what takes place in church in terms of its impact on their own spiritual growth and development need to recover Paul's perspective. Nevertheless, if the focus of the meeting is on the edification of the church, this should enable God's people individually to engage with him afresh and to offer themselves to him in the way that he requires and himself makes possible through the Holy Spirit. Thus, the 'vertical' and the 'horizontal' dimensions of what takes place should not be artificially separated. One part of the meeting cannot be 'the worship time' (*e.g.* prayer and praise) and another part 'the edification time' (*e.g.* preaching), since Paul's teaching encourages us to view the same activities from both points of view.

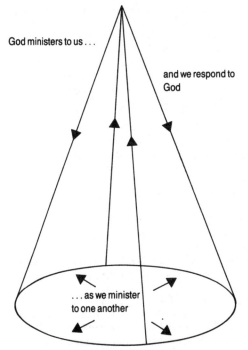

God ministers to us . . .

and we respond to God

. . . as we minister to one another

When the church gathers

The God-directed ministry of prayer or praise and the notion of edification are intimately linked in the New Testament (*e.g.* Col. 3:16; Eph. 5:19). Even 'psalms and hymns and spiritual songs' (RSV), which are expressions of faith and thankfulness to God, are to be considered simultaneously as the means of teaching and admonishing one another. This does not mean that prayer or praise is a means to an end, namely edification. We worship God because of who he is and because of his grace towards us. Participating in the edification of the church, however, is an important expression of our devotion and service to God.

Notes

[1] This could be concluded from the statement of E. Käsemann ('Worship and Everyday Life', p. 191) that 'Sacred times and places are superseded by the eschatological public activity of those who at all times and in all places stand "before the face of Christ" and from this position before God make the everyday round of so-called secular life into the arena of the unlimited and unceasing glorification of the divine will. At this point the doctrines of worship and Christian "ethics" converge.'

[2] Bending the knee to God is a figure for prayer in Eph. 3:14 (*cf.* Acts 7:60; 9:40; 20:36), but *proskynein* is never used in the New Testament with specific reference to prayer. H. Greeven (*TDNT* 6. 765) goes beyond the evidence when he suggests that 'proskynesis demands visible majesty before which the worshipper bows'.

[3] *Cf.* W. A. Grudem, *The Gift of Prophecy in 1 Corinthians* (Lanham/New York/London: University Press of America, 1982), pp. 43–54. Note the critique of Grudem's argument by D. A. Carson, *Showing the Spirit: A Theological Exposition of 1 Corinthians 12 - 14* (Grand Rapids: Baker; Homebush West: Lancer, 1988), pp. 91–100, 160–165.

[4] W. A. Grudem, *The Gift of Prophecy*, pp. 54–73. Grudem argues that the sort of revelation given to these 'prophets' only gives 'a kind of divine authority of general content'. M. M. B. Turner ('Spiritual Gifts Then and Now', pp. 15–16) sees rather 'a spectrum of authority of charisma' in the NT, 'extending from apostolic speech and prophecy (backed by apostolic commission) at one extreme, to vague and barely profitable attempts at oracular speech such as brought "prophecy" as a whole into question at Thessalonika (1 Thes. 5:19f) at the other'.

[5] W. A. Grudem, *The Gift of Prophecy*, pp. 184–185. D. Hill, 'Christian Prophets as Teachers or Instructors in the Church', in J. Panagopoulos (ed.), *Prophetic Vocation in the New Testament and Today* (Leiden: Brill, 1977), pp. 122–123, 127–128, does not distinguish prophecy from teaching as sharply as Grudem and Turner do.

[6] Something of the synagogue pattern may be reflected in the injunction to Timothy to attend to the public reading of Scripture, to preaching (*tē paraklēsei*) and to teaching (*tē didaskalia*, 1 Tim. 4:13) and in the guidelines for public prayer in 1 Tim. 2:1–8.

[7] The lengthy clause in Col. 3:16 beginning with the words *en pasē sophia didaskontes kai nouthetountes heautous* gives a definition of the way in which they are to let the word of Christ dwell richly in their midst (so NIV, 'as you teach and admonish one another with all wisdom...', against RSV). *Ho logos tou Christou* is probably 'the message that centres on Christ', though it is possible to read the genitive to mean that it is the word spoken by Christ. *En hymin* is best taken in the context as a reference to Christ's presence amongst his people as they minister to one another. *Cf.* P. T. O'Brien, *Colossians, Philemon*, WBC 44 (Waco: Word, 1982), pp. 206–210.

[8] I have explored different aspects of New Testament teaching about the ministry of *paraklēsis* in P. T. O'Brien and D. G. Peterson (eds.), *God who is Rich in Mercy* (Homebush West: Lancer; Grand Rapids: Baker, 1986), pp. 235–253.

Note also what was said in the last two chapters about the significance of preaching Christ.

9 J. D. Crichton, 'A Theology of Worship', in C. Jones, G. Wainwright and E. Yarnold (eds.), *The Study of Liturgy* (London: SPCK, 1978), p. 10.

10 *Cf.* D. G. Peterson, 'Prayer in the Writings of Paul', in D. A. Carson (ed.), *Teach us to Pray: Prayer in the Bible and in the Church* (Grand Rapids: Baker; Exeter: Paternoster, 1990), pp. 84–101.

11 G. P. Wiles, *Paul's Intercessory Prayers*, p. 167.

12 *Cf.* P. T. O'Brien, 'Thanksgiving and the Gospel in Paul', *NTS* 21, 1974–75, p. 150.

13 Translation of C. K. Barrett (*A Commentary on the First Epistle to the Corinthians, BNTC*, London: Black, ²1971, p. 86), based on the observation that in Plato (*Statesman* 259E, 260A) an *architektōn* contributes knowledge, not manual labour, but also assigns their task to individual workmen.

14 The implication of 'Do you not know...' (1 Cor. 3:16) may be that such teaching was already familiar to the Corinthians.

15 R. J. McKelvey (*The New Temple*, p. 104) rightly notes that Paul differs from the teaching of Philo and the Stoics in this respect by making the Christian community, not the individual his starting point, by his focus on the human body as the sphere of God's indwelling, and by introducing the note of redemption (6:19–20), indicating that God's indwelling is the result of his gracious, saving work in Jesus Christ. *Cf.* his discussion of the Jewish background of Paul's teaching (pp. 120–123) and R. Corriveau, *The Liturgy of Life*, pp. 64–72.

16 In the LXX, but not necessarily in Greek usage more generally, *naos* refers to the sanctuary as the place where God dwells, whereas *hieron* refers to the whole temple complex (including the sanctuary). *Cf.* O. Michel *TDNT* 4. 880–890.

17 R. J. McKelvey, *The New Temple*, p. 101. *Cf.* R. Y. K. Fung, 'Some Pauline Pictures of the Church', *EQ* 53, 1981, p. 101, and G. D. Fee, *The First Epistle to the Corinthians*, pp. 147–150.

18 Critical issues, such as the origin of this passage and its relation to the surrounding context in 2 Corinthians, are helpfully analysed by V. P. Furnish, *II Corinthians*, AB 32A (Garden City, NY: Doubleday, 1984), pp. 367–383. The warning against being 'yoked together with unbelievers' cannot refer to involvement with Paul's opponents. Against Furnish, there is some support in the immediate context for the view that Paul is warning against involvement in pagan idolatries (vv. 15–16). *Cf.* C. K. Barrett, *The Second Epistle to the Corinthians, BNTC* (London: Black, 1973; San Francisco: Harper, 1974), pp. 195–199.

19 R. J. McKelvey, *The New Temple*, p. 94. He observes that the addition of the words *enoikēsō en autois* ('I will live in/among them') means that 'God no longer dwells *with* his people in a sanctuary which they make for him; he dwells *in* them, and *they* are his temple' (p. 95).

20 *Cf.* M. Barth, *Ephesians 1 – 3*, AB 34 (Garden City, NY: Doubleday, 1974), p. 238. His extended note on this verse is very helpful (pp. 236–238). The Pauline origin of Ephesians is well argued by Barth (pp. 36–50) and will be assumed in my discussion of the letter.

21 A. T. Lincoln, *Paradise Now and Not Yet*, SNTSMS 43 (Cambridge, London,

New York and Melbourne: Cambridge University Press, 1981), p. 150. He goes on to argue that *sympolitai tōn hagiōn* means 'fellow-citizens of the angels' (rather than fellow-citizens with Jewish Christians). If this is correct, the notion of the church as a heavenly assembly is further strengthened.

22 R. J. McKelvey, *The New Temple*, p. 117. Contrast R. Corriveau, *The Liturgy of Life*, p. 189. In reality he takes this to be a way of describing the growth which is that of the Christian life, reading Eph. 4:15–16 in individualistic terms.

23 The debate continues about the meaning of *akrogōniaios*. R. J. McKelvey (*The New Temple*, pp. 195–204) and W. A. Grudem (*The Gift of Prophecy*, pp. 85–87) defend the view that Christ is the cornerstone, meaning the primary stone of the foundation. J. Jeremias (*TDNT* 1. 792; 4. 275) and A. T. Lincoln (*Paradise Now and Not Yet*, pp. 152–154) are proponents of the view that Christ is the top or final stone which holds together the building. The latter view is certainly appropriate to the emphasis of Ephesians on the role of the exalted Christ in relation to the church (*cf.* 1:22–23; 4:7–16).

24 R. Corriveau, *The Liturgy of Life*, p. 188, taking the prophets as another way of referring to the apostles. W. A. Grudem (*The Gift of Prophecy*, pp. 93–101) also argues that the reference is to 'the apostles who are also prophets'. Against this view see F. F. Bruce, *The Epistles to the Colossians, to Philemon and to the Ephesians*, *NICNT* (Grand Rapids: Eerdmans, 1984), pp. 304, 315 n. 29.

25 *Cf.* P. T. O'Brien, 'The Church as a Heavenly and Eschatological Entity', in D. A. Carson (ed.), *The Church in the Bible and the World* (Exeter: Paternoster, 1987), p. 116. He rightly argues that the New Testament rules out the view of the local church as simply a 'part' of some universal or heavenly reality. *Cf.* also R. J. Banks, *Paul's Idea of Community*, pp. 51–60.

26 *Cf.* P. Vielhauer, *Oikodomē. Aufsätze zum Neuen Testament* Band 2, Theologische Büchere, Neues Testament Band 35 (Munich: Kaiser Verlag, 1979), pp. 4–52, and O. Michel, *TDNT* 5. 137–138.

27 On the authenticity of this text and its meaning in the context of Matthew's Gospel *cf.* D. A. Carson, 'Matthew', pp. 366–370.

28 M. Barth, *Ephesians 4 – 6*, p. 439, notes that the noun *katartismos* ('preparation'), which occurs only here in the NT, describes 'the dynamic act by which persons and things are properly conditioned'. Pastor-teachers in particular have the task of preparing God's people for their work of service (on the punctuation and structure of this verse *cf.* his Comment VI, pp. 477–484).

29 P. Vielhauer, *Oikodomē*, p. 72. *Cf.* H. Ridderbos, *Paul: An Outline of his Theology* (ET, Grand Rapids: Eerdmans, 1975), pp. 429–438, where the point is similarly made that edification involves both the increase and the consolidation of the church.

30 Many commentators consider that when Paul wrote to the Christians in Rome they were scattered throughout that city in various house churches, rather than being members of a single congregation (*cf.* Rom. 16:3–16). Consequently, the body metaphor in Rom. 12:4–5 might have reference to relationships and ministries within and between diverse groups of Christians in the one city.

31 Perhaps there is a parallel here with the notion of the church as a temple: the body of Christ is a heavenly reality, with particular local manifestations. *Cf.*

P. T. O'Brien, 'The Church as a Heavenly and Eschatological Entity', pp. 106–107, 112.

[32] Translation of M. Barth, *Ephesians 4 - 6*, pp. 440–441. He argues that one goal is described by three parallel expressions beginning with *eis*. The verb *katantaō* implies movement towards an object (*cf.* 1 Cor. 14:36) and may suggest in this context a 'solemn meeting' with Christ at his second coming, when the church will be conformed to his glory (*cf.* Eph. 5:27; Phil. 3:20–21; Rom. 8:29–30; Col. 3:4). *Cf.* his Comment VII.

[33] M. Barth, *Ephesians 4 - 6*, p. 441. He rightly observes that vv. 14–16 form the second half of a long sentence running from v. 11. The dependent clause in v. 13 describes the goal towards which the church is moving and the second dependent clause in vv. 14–16 puts the focus back on present responsibilities.

[34] M. Barth (*Ephesians 4 - 6*, p. 444) rightly observes: 'the passage calls for the right confession and it urges the whole church and all its members to be a confessing church'. Nevertheless, Eph. 4:19, with its emphasis on the right choice of language suggests that everyday conversation amongst believers can also be the means of building up one another in Christ.

[35] R. Y. K. Fung, 'Some Pauline Pictures of the Church', pp. 95–96. *Cf.* H. Ridderbos, *Paul*, pp. 432–438.

[36] This translation by M. Barth is justified by his detailed analysis of the key words in this text and their relationship to each other (*Ephesians 4 - 6*, pp. 447–450).

[37] P. T. O'Brien, 'The Church as a Heavenly and Eschatological Entity', p. 111.

[38] W. Richardson ('Liturgical Order and Glossalalia in 1 Corinthians 14. 26c–33a', *NTS* 32, 1986, p. 147) overstates his case when he argues that 'Paul's over-riding concern in chapter 14 is that of missionary witness'. So also E. Schweizer, *Church Order in the New Testament*, p. 226.

[39] *Cf.* D. A. Carson, *Showing the Spirit*, pp. 100–101.

[40] So W. Richardson, 'Liturgical Order and Glossalalia', p. 147. *Contra* E. Schweizer ('The Service of Worship', *Interpretation* 13, 1959, p. 404), who overstates his case by arguing that 'Paul never speaks of edifying oneself; he always means edifying the congregation.'

[41] R. P. Martin, *The Spirit and the Congregation* (Eerdmans: Grand Rapids, 1984), p. 70. Martin incorrectly concludes that Paul's concession here opposes any concentration on personal experiences. It is the chapter as a whole that leads to Martin's conclusion.

[42] G. Delling, *Worship in the New Testament* (ET, London: Darton, Longman and Todd, 1962), p. 40.

[43] J. D. G. Dunn, 'The Responsible Congregation (1 Cor. 14:26–40)', in P. Benoit *et al* (eds.), *Charisma und Agape (1 Kor 12-14)* (Rome: St Paul vor den Mauern, 1983), p. 213. Dunn rightly challenges Cullmann's view that in the New Testament the Lord's Supper was 'the basis and goal of every gathering'. *Cf.* O. Cullmann, *Early Christian Worship*, SBT 10 (ET, London: SCM, 1953), p. 29.

[44] At the Supper, 'the participants have fellowship with God as their host because it is his table and he provides the spiritual blessings (*cf.* 1 Cor. 10:4). But this communion with God is not the same thing as participation in the

body and blood of Jesus, and it is not achieved through eating bread and drinking wine in the sense that we somehow partake of Christ or God in so doing' (I. H. Marshall, *Last Supper and Lord's Supper*, Exeter: Paternoster, 1980, p. 123).

[45] J. Jeremias, *Eucharistic Words*, pp. 86–88. H. W. Beyer (*TDNT* 2. 760) gives some evidence for the more general use of the expression 'the cup of blessing' with reference to the final cup at any Jewish meal.

[46] C. K. Barrett, *First Corinthians*, p. 232. He suggests that *koinōnia* must be translated 'common participation' to bring out its true meaning.

[47] G. D. Fee, *First Corinthians*, p. 468.

[48] C. K. Barrett, *First Corinthians*, p. 233. It is possible that Paul intended a double reference to the crucified body of Christ and the body of his people, without confusing those entities. *Cf.* J. A. T. Robinson, *The Body: A Study in Pauline Theology*, SBT 5 (London: SCM, 1952; Philadelphia: Westminster, 1977), p. 478.

[49] *Cf.* B. W. Winter, 'The Lord's Supper at Corinth: An Alternative Reconstruction', *RTR* 37, 1978, pp. 73–82, for the argument that the division was not so much between rich and poor as between 'the secure' (those guaranteed security, and thus food, by reason of membership of a household) and 'the insecure' (those who had no protection from a patron) in the social structure of Roman Corinth. For further discussion of various sociological factors that have been suggested *cf.* G. D. Fee, *First Corinthians*, pp. 533–534, 540–541 (and references).

[50] *Cf.* G. D. Fee, *First Corinthians*, pp. 539–540. The holding of a *deipnon* in honour of a god was common in the Greco-Roman world (*cf.* J. Behm, *TDNT* 12. 34–35).

[51] J. Jeremias (*Eucharistic Words*, pp. 49–50) points out that, at the Passover, the blessing and distribution of the bread came during the meal (*cf.* Mk. 14:18–22; Lk. 22:17–19), after the liturgy expressing the meaning of the ritual. Against the common assumption that there was an ordinary meal at Corinth and then the formal 'Lord's Supper', *cf.* G. Theissen, *The Social Setting of Pauline Christianity: Essays on Corinth* (ET, Philadelphia: Fortress, 1982), pp. 152–153.

[52] G. D. Fee, *First Corinthians*, p. 557. *Cf.* his helpful discussion of what Paul means by 'not recognizing the body' (pp. 562–564).

[53] The verb *ekdechomai* in 11:33 carries its primary meaning of 'receive' here, which it often does in the context of hospitality (hence, 'welcome' or 'entertain'). NIV 'wait for each other' would normally be conveyed by *apekdechomai*. *Cf.* G. D. Fee, *First Corinthians*, pp. 567–568 and B. W. Winter, 'The Lord's Supper', pp. 79–80.

[54] H. Ridderbos, *Paul*, p. 481.

[55] R. J. Banks (*Paul's Idea of Community*, p. 92) overstates the case when he says that it cannot be worship as such but edification that 'marks off their coming together from everything else that they are doing'. This ignores the fact that edification also takes place outside the assembly and that, from one point of view, the purpose of the assembly is also worship.

[56] I. H. Marshall ('How far did the early Christians worship God?', *Churchman* 99 (1985), pp. 226–229) does not take adequate account of this, restricting the notion of worship to response, in order to avoid any suggestion that we can benefit God by what we do in church.

[57] H. Ridderbos, *Paul*, p. 486.
[58] C. E. B. Cranfield, *Romans* II, p. 602. Against Käsemann, he insists on talking about 'a Christian cultic worship', without explaining or justifying the use of such terminology. Whether it is valid or helpful to describe the activities of Christian assembly as 'cultic', in view of Paul's radical transformation of cultic concepts, must be argued, not assumed.

CHAPTER EIGHT

The book of Hebrews and the worship of Jesus

In the whole New Testament there is but one cult,
one priesthood, namely that rendered by Jesus Christ
himself to his church, which flows over from it to the
world.[1]

Hebrews presents the most complete and fully integrated theology of worship in the New Testament. All the important categories of Old Testament thinking on this subject – sanctuary, sacrifice, altar, priesthood and covenant – are taken up and related to the person and work of Jesus Christ. More than any other New Testament document, Hebrews makes it clear that the inauguration of the new covenant by Jesus means the fulfilment and replacement of the whole pattern of approach to God established under the Mosaic covenant. The writer proclaims the end of that earthly cult, by expounding Christ's work as the ultimate, heavenly cult.

The idea that Jesus' life was the expression of perfect worship, culminating in his sacrificial death for others, has already been noted in the gospels and the writings of Paul. More fully than in any of these other sources, the ministry of Christ – past, present and future – is portrayed in Hebrews as the only basis on which we can relate to God and offer him acceptable worship. What others mention briefly, Hebrews makes central to its message.

Cultic imagery is used to stress the immediate benefits available to those who draw near to God through Jesus Christ and to indicate the response we should make to the gospel in our everyday lives. Paradoxically, however, Christians are liberated from cultic obligations in any earthly sense, to serve God in a new way. As Hebrews interprets the work of Christ and the response of believers, it develops a theology of the congregational gathering that has much in common with the teaching of Paul.

The definitive worship of Jesus

A first hint of the writer's cultic viewpoint is presented in 1:3, where it is briefly mentioned that the Son of God 'made purification for sins' (RSV). This expression portrays humanity's fundamental problem as defilement due to sin, recalling the perspective of Leviticus. Jesus has provided the purification necessary to enable those corrupted and stained by sin to draw near to God in his awesome holiness. However, the high-priestly dimension of Christ's work is not made explicit until we are told that he had to become 'a merciful and faithful high priest in service to God', so that he might 'make atonement for the sins of the people' (*eis to hilaskesthai tas hamartias tou laou*, 2:17).

Jesus as high priest

The role of the high priest on the Day of Atonement was to deal with the problem of sin by means of the appropriate rites and thereby to remove from the Israelite community what provoked God's anger (*cf.* Lv. 16). This annual ministry, which was a central feature of the Old Testament cult, is one of several inspirations for our writer's portrait of the priesthood of Christ (*e.g.* Heb. 9:11–12, 23–28; 10:1–10). In Hebrews it is clear that the blood or death of Jesus is what actually removes sin and makes it possible for sinners to draw near to God (*e.g.* 9:12–14, 15–22; 10:19, 29; 12:24; 13:12). Yet it is because he offered himself as a perfectly obedient and unblemished sacrifice to God that his death has atoning significance (*cf.* 5:7–9; 7:27; 9:14, 28).[2] The perfection of his sacrifice makes it possible for him to enter heaven itself, 'now to appear for us in God's presence' (9:24).

The victim is the priest himself and this unity of the priest and the sacrifice brings the Mosaic cult to an end because its ideal has been fulfilled in Jesus (cf. 10:5–14). Hebrews regularly insists on the unique and unrepeatable character of Jesus' sacrifice (cf. 7:27; 9:24–28; 10:10, 12, 14), using expressions like 'once for all' ([eph]apax), to emphasize the contrast with the numerous and repeated offerings prescribed in the Old Testament. These included the daily offerings as well as the annual rituals. It is important to note, however, that Jesus fulfilled the functions of the Old Testament priesthood as the priest of another order.

Our writer sees Psalm 110:4 as a prophecy of the unique priesthood of the Messiah ('The Lord has sworn and will not change his mind: "You are a priest for ever, in the order of Melchizedek" '). This text is used to establish Jesus' calling by God to priesthood (Heb. 5:4–6), and to counter the objection that he was descended from Judah, rather than the priestly tribe of Levi (7:11–19). Moreover, it is the basis for asserting that his is an eternal and heavenly priesthood, guaranteed by God's oath, transcending and replacing the levitical priesthood of the Old Testament (7:20–25).

As the messianic or eschatological priest, who reigns at God's right hand, Jesus is 'able to save completely those who come to God through him, because he always lives to intercede for them' (7:25; cf. Rom. 8:34; 1 Jn. 2:1–2). With this assurance, the practical implication of the complex argumentation in Hebrews 7 becomes clear. The image of the heavenly intercessor is used to portray Christ's willingness and ability to go on applying the benefits of his once-for-all sacrifice to believers, in the midst of all their trials and temptations (cf. 4:14–16; 10:19–22).[3] Such encouragements were particularly necessary for those readers tempted to drift from Christ and the fellowship of his people (e.g. 2:1; 3:7 – 4:11; 10:24–39).

Mediator of the new covenant

The exposition of Christ's heavenly priesthood in Hebrews 7 leads into the portrayal of his work as a sacrificial liturgy performed with reference to the heavenly sanctuary in Hebrews

8 – 10. Jesus is a 'minister' (*leitourgos*) of 'the sanctuary, the true tabernacle, set up by the Lord, not by man' (8:2). As such, his 'ministry' (*leitourgia*) is superior to that of earthly priests (8:6), since they serve (*latreuousin*) only 'at a sanctuary that is a copy and shadow of what is in heaven' (8:5; *cf*. 9:24; 10:1). This is said to have been indicated by the command in Exodus 25:40 for Moses to construct the earthly tabernacle according to the pattern given to him by God.[4] The point of the contrast is that Jewish priests served in a God-ordained, but humanly constructed sanctuary. In this ministry they only foreshadowed the definitive priestly work of Jesus Christ, in his death and exaltation to the very presence of God. Now that the ultimate priestly liturgy has been performed, there is no place for the operation of any human priesthood in an earthly sanctuary.

The priestly ministry of Jesus is superior because it involved the offering of himself as a perfect sacrifice to God (7:26–27) and because it inaugurates the new covenant, which is 'founded on better promises' (8:6). The prophecy of Jeremiah 31:31–34, which is cited fully in Hebrews 8:8–12 and then in an abbreviated form in Hebrews 10:16–17, is the controlling text in the argument of chapters 8 – 10.[5] In between these two citations the writer proclaims that the heavenly eschatological 'cult' effected by Jesus' death and exaltation to the right hand of God is the means by which Jeremiah's prophecy has been fulfilled. Understanding this, we may discover the ultimate purpose and application of the writer's cultic argument in this central section.

Although Jeremiah 31:31–34 says nothing about a new priesthood or a transformation of the worship of God's people, it is clear that the final and foundational promise of that prophecy implies some definitive act on God's part to deal with the problem of Israel's sin ('For I will forgive their wickedness and will remember their sins no more', Je. 31:34). Because of what Christ has achieved, the Old Testament system of approach has been 'set aside' and a new basis of relationship with God has been established (Heb. 10:9–14; *cf*. 8:13). Even before that prophecy comes into focus, it is stated that a change of priesthood necessitates 'a change of the law' (7:12) and this implies a new covenant.

With a single sacrifice for sins, Christ has removed the necessity for the old covenant sacrificial system, providing the final and decisive forgiveness of which Jeremiah spoke (10:17–18). By this means also he has consecrated believers to God in the relationship of heart-obedience envisaged by Jeremiah (9:14; 10:10, 22), cleansing from sin at the level of the conscience. Moreover, his death has made it possible for those who are called to receive 'the promised eternal inheritance' (9:15), which is later described as 'the heavenly Jerusalem, the city of the living God' (12:22–24), or 'the city that is to come' (13:14). In other words, the sacrifice of Christ inaugurates all the blessings of the messianic era envisaged in the prophetic literature.

In line with Old Testament thinking, the writer understands covenant, worship and the enjoyment of a God-given inheritance to be inextricably linked together. When it is affirmed that Christ has 'made perfect for ever' those who are being sanctified (10:14, *teteleiōken eis to diēnekes*), the meaning is that he has achieved all that is necessary for believers to enjoy in the present the benefits of a direct and personal relationship with God and to share the glory of his eternal kingdom.[6]

The 'cult' of the new covenant

A detailed exposition of the work of Christ in cultic terms begins in Hebrews 9, with various assertions about the limitations of the old levitical system (vv. 1–10). The writer first stresses the earthly nature of the Mosaic sanctuary and its furniture (vv. 2–5), suggesting its insufficiency as a means of relating to God. As a preparation for the argument to follow, he brings out as strongly as possible the distinction and independent significance of the two chambers in the tabernacle, 'the Holy Place' and 'the Most Holy Place'.

Worship by means of such a sanctuary is then shown to be inadequate on several grounds (vv. 6–10). The system allowed the people to approach God, but only through their representatives the priests (v. 6). The ritual of the Day of Atonement stressed that only the high priest could enter the inner sanctuary, symbolic of the actual presence of God, and there but once a year, with the appropriate sacrificial blood (v. 7). The very existence of such a sanctuary, with its two divisions and rigid regulations, witnessed constantly to the possibility of drawing near to God, but *only on his terms*. The worshipper 'could not penetrate to that innermost sanctuary to which he necessarily looked, and from which blessing flowed'.[7]

In view of the law's fulfilment in Christ, the writer claims special insight from the Holy Spirit into the meaning and purpose of these provisions (vv. 8–9a). As long as the 'outer tent' (RSV) or first tent, continued to have the status of a sanctuary, 'the way into the Most Holy Place' remained unrevealed. At a literal level, of course, the outer tent obscured the way into the second tent. The way into the true, heavenly sanctuary, however, has now been disclosed and opened by Jesus in his death and heavenly exaltation (vv. 11–12). So, at a symbolic level, the outer tent represents the whole system of Jewish worship, which actually stood in the way of direct and permanent access to God.[8]

The writer stresses elsewhere that the Old Testament cult functioned as an anticipation or 'shadow of the good things to come' (10:1, RSV; *cf.* 8:5). The implication of 9:8–9a, however, is that God has only made its anticipatory function clear in New Testament times. The cult enabled Israel to draw near to God in a limited sense, but its strengths and weaknesses have really only come to light with its fulfilment in Christ.

A particular weakness of the old covenant is then emphasized (9:9b). In the worship of the earthly sanctuary, gifts and sacrifices were offered which were literally not able 'to perfect the worshipper with respect to conscience' (*kata syneidēsin teleiōsai ton latreuonta*). 'Conscience' is a rare term in the LXX but was coming into common use in Greek literature in the first century BC.[9] Hebrews is fundamentally concerned with conscience as a register of our guilt before God. The writer insists that the Jewish cult left the participants with 'a consciousness of sins' (10:2, lit.: *syneidēsin hamartiōn*), because it did not provide a definitive cleansing from sin. This failure is explained in terms of the external operation of the Mosaic cultus (9:10). Food laws, libations to accompany sacrifices, various rites for bodily cleansing and the sacrifices themselves are all described as 'external regulations' (*dikaiōmata sarkos*). This whole earth-bound system was only a temporary provision in the outworking of God's plans, being in force 'until the time of the new order'.

Against this background, the efficacy of Christ's high-priestly work is expounded (9:11–28). As 'high priest of the good things that are already here' (9:11),[10] Jesus Christ instituted 'the time of the new order' (9:10). His achievement is described in an extended comparison with the task of Jewish high priests on atonement day. The sphere of his ministry is superior because he went through 'the greater and more perfect tabernacle that is not man-made, that is to say, not a part of this creation'. Instead of passing through an earthly tent to fulfil his ministry, Christ passed through various heavenly realms (*cf.* 4:14; 7:26) to enter 'the Most Holy Place' (9:12), which is later identified as 'heaven itself', the actual dwelling place or presence of God (9:24).[11] The means of his atoning work is also superior because it is 'his own blood', rather than 'the blood of goats and calves' (9:12). Finally, the writer is able to speak of the issue of Christ's atoning work as superior: he obtained 'an eternal redemption' (9:12, *aiōnian lystrōsin*), in contrast with 'the limited, recurrent redemption of the yearly atonement'.[12]

A number of the writer's key ideas and emphases are then brought together as he begins to spell out the implications of Christ's perfect and definitive worship for believers:

> For if the sprinkling of defiled persons with the blood
> of goats and bulls and with the ashes of a heifer
> sanctifies for the purification of the flesh, how much
> more shall the blood of Christ, who through the
> eternal Spirit offered himself without blemish to God,
> purify your conscience from dead works to serve the
> living God (Heb. 9:13–14, RSV).

Once more there is a claim that the old covenant rituals only provided outward or ceremonial purification and sanctification. The perfection of Christ's self-offering as the sacrifice to end all sacrifices is indicated. The power of his blood to effect purification at the level of the conscience, to liberate people from the guilt associated with 'dead works',[13] and to set them free to serve God in a new way is affirmed. The meaning and significance of these particular assertions will now be discussed under several headings.

The blood of Jesus

A significant reason for affirming the superiority of the new covenant is conveyed by the use of the word 'blood', which is found fourteen times in Hebrews 9 – 10. The overriding axiom of this section is that 'without the shedding of blood there is no forgiveness' (9:22).[14] We are told that the first covenant could not be inaugurated 'without blood' (9:18–21) and the Mosaic law required nearly everything to be cleansed with blood. Most importantly, the high priest could not enter the inner sanctuary on atonement day without blood, which he offered for himself and for the 'sins of the people (9:7). Yet animal blood is said to have been effective only at an outward or ceremonial level, literally 'for the purification of the flesh' (9:13, RSV, *pros tēn tēs sarkos katharotēta*). Indeed, 'it is impossible for the blood of bulls and goats to take away sins' (10:4).

The power of Christ's 'blood' is demonstrated in two fundamental ways. Firstly, it enabled him to gain access to the heavenly sanctuary (9:12), to open the way for believers to enter that 'Most Holy Place' with confidence (10:19). Secondly, only the blood of Jesus Christ can cleanse the conscience of believers and equip them to serve God in the way that he desires (9:14). There is thus a close connection in Hebrews between the cleansing of the conscience and acceptable worship.

Even the 'heavenly things' had to be cleansed by means of 'better sacrifices' (9:23). In the Old Testament, the sanctuary was a sort of prism through which the relations between God and his people were refracted: 'when the sanctuary was cleansed, the sins of the people were objectively expiated and contact between God and the people re-established'.[15] Heaven itself can hardly be defiled by human sin, otherwise God would have to leave it! Hebrews, however, appears to be saying that the sacrifice of Christ had cosmic significance, removing a barrier to fellowship with God that existed at the level of ultimate reality and not simply in human hearts. The blood of Christ is the medium by which we are consecrated to God under the new covenant (10:29; *cf.* 13:12, 20) and, because of the shedding of his blood, the blessings of the new covenant are freely available for all who will draw near to God through him.

In 9:26–28 the language of blood recedes into the background and Christ's death is portrayed more generally as the sacrifice 'at the end of the ages to do away with sin' (9:26). Using the language of Psalm 40:6–8, the writer then asserts that this eschatological sacrifice has fulfilled and replaced every kind of offering prescribed in the levitical ritual (10:5–10).[16] In this context it is affirmed that we are consecrated to God 'through the offering of the body of Jesus Christ once for all' (10:10, RSV). Psalm 40 points to the powerlessness of animal sacrifices in themselves to please God and bring about a right relationship with God. What really pleases God is the willing self-offering of his people, in obedience to his will. One of the purposes of the sacrificial system was to promote such obedience from the heart, but Jesus was the only one in whom it was perfectly expressed.

The new covenant, which provides for the writing of God's law on the 'heart' (Je. 31:33; Heb. 8:10; 10:16), is thus significantly established by the action of one in whom the ideal of Psalm 40:8 has been fulfilled. While it is true that the obedience of a lifetime made Jesus' offering to God so pure and blameless (4:15; 7:26–27; 9:14), in the writer's perspective it is still the actual death of Jesus that achieves our consecration to God.[17] In the concluding appeal of this section (10:19–39), Christ's blood and its effects return to the foreground (vv. 19, 29).

At first sight it is puzzling to see how Hebrews lumps together the daily sacrifices of Judaism (7:27; 10:5–6, 8), the annual Day of Atonement sacrifices (9:6, 7, 12, 21, 23, 25; 10:1–3), the sacrifices inaugurating the Sinai covenant (9:18–20) and allusions to the red heifer ceremony (9:13; 10:22). What all these sacrifices have in common, however, is the single point of blood: 'blood provides the medium of drawing near to God'.[18] Blood cleanses from defilement, bringing life instead of the judgment of death, and a renewal of the relationship with God. Without blood there is no access to God, no inauguration of the covenant and no forgiveness. In the writer's thought-world, blood has a direct, immediate potency. The blood of Christ is the most powerful of all, because he offered himself without blemish to God, as the true and final offering for sin ordained by God (10:5–10).

Christ's blood breaks the old oscillating pattern of defilement and cleansing. The ongoing problem of sin made it necessary for rites of cleansing and reconsecration to be repeated under the old covenant, year after year (*cf.* 10:1–4). The blood of Jesus, however, provides a once-for-all cleansing and consecration to the service of God under the new covenant (*cf.* 9:14; 13:12). Thus, the sacrifice of Christ is foundational to a Christian theology of worship.

Worship as homage to God's Son

As the writer develops his complex argument, there are various ways in which he uses transformed worship terminology to indicate what it means for believers to be the beneficiaries of the new covenant. The important Old Testament word *proskynein* is used only once, in a passage claiming that the role of the angels is to pay homage to Christ as the Son enthroned at God's right hand (1:6; *cf.* Rev. 5:11–14). The text cited here appears to be a conflation of the LXX version of Psalm 96:7 and Deuteronomy 32:43 – 'Let all God's angels worship him.' One of the writer's aims in portraying the homage of the angels to Christ in the heavenly realm is apparently to encourage disciples on earth to honour him appropriately.[19] The immediate context suggests how this can be done.

The exhortation to 'pay the closer attention to what we have heard, lest we drift away from it' (RSV) is clearly the consequence (*dia touto*, 2:1) of the teaching about Christ in 1:1–13. God has spoken 'in these last days' by means of his Son and has acted to redeem humanity through his death and heavenly exaltation. The message 'first announced by the Lord' and then attested by those who heard him is a message of salvation (2:3–4). Only by receiving that message with faith and obedience can we benefit from what he offers (*cf.* 5:9). Only as we 'hold on to our courage and the hope of which we boast' can we count ourselves as God's 'house', over which Christ rules as Son (3:6). The way we share on earth in the homage of the angels is not in some cultic activity but in a life of faith and obedience to Christ and his message.

As in other parts of the New Testament, there is an indication in Hebrews 1 that the exalted and glorified Son of God is properly the object of Christian worship. However, the writer's use of other worship terminology introduces a further perspective. The high-priestly work of Christ makes it possible for us to draw near to God on a new basis and, in effect, to share in the Son's relationship with the Father. It is 'by the blood of Jesus' that we are to approach God (10:19; *cf.* 7:25) and it is 'through Jesus' that we are to offer the praise and obedience that is pleasing to God (13:15–16). So Christ is more often portrayed as the means of acceptable worship in this book.

The participation of believers in the worship of Jesus

The primary focus of Hebrews is on the perfect worship that Jesus offers to the Father in his life, death and heavenly exaltation. On the basis of his high-priestly work, however, Christians themselves can draw near to God and serve him in a way that fulfils the promises of the new covenant.

Drawing near to God

In two important passages of exhortation, preceding and concluding the main doctrinal argument, Hebrews issues the challenge to hold fast the Christian confession and to 'draw near' to God with confidence (4:14–16; 10:19–23). In both cases, the appeal is based on the fact that Christ is the perfected and enthroned high priest, who has entered the heavenly sanctuary by means of his sacrificial death and heavenly exaltation and opened up 'a new and living way' into that sanctuary for us. This challenge brings us to the heart of the writer's concern.

The verb *proserchesthai* occurs at a number of points in the argument (4:16; 7:25; 10:1, 22; 11:6; 12:18, 22) and the synonym *engizein* once (7:19). This terminology is clearly a key to understanding the way believers should respond to the person and work of Christ. In non-biblical Greek, *proserchesthai* meant 'to come before', or 'to approach' someone such as a judge or a god. Since this verb was commonly used in the LXX to describe the priestly approach to God in sacrificial ministry (*e.g.* Lv. 21:17, 21;

22:3), some commentators understand the usage of Hebrews to imply that the right of priestly approach is now extended to Christians.[20]

There is certainly a hierarchy of drawing near to God in such references as Exodus 19:21–22, where only the priests who consecrate themselves for this purpose may draw near to God on Mount Sinai, and Exodus 24:2, where Moses alone is to draw near to God at the top of the mountain, leaving the elders (including Aaron!) to worship 'afar off' (Ex. 24:1, RSV). However, this terminology is also used in the LXX to describe the relationship which all Israel could enjoy with God, either in cultic ritual or in prayer.[21] In Hebrews 11:6, where there are no specifically cultic associations, drawing near to God means having a relationship with him by faith (cf. Jas. 4:8; 1 Pet. 2:4). Even in cultic contexts, it is most likely that this is the reality behind the writer's use of the imagery of drawing near to God.

Thus, it is simplistic to say that our writer uses this terminology to expound the view that the privileges of the Old Testament priesthood find their fulfilment in a priesthood of all Christian believers. The people of God may now draw near without the aid of human priesthood, but only because they rely on the priestly mediation of Jesus Christ. This directness of approach to God comes about because the office of priesthood is fulfilled in Christ rather than in us. In 10:1–2, the Israelites generally are described as those who drew near to God by means of the sacrificial system. The writer clearly affirms, however, that the system was not able to 'perfect' those who sought to relate to God in this way. On the other hand, the high-priestly ministry of Jesus has 'made perfect for ever those who are being made holy' (10:14).

Similarly, in 7:11–19, the replacement of the levitical priesthood by the high-priesthood of Christ involves the introduction of 'a better hope...by which we draw near to God' (7:19). This better hope with which the Christian encounters God is due to the 'better covenant' of which Jesus is surety (7:22) and mediator (8:6; 12:24): it is enacted on 'better promises' (8:6) and is eternal in its consequences (13:20). In short, the contrast in these passages is between the limited effectiveness of the former priesthood and the absolute effectiveness of the priesthood of Christ to bring about a right relationship with God (*cf.* 7:25). The work of Christ means that 'the certainty of the actualisation of the drawing near is now stronger and surer and more complete than in the O.T. and later Judaism'.[22]

Consequently, 4:16 and 10:22 must be understood as encouragements to realize the benefit of the new relationship with God made possible by Christ. In both verses, the Greek implies the need for this to be an ongoing activity (*proserchōmetha*, 'let us draw near', being in the present tense). Christians have already drawn near by faith to 'the heavenly Jerusalem' (note the perfect tense of *proselēlythate* in 12:22, 'you have come'), which is another way of talking about the heavenly sanctuary (12:22–24). Responding to the gospel, they have received the gift of salvation and all it entails. Even so, they are to 'keep on drawing near with confidence to the throne of grace' (4:16, lit.). This 'throne' represents God as ruler,[23] but it is particularly a 'throne of grace' for us since Jesus sits there, 'at the right hand of the throne of the Majesty in heaven' (8:1), the eternal source of mercy and grace because of his atoning work.

The direct approach to God 'with confidence' (*meta parrēsia*, 4:16; *cf.* 3:6; 10:19, 35),[24] which is the essence of Christian faith, needs to be expressed continually as an ongoing relationship of trust and dependence (10:22, RSV, 'with a true heart in full assurance of faith'). A true heart is one which 'expresses completely the devotion of the person to God. There is no divided allegiance: no reserve of feeling.'[25] With such terms the writer apparently proclaims the fulfilment of Jeremiah's promise about God renewing the hearts and minds of his people and causing them all to know him, 'from the least of them to the greatest' (Je. 31:33–34; *cf.* Ezk. 36:26–27). The alternative is to 'throw away your confidence' (10:35) and 'shrink back' (10:39), which is another way of describing apostasy. The ultimate joy of the faithful will be to draw near to God in the reality of the heavenly sanctuary, which is still for us 'the city that is to come' (13:14). The right of approach we enjoy now is only an anticipation of the final outworking of Jesus' high-priestly work.

Fundamentally, then, drawing near to God means believing the gospel and making 'personal appropriation of salvation'.[26] The language of 10:22 confirms this ('having our hearts sprinkled to cleanse us from a guilty conscience and having our bodies washed with pure water'). This verse highlights the cleansing effect of the sacrifice of Christ, applied to individuals at some decisive moment in the past, and continuing to qualify them to draw near to God.[27] The 'sprinkling' of the heart from an evil conscience recalls the imagery of 9:18–22, where the sprinkling of the people with blood was associated with the inauguration of the old covenant. The sprinkling of the people of the new covenant is associated with Jesus' opening of the new way to God through his death (10:20; cf. 9:18), but the phrase 'with our bodies washed with pure water' probably points to Christian baptism as the moment when the benefits of his sacrifice are first appropriated.[28]

Drawing near to God on this basis will mean constantly expressing trust in Jesus and his saving work. Prayer through the mediation of our heavenly high priest is particularly in view in 4:14–16. Here the challenge is to approach God 'so that we may receive mercy and find grace to help us in our time of need' (4:16). The reference is not to prayer in a general sense but more specifically to confession of sin, seeking mercy for past failures, and petition for timely help in running the Christian race (cf. 2:18). Such prayer will be the means by which the benefits of Christ's high-priestly work will first be grasped in conversion/ baptism. Such prayer will also be the means by which genuine disciples continue to express their dependence upon God through Christ. The implications of this teaching for the congregational gathering will be considered shortly. When all is said and done, one of the main points of the writer's complex presentation is to urge Christians to continue to draw on all the spiritual resources available to them through Jesus Christ and not to fall away.

Worship as service to God

At two key points in the argument of Hebrews (9:14; 12:28), the worship term *latreuein* is employed in a new way to highlight what it means to be a Christian.[29] The sacrifices of the old covenant were not able to perfect 'the worshipper' (*ton latreuonta*) by dealing with the fundamental problem of a guilty conscience (9:9; cf. 10:1–4). The all-sufficient sacrifice of Christ for the forgiveness of sins, however, makes such cleansing possible. The blood of Christ is able to cleanse our consciences from the defilement caused by sin, so that we might serve the living God (9:14, *eis to latreuein theō zōnti*). Conscience must be 'cleansed' by the assurance that the blood of Christ provides the necessary forgiveness before one can worship or serve God effectively (*cf.* 10:19–22).

But what exactly is the nature of the service that Christ makes possible? A key to the interpretation of 9:14 is a later passage:

> Therefore, since we are receiving a kingdom that
> cannot be shaken, let us be thankful, and so worship
> God acceptably (*latreuōmen euarestōs tō theō*) with
> reverence and awe, for our 'God is a consuming fire'
> (Heb. 12:28–29).

Acceptable worship is clearly related here to the reception of 'an unshakable kingdom'. Thanks to the work of Christ, Christians are already participants by faith in the eschatological kingdom of God,[30] having already 'drawn near' to the heavenly Jerusalem, where God is in the midst of his angels and the perfected saints of all generations (12:22–24). At first glance it may appear from 12:28 that acceptable worship is simply defined in terms of expressing gratitude for this great gift: 'let us be grateful...and thus (*di' hēs*) let us offer to God acceptable worship'.[31] Since chapter 13 follows immediately, with its many exhortations to faithfulness and obedience, however, it is more likely that the writer is indicating that the words and actions that flow from such gratitude are the worship that is pleasing to God.[32] That is certainly the meaning of 13:15–16.

As in Romans 12:1, Christian worship is the service rendered by those who have truly grasped the gospel of God's grace and its implications. The motivation and power for such service in Hebrews is quite specifically the cleansing that derives from the finished work of Christ (9:14) and the hope which that work sets before us (12:28). Gratitude expressed in service is the sign that the grace of God has been apprehended and appreciated. The writer introduces a more serious note, however, when he asserts that acceptable worship is characterized by 'reverence and awe' (*meta eulabeias kai deous*), and supports his challenge with an allusion to the coming judgment of God ('for our "God is a consuming fire" ').

In the Old Testament, reverence or fear of the Lord regularly meant faithfulness and obedience to the revealed character and will of God.[33] Jesus is presented in Hebrews 5:7 as the one who pre-eminently displayed such godly fear or 'reverent submission' (*eulabeia*), and in 12:28 we are exhorted to pursue the same lifestyle of trust and loyalty (*cf.* 12:1–3). The description of God as 'a consuming fire' (12:29) recalls Deuteronomy 4:24 (*cf.* Dt. 9:3; Is. 33:14), where Moses warns Israel not to indulge in idolatry, but to remain faithful to the LORD and to serve him exclusively, lest they provoke him to anger. Warning believers to remain faithful to Jesus and his covenant, Hebrews speaks of the fearful prospect of judgment that will consume those who turn out to be the enemies of God (10:26–31). The same pattern emerges in Hebrews 12, where the challenge to respond with gratitude to the grace of God is blended with the warning to keep heeding the voice of 'him who warns us from heaven' (12:25–27), lest we encounter God as 'a consuming fire'. The certainty of God's grace must not obscure for us the truth that a terrible judgment awaits the apostate (*cf.* 2:2–3; 6:4–8; 12:14–17).

The practicalities of Christian service

A wide range of instructions in 13:1–7 offers a challenge to persist with the sort of practical expressions of love and patient faith previously commended (*cf.* 6:10–12; 10:32–36). Here we begin to see what Christian worship means in the context of everyday life: it has to do with entertaining strangers, visiting prisoners, being faithful in marriage, trusting God to provide material needs and imitating the faith of Christian leaders! A negative note is then struck with the warning not to be 'carried away by all kinds of strange teachings' (13:9).

The writer touches on matters more commonly associated with religion or worship in common parlance when he refers to 'foods' which are 'of no value to those who eat them'. The practice in question may have involved some kind of ritual meal, as in various traditions of Judaism and paganism. Whether its roots were purely Jewish or not, it was presumably being presented as a helpful Christian activity.[34] Yet, it is by God's grace, and not rules about food, that the heart – that is to say, the spiritual life – is to be nourished (*cf.* Rom. 14:17; 1 Cor. 8:8; Col. 2:16, 20–23). Food laws are among the 'external regulations', now surpassed and outmoded by the work of Christ (*cf.* 9:10). The following verses suggest that such practices are a hindrance to true Christian worship:

> We have an altar from which those who minister at
> the tabernacle have no right to eat. The high priest
> carries the blood of animals into the Most Holy Place
> as a sin offering, but the bodies are burned outside
> the camp. And so Jesus also suffered outside the city
> gate to make the people holy through his own blood.
> Let us, then, go to him outside the camp, bearing the
> disgrace he bore. For here we do not have an
> enduring city, but we are looking for the city that is
> to come (Heb. 13:10–14).

Some commentators have taken the statement about the Christian 'altar' as a reference to 'the Lord's table' (*cf.* 1 Cor. 10:21), viewing the Lord's Supper as a sacrificial meal.[35] To locate the altar of 13:10 in the Christian community, however, is to misunderstand the way the writer employs typology. The whole burden of Hebrews is that the high-priesthood, sacrifices and sanctuary of Judaism find their fulfilment in the person and work of Jesus Christ, not in the activities of the church or Christian ministers (*cf.* 4:14; 8:1; 10:19–21). 'Altar' is another cultic term used in a shorthand and figurative way for the sacrifice of Christ in all its complexity.[36] Those Jewish priests who continue to 'minister at the tabernacle' (*hoi tē skēnē latreuontes, cf.* 8:5), and who are authorized to benefit from its sacrifices (*e.g.* Lv. 7:5–6; Nu. 18:9–10), have no authority to 'eat' from the altar of the new covenant. They, along with anyone else attached to a material cult, are pursuing the 'shadow' instead of the reality (8:5; 10:1).

Hebrews does not here draw the inference that Christians may even metaphorically 'eat' from their 'altar', or sacramentally benefit from Christ's once-for-all sacrifice. It is remarkable that there is no treatment of the Lord's Supper in this context, even at the level of correcting false views of the community meal.[37] The motif of food or eating is left behind as the argument moves to a further comparison between the ritual of the Day of Atonement and the death of Jesus. The detail in that ancient ritual which our writer finds especially significant in this context is the burning of the bodies of the sacrificial victims 'outside the camp' (13:11; cf. Lv. 16:27). To leave the camp, even for this sacred duty, rendered a person unclean and necessitated a rite of purification before the camp could be re-entered (Lv. 16:28).

The point is that the sacrifice of Jesus was offered outside the holy city of Jerusalem, and it is this 'unholy' sacrifice, 'outside the camp', which paradoxically 'sanctifies' us under the new covenant (Heb. 13:12). Such an interpretation of the death of Jesus suggests that it marks 'the abolition of the necessity of holy places for sanctification'.[38] Christians who have been cleansed and consecrated to God by the sacrifice of Christ must no longer take refuge in holy places and cultic performances but must 'go to him outside the camp, bearing the disgrace he bore' (13:13). The place of Christian service or worship is in the uncleanness of the world, where there is unbelief and persecution! True participation in the Christian 'altar' is to be found in accepting the disgrace of identifying with a crucified and rejected Messiah.[39] Furthermore, since there is no abiding sacred refuge for Christians here, the challenge to confess Christ and serve him in the world is coupled with the challenge to seek the city which is to come (13:14; cf. 11:8–16).

Another reference to the worship that is 'pleasing to God' then follows (13:15, RSV; cf. 12:28; 11:5–6). Christians are continually to offer to God a 'sacrifice of praise' (*thysian aineseōs*) through Jesus. In language borrowed from Hosea 14:2 (LXX) this sacrifice is described as 'the tribute of lips which acknowledge his name' (NEB). In other words, this 'sacrifice of praise' is a sacrifice consisting of praise or the public acknowledgment of the name or character of God.[40] The 'name' to be confessed could be specifically that of Jesus, since the focus of Christian confession in 3:1; 4:14 and 10:23 is Jesus as Son of God and high priest of his people. Confession of Christ in personal or corporate acts of praise could thus be in view in 13:15.

The writer's meaning here, however, cannot simply be restricted to such activities. The verb 'to acknowledge' (*homologountōn*) can be understood in a non-cultic and non-liturgical way to refer to the confession of Christ before unbelievers.[41] Our writer's concern in the immediate context is to exhort believers to acknowledge Christ in the world, in the face of opposition and suffering. In its widest sense, this sacrifice of praise will be rendered by those who confess Jesus 'outside the camp', in various forms of public testimony or evangelism. The offering up of praise to God is certainly not just a matter of singing hymns or giving thanks in a congregational context, though these activities can be a stimulus to effective proclamation in other contexts.[42]

'To do good' and 'to share with others' is also acceptable worship, for 'with such sacrifices' (*toiautais thysiais*, 13:16) God is pleased. The writer employs transformed cultic language to show the centrality of these activities to genuine religion (*cf.* Jas. 1:26–27).[43] Such 'sacrifices' cannot be regarded as cultivating God's favour, since Christian worship is meant to be an expression of gratitude for the care that he first showed us (*cf.* 12:28). Although the writer is concerned about practical expressions of fellowship among believers (*cf.* 10:32–34; 13:1–3), it is doubtful that he used the word *koinōnia* ('sharing' or 'fellowship') in the narrow and technical sense of 'the Christian fellowship' in 13:16. There can be no boundaries to doing good and there are many opportunities for sharing what we have in relationships and situations outside of the Christian fellowship.

The note of pleasing God is sounded once more in the closing benediction of Hebrews. There it is asserted that God himself must equip us with everything good for doing his will and must 'work in us what is pleasing (*to euareston*) to him, through Jesus Christ' (13:20–21).[44] Thus, the writer's final affirmation on the subject is that acceptable worship in all its dimensions can only be offered through Christ, by God's enabling.

The congregational gathering in Hebrews

When the writer details with the meeting together of the particular group of Christians he addresses, he uses the word *episynagōgē*. Like *ekklēsia*, this word refers to the act of gathering and is not yet a technical term for their group or its place of assembly.[45] Since the nearness of the Lord's return is used to highlight the importance of such gatherings (10:25; *cf.* 9:28), it seems that our writer understood them as an anticipation of the ultimate, eschatological assembly of God's people portrayed in 12:22–24.[46] Put another way, local congregations or house-groups may be viewed as earthly manifestations of that heavenly assembly already gathered around God and Christ. The congregational meeting should thus be a way of expressing our common participation in that eschatological community, gathered, cleansed and consecrated to God by Messiah's work.

Unlike Paul, who identifies the community of God's people on earth with the new temple, Hebrews locates temple imagery in the heavenly realm.[47] Cultic imagery is used to stress the immediate benefits available to those who approach God through the crucified and exalted Lord Jesus Christ and to indicate the response we should make to the gospel in our everyday lives.

Mutual encouragement

Hebrews does not apply the language of worship specifically to what goes on when Christians meet together. As in the Pauline writings, there is an emphasis on gathering for the benefit of the believing community (3:12–15; 10:24–25). Our writer has nothing of the elaborate teaching of Paul about spiritual gifts, but he is no less insistent on the importance of mutual ministry in the congregation. There are leaders in the church, charged with the responsibility of watching over them, whom they must obey and to whose authority they must submit (13:17). The focus of Hebrews, however, is on the care that believers in general must exercise for one another. Anyone who has been instructed for a time in the faith should be able to explain its implications to others (*cf.* 5:12).[48] The specific terminology of edification is not used, but related concepts are found in key contexts. Particular point and purpose is given to their meetings by the pilgrimage motif. Christians are on a journey of faith to their ultimate destination in the city of God and nothing must be allowed to deflect them from that goal.

In the midst of the warning passage in 3:7 – 4:14 the writer warns: 'See to it, brothers, that none of you has a sinful, unbelieving heart, that turns away from the living God. But encourage one another daily, as long as it is called Today, so that none of you may be hardened by sin's deceitfulness' (3:12–13). The context really demands that the key word *parakaleite* be translated 'exhort' (so RSV), instead of 'encourage' (NEB, NIV).[49] The need for warning on the basis of scriptural teaching is in view, together with the sort of encouragement to persevere suggested by the writer's own arguments. His use of Psalm 95 as a means of exhorting the readers in Hebrews 3 – 4 provides an immediate example. As they read the Scriptures together and apply them in the manner illustrated in his own 'word of exhortation' (13:22), they will be challenged and encouraged to hold 'firmly to the end' the confidence they had at first (3:14, RSV).

In no other context in the New Testament is mutual exhortation highlighted as a means of dealing with 'a sinful, unbelieving heart',[50] and the possibility of apostasy. The purpose of this ministry is to avoid being 'hardened by sin's deceitfulness' (3:13). To put it more positively, Christians need to expose themselves to the warnings and encouragements that will help them persevere in the faith and grow to maturity (*cf.* 5:11 – 6:3). It is possible that the writer envisaged a regular 'daily' meeting of the readers for teaching and prayer (3:13, *kath' hekastēn hēmeran*). The giving and receiving of exhortation is undoubtedly a key factor in his view of the Christian assembly (*cf.* 10:24–25). More likely, his meaning in 3:13 was that each new day provided opportunities for informal exhortation of one another and the chance to 'heed the psalmist's warning to hear the voice of God and render him heart-obedience'.[51]

One of the features of Hebrews is its emphasis on the care that members of the congregation should have for each other. They should take care lest any of their number has a sinful, unbelieving heart (3:12), and exhort one another lest any should be hardened by the deceitfulness of sin (3:13). The writer's desire for each one of them to show 'the same earnestness in realizing the full assurance of hope until the end' (6:11, RSV) leads him to challenge them to minister to one another again in 10:24–25, and in 12:12–17. The last passage particularly echoes the sentiment of 3:12–13 by challenging them to 'take care' (*episkopountes*, 12:15) lest anyone 'misses the grace of God' and any 'bitter root grows up to cause trouble and defile many'.[52]

In 10:24 the writer urges: 'let us consider (*katanoōmen*) how we may spur one another on towards love and good deeds'. This implies thoughtful reflection on the needs of other believers and recalls the challenge of 3:12 to 'take care' (*blepete*, RSV) with respect to the spiritual health of the congregation.[53] The following expression (*eis paroxysmon agapē kai kalōn ergōn*) shows that the purpose of this reflection is to rouse or provoke one another to godly living. Later on, the readers are commended for having demonstrated such love and good works in the past (*cf.* 10:32–34). Their zeal needed to be renewed, however, so that they did not tire of expressing their faith in such practical ways (*cf.* 6:10–12). Such a stimulus to godliness will not simply come by the setting of a good example.

The exhortation to 'consider how we may spur one another on towards love and good deeds' is followed by two clauses, indicating how this ministry is to be conducted. Negatively it will mean not forsaking the local gathering of believers,[54] as some professing Christians do. Positively it will mean using such occasions as a means of mutual encouragement or exhortation (*parakalountes*). Encouragement can be given to other Christians at the most basic level by not abandoning the assembly. However, remembering what was said above, it would seem that the writer intended them to use their meetings for mutual teaching and exhortation (*cf.* 3:12–13; 5:12). In 10:24–25 the focus is not simply on avoiding hardness of heart but on promoting the sort of everyday living that brings praise to God.

The purpose of the congregational gathering in Hebrews may be thus defined as mutual ministry with an eschatological focus ('encourage one another – and all the more as you see the Day approaching', 10:25). Christians ought to gather together regularly to *give* in ministry, and not simply to receive. The ministry they share with one another should be focused on the promises of God and the encouragement the gospel can bring for godly living in the present. Public preaching and teaching in the congregation should thus combine a thoughtful restatement of biblical truths with reflection on the needs of those present. As noted in the last chapter, however, there is also a need in contemporary church life to encourage congregational members to exhort one another in informal and less structured ways.

Drawing near to God together

Although the writer puts the emphasis on meeting together for mutual encouragement, his wider teaching challenges us to consider the vertical dimension to the congregational gathering. There are three key exhortations linked together in 10:22–24 – 'let us draw near to God... let us hold unswervingly to the hope we profess... let us consider how we may spur one another on towards love and good deeds.' These identify the sort of response that the people of God should make to the covenant mercies previously outlined and summarized (10:15–21). They challenge us to express faith, hope and love in every sphere of life, indicating 'the threefold nature of the activities of the church in the world'.[55] But to what extent are these exhortations applicable to the congregational meeting itself?

The emphasis in 10:19–22 is on our approach to God through Jesus Christ in the heavenly sanctuary. That initial encounter with God in Christ, portrayed so vividly in 12:22–24 in similar terms, needs to be constantly renewed and expressed. Drawing near to God in both contexts essentially describes an act of personal faith or appropriation of the gift of salvation in Christ. Yet drawing near to God is not merely something we do on our own. The writer and his readers are among those who have come together into the heavenly presence, to join in the celebration of the heavenly assembly. It seems logical to assume that a corporate dimension is also implied in 10:22. Meeting together as the household of God on earth (10:21), we are to keep on drawing near to God in the midst of his people in the heavenlies (10:22):

Through Christ, their high priest, Christians may

250

approach God in the sanctuary of heaven and of the
world to come. In their worship they participate in
the heavenly worship of the angels and of the perfect
saints.[56]

It is certainly obvious from the flow of the argument in 10:24–
25 that gathering together is an important means of encouraging
one another to express love and good deeds, until the Day of the
Lord dawns and believers share in the unspoiled fellowship of
the city which is to come. The writer has already established in
3:12–14 that mutual exhortation is essential for maintaining
confidence in Christ 'firmly to the end', RSV. One of the ways in
which we continue to draw near to God is to expose ourselves to
the ministries of others. In particular, God continues to confront
his people through the Scriptures, as Hebrews itself testifies (*e.g.*
3:7–11; 4:12–13; 12:5–6). Responding appropriately to the reading and exposition of Scripture, or to exhortations based on
Scripture, we may engage with him as the family of God
together.

If the congregational meeting is truly the context in which the
participants may draw near to God collectively, to realize afresh
the benefits of the gospel, some form of public confession of sin,
coupled with an appeal for pardon and a prayer for strength to
live godly lives, would logically be part of the proceedings.[57]
This would be a most obvious way of putting into practice the
specific challenge of 4:14–16 (*cf.* 1 Jn. 1:9–10). Although there is
no good ground for thinking that the writer was actually alluding
to the Lord's Supper here or in 10:19–22,[58] it is certainly legitimate to see the Supper as a means of corporately drawing near to
God, in the way that I have suggested.

There is always the danger, however, that public confession of
sin or the Lord's Supper can become occasions for morbid
introspection, reinforcing for people a sense of guilt, as the
sacrificial rituals of Judaism apparently could (*cf.* 10:1–4). We
may give the impression that the Christian life is all about
discovering the depth of your own sinfulness and the difficulty of
serving God! The writer's challenge to go on seeking God's
mercy and help to run the Christian race has to be set firmly
within the context of his emphasis on definitive cleansing and

sanctification through the death of Jesus. Our approach to God must demonstrate confidence in such promises ('with a sincere heart in full assurance of faith', 10:22) and be characterized by joy and thanksgiving. It is not honest or appropriate to ignore our failure and disobedience when we come before God, but the finality and perfection of Christ's atoning work should be at the forefront of our thinking and practice.

Maintaining the hope we profess

It was argued above that Hebrews 13:15 could refer to the acknowledgment of Christ in personal or corporate acts of praise as well as in the world, in the face of opposition and suffering. Does the challenge to 'hold unswervingly to the hope we profess' in 10:23 have a similar application? This verse links up with earlier exhortations to fix our thoughts on Jesus, 'the apostle and high priest whom we confess' (3:1), to 'hold on to our confidence and the hope of which we boast' (3:6, lit.) and to 'hold firmly to the faith we profess' (4:14).

It should first be noted that the noun *homologia* ('confession') in 3:1; 4:14 and 10:23 is translated verbally in the NIV ('we confess, profess'). In each context, the readers are being exhorted to hold firm to a confession already made, and not to make or express a new confession. While some argue that the reference is to a solemn liturgical formula, such as a baptismal confession, a creed, or a hymnic confession of Christ,[59] the term could just as easily refer to a free and unstructured confession of Christ and the Christian hope. Certainly the concern of our writer is not with the original situation in which the confession was made, but with the need for the readers to 'cling to their faith as expressed in the *homologia*, which they once accepted and have openly declared'.[60]

This will mean maintaining confidence in Jesus and his promises before unbelievers in everyday life situations (*cf.* 10:35). If this is so, it could be argued that believers need to express and regularly affirm that confidence to one another, when the church gathers. Once again we may say that the praise of Christ for what he has accomplished, either in credal form or in hymns and songs, will rightly be at the heart of the congregational meeting. Such praise will glorify God in the midst of his people and encourage believers to express gratitude in word and deed in other contexts.

Conclusion

Hebrews is truly essential reading for those who would establish a Christian theology of worship. The writer takes up a number of Old Testament themes and shows how they remain an essential foundation for our thinking. In a variety of ways he demonstrates that acceptable worship is only possible on God's terms and in the way that he makes possible. God initiates and sustains a relationship with his people on the basis of the covenant he makes with them. His chosen sanctuary is a focuspoint for that engagement, but genuine worship will be offered in every sphere of life. A God-ordained priesthood, authentic sacrifices, and effective cleansing and sanctification must be provided for those who would draw near to God and serve him.

The writer also shows us, however, how these foundational Old Testament themes must be re-interpreted in the light of their fulfilment in Christ. Indeed, our understanding of the person and work of Christ can be greatly enriched by viewing the central truths of the gospel in terms of transformed worship categories. The perfect sacrifice of Jesus provides the basis for relating to God under the new covenant. His high-priestly work secures a once-for-all atonement for sin, the cleansing of our consciences and continuing right of direct access to God. Expressed in other terms, this means participation by faith now in the joyful assembly of all God's people in the heavenly Jerusalem. This certainty of access to God in the present is the guarantee of literal participation in the coming kingdom or city of God. In other words, Hebrews uses the language of worship to emphasize the realized or inaugurated aspect of Christian eschatology.

What has previously been described as the 'vertical' dimension to the Christian life is mostly expressed in Hebrews in terms of drawing near to God. This is central to the writer's exhortation and has its place in the congregational gathering as well as in the everyday experience of believers. Other worship terms are used to describe more generally our response to the high-priestly work of Jesus. The service pleasing to God under the new covenant is the obedience offered through Jesus Christ, motivated by gratitude for all that he has achieved on our behalf. Such worship will find expression in deeds of love and various forms of ministry to others, as well as in prayer, praise and confessions of faith.

As in the Old Testament, the locus of life and worship is to be the sanctuary. However, under the new covenant, that sanctuary is the heavenly Jerusalem, where Christ is seated at the right hand of God. Christians are pilgrims, still treading the road to that heavenly city, yet through Christ we may enjoy the fellowship of that joyful assembly in advance. What we experience now in our relationship with God, in the company of his people, is an anticipation of the ultimate reality. The whole of life is to be lived with reference to that unshakable kingdom and the prospect of living in God's presence for ever. Meanwhile, there is a special need to encourage fellow believers in faith, hope and love, lest any should fall by the wayside and fail to share in what God has promised.

The motivation and power for everyday service is the cleansing that derives from the finished work of Christ (10:19–22; cf. 9:14), together with the hope which that work sets before us (10:23; cf. 12:28–29). Christians need to be reminded of these truths whenever they meet together and to exhort one another to love and good works on that basis. In its own distinctive way, Hebrews affirms the truth of certain observations that I have made elsewhere in this book. The Christian gathering ought to focus on the finished work of Christ, the needs of his people as they seek to serve him in the present, the resources that are available from our heavenly high priest for running the Christian race, and the joyful hope of sharing with him in the perfection of 'the world to come'.

Notes

[1] E. Schweizer, 'Divine Service in the New Testament and Today', *St. Mark's Review* 66, 1971, p. 16.

[2] This suggests that the idea of Jesus as Servant of the Lord is another one of 'several converging elements that bring the author to see Jesus' death as a priestly act'. (J. R. Schaefer, 'The Relationship between Priestly and Servant Messianism in the Epistle to the Hebrews', *CBQ* 30, 1968, p. 382). Is. 53:12 appears to be reflected in the language of Heb. 9:28, but Schaefer (pp. 377–381) also argues that various themes associated with the figure of the servant in Isaiah are prominent more generally in the portrayal of Jesus and his work in Hebrews. He suggests that Servant Christology provides 'the point of contact between the singular teaching of Heb. on the priesthood of Christ and the Apostolic *kerygma*...' (p. 383).

[3] There is no justification for the view that, by some continuous liturgical action in heaven, Christ pleads the sacrifice made on the cross. The presence of the crucified and glorified Christ with God is the reality behind the concept of his heavenly intercession (*cf.* 9:24). *Cf.* D. G. Peterson, *Hebrews and Perfection*, SNTSMS 47 (Cambridge, London, New York and Melbourne: Cambridge University Press, 1982), pp. 113–116; and A. Cody, *Heavenly Sanctuary and Liturgy in the Epistle to the Hebrews: The Achievement of Salvation in the Epistle's Perspective* (St. Meinrad, IN: Grail, 1960), pp. 168–202.

[4] Despite the attempt of various commentators to draw parallels here with Platonic idealism, particularly as it is expressed in the writings of Philo of Alexandria, our writer's distinction between the earthly and heavenly is eschatologically controlled, rather than philosophically inspired. *Cf.* D. G. Peterson, *Hebrews and Perfection*, pp. 131–132. The heavenly sanctuary is not a part of the heavenly topography but a way of describing the presence of God (*cf.* 9:24).

[5] *Cf.* G. B. Caird, 'The Exegetical Method of the Epistle to the Hebrews', *Canadian Journal of Theology* 5, 1959, pp. 44–51. S. Kistemaker, *The Psalm Citations in the Epistle to the Hebrews* (Amsterdam: van Soest, 1961), pp. 101, 124–133, argues that Ps. 40:6–8 is the basis of the argument in Hebrews 8 – 10, but this text is best regarded as supportive of Je. 31:31–34, which forms an 'inclusion' or 'bracket' around the material about Christ's sacrificial work.

[6] The terminology of perfection does not derive from the cultic realm and is not to be equated with consecration or initiation. The perfecting of believers in Hebrews refers to their 'consummation' or 'completion' in a relationship with God, accomplished by the work of Christ. *Cf.* D. G. Peterson, *Hebrews and Perfection*, pp. 126–130, 136–140, 144–156, 166–167.

[7] B. F. Westcott, *The Epistle to the Hebrews*, (London: Macmillan, [3]1914), p. 252.

[8] *Cf.* D. G. Peterson, *Hebrews and Perfection*, p. 133. H. W. Attridge, *The Epistle to the Hebrews* (Philadelphia: Fortress, 1989), pp. 240–242, opposes the view that the first tent in 9:8–9 represents the whole Mosaic system.

[9] C. Maurer (*TDNT* 7. 898–919) rightly argues that the Old Testament view of human nature in general, and of the 'heart' in particular, must be taken into account when assessing New Testament teaching about the conscience. Hebrews certainly links the concepts of conscience and heart together, most importantly in 10:22 ('hearts sprinkled clean from a guilty conscience').

[10] *tōn genomenōn agathōn* ('the good things that are already here') is more likely to have been the original reading on the score of age and diversity of text type. The alternative (*tōn mellontōn agathōn*, 'the good things that are to come') appears to have arisen under the influence of 10:1. The good things that were still to come from the point of view of the Old Testament have now come with Christ.

[11] I have discussed alternative interpretations of 'the greater and more perfect tabernacle' in *Hebrews and Perfection*, pp. 140–144.

[12] B. F. Westcott, *Hebrews*, p. 261. The comparison of Christ's work with the ritual of the Day of Atonement suggests that the redemption in view is 'a once-for-all and standing offer of forgiveness for mankind', O. Michel, *Der Brief an die Hebräer*, Meyers Kommentar (Göttingen: Vandenhoeck & Ruprech, [7]1975), pp. 312–313. The reference to 'redemption from transgressions' in 9:15 (*apolytrōsin tōn...parabaseōn*) supports this interpretation. However, it is interesting to note from 9:15 that redemption from transgressions is the preliminary to receiving the further blessing of 'the promised eternal inheritance'.

[13] The 'dead works' (NIV 'acts that lead to death') from which the conscience needs cleansing, must include those offences from which a person had to break away in order to become a Christian (*cf.* 6:1, 'repentance from dead works'). Against Westcott (*Hebrews*, p. 146), the writer cannot mean 'all the works corresponding with the Levitical system', since those 'works' were not such as would give a person a guilty conscience.

[14] W. G. Johnsson, 'Defilement and Purgation in the Book of Hebrews' (Unpublished dissertation, Vanderbilt University, Nashville, TN, 1973), p. 225, argues that the 'blood rule' of 9:22 controls the logic by both exclusion and inclusion: 'on the one hand, all means of purgation other than blood are ruled out of court as being ultimately ineffective: on the other hand, animal sacrifices here find their common ground with the self-offering of Christ'.

[15] A. Cody, *Heavenly Sanctuary and Liturgy*, p. 188. *Cf.* W. G. Johnsson, 'Defilement and Purgation', pp. 330–337. In its immediate context, 9:23 cannot simply be a figurative restatement of the effect of Christ's death on believers. *Cf.* the contrary argument of F. F. Bruce, *The Epistle to the Hebrews* (London and Edinburgh: Marshall Morgan and Scott; Grand Rapids: Eerdmans, 1964), pp. 218–220.

[16] Note the range of technical terms used in the citation from Ps. 40:6 (LXX 39:7). *thysia* ('sacrifice'), while capable of referring to any kind of animal sacrifice, is used in the Old Testament with more special reference to the peace-offering. *prosphora* ('offering'), while also used in a general sense, is restricted in the levitical terminology to the 'cereal offering'. *holokautōma* is the standard Greek term for the 'holocaust' or 'burnt offering' and *peri hamartias* is the usual technical translation for the 'sin offering'. *Cf.* F. F. Bruce, *Hebrews*, pp. 233–234, and my discussion of these different forms of sacrifice in chapter one.

[17] As J. Denney, *The Death of Christ* (1902), edited by R. V. G. Tasker (London: Tyndale; Grand Rapids: Kregal, 1951), pp. 131–132, rightly observes, the redemptive value of Christ's obedience 'belongs to it not simply as obedience, but as obedience to a will of God which requires the Redeemer to take upon himself in death the responsibility of the sin of the world'.

[18] W. G. Johnsson, 'Defilement and Purgation', p. 228.

[19] Against all attempts to find a special polemic in the comparison of Christ with the angels, O. Michel (*Hebräer*, pp. 107–109) rightly argues that we have in these verses a logical development of the writer's apocalyptic framework of thought. *Cf.* B. F. Westcott, *Hebrews*, p. 16.

[20] *Cf.* B. F. Westcott, *Hebrews*, p. 110. Again, noting the particular application of *engizein* in the LXX to the ministry of the priests (*e.g.* Ex. 19:22; Lv. 10:33; Ezk. 42:13; 43:19), Westcott (p. 189) argues in connection with Heb. 7:19 that all believers are, in virtue of their Christian faith, priests: 'that which was before (in a figure) the privilege of a class has become (in reality) the privilege of all'.

[21] *Engizein* is used of Abraham's drawing near to God in prayer (Gn. 18:23) and in Ec. 4:17 (ET 5:1); Ho. 12:7 (ET 12:6); Zp. 3:2; Hg. 2:15; Is. 29:13; 58:2, all Israel draws near to God, either in cultic worship or in prayer. Indeed, the people of God are characterized in Ps. 148:14 as 'those who draw near to him' (*cf.* Judith 8:27). Similarly, *proserchesthai* is used to describe the action of Israelites in general, coming before the Lord in solemn assembly (*e.g.* Ex. 16:9; 34:32; Nu. 10:3–4), or simply in prayer (*cf.* Je. 7:16 [LXX]; Ps. 33:6 [LXX]). In Sirach 1:28, 30; 2:1 and Philo (*e.g. Op. Mund.* 144, *Deus Imm.* VIII. 161, *Plant.* 64), *proserchesthai* is used in the more general sense of having a relationship with God.

[22] H. Preisker, *TDNT* 2. 331.

[23] The 'throne of grace' is really 'a Hebraic periphrasis for God himself' (O. Michel, *Hebräer*, p. 209, *cf.* Heb. 8:1). The earthly counterpart of the heavenly throne in Old Testament thought was the 'mercy seat' (*hilastērion, cf.* Heb. 9:5) in the inner sanctuary of the tabernacle, where the rites of expiation on the Day of Atonement were conducted.

[24] W. C. van Unnik ('The Christian's Freedom of Speech in the New Testament', *BJRL* 44, 1961–62, p. 485), argues that the term *parrēsia* points to 'the free right to approach God, given in the sacrifice of Christ'.

[25] B. F. Westcott, *Hebrews*, p. 324.

[26] O. Michel, *Hebräer*, p. 346. Michel (p. 460, n. 2) rightly argues in connection with 12:22–24 that 'one draws near to the good things of salvation by first grasping the word of God'. *Cf.* 1 Pet. 2:4.

[27] Note the two perfect participles in 10:22, *rherantismenoi* ('having been sprinkled') and *lelousmenoi* ('having been washed').

[28] J. D. G. Dunn, *Baptism in the Holy Spirit* (London: SCM, 1970; Philadelphia: Westminster, 1977), pp. 211ff., sees a 'complementary parallelism' in 10:22, viewing Christian conversion-initiation in its inward and outward aspects (so also F. F. Bruce, *Hebrews*, pp. 250–251).

[29] It was noted previously that, in the LXX, *latreuein* regularly denotes the service or worship of the people in general, and that *leitourgein* has special reference to the priestly ministry. In Hebrews this fine distinction is not observed. Although *latreuein* is used in 9:9 and 10:2 in the normal LXX sense, to describe the service of all who sought to draw near to God by means of the Old Testament cult (contra H. Strathmann *TDNT* 4. 63 and O. Michel, *Hebräer*, p. 308), in 8:5 and 13:10 it apparently refers more specifically to the sacrificial ministry of Jewish priests (*cf.* 9:6).

[30] F. F. Bruce (*Hebrews*, p. 383, n. 199) suggests that the present participle in 12:28 *paralambanontes* ('receiving') indicates that 'the people of Christ have not

entered into their royal heritage with (Christ), although it is already theirs by promise'. This is consistent with the perspective of 13:14.

[31] The expression *echōmen charin* is a common idiom for gratitude and should not be rendered 'let us hold on to (God's) grace'. *Cf.* H. W. Attridge, *Hebrews*, p. 382, especially n. 69.

[32] F. F. Bruce, *Hebrews*, p. 384. According to H. Strathmann (*TDNT* 4. 64), the essence of this service or worship is 'a manner of life which is pleasing to God and which is sustained both by gratitude and by a serious sense of responsibility'. Michel (*Hebräer*, p. 477) inclines to the view that thanksgiving itself is the worship acceptable to God but acknowledges the possibility of the alternative understanding. *Cf.* H. W. Attridge, *Hebrews*, pp. 13–14, 384–385, regarding the authenticity of Hebrews 13 and it relation to the rest of the work.

[33] Terror and trembling are appropriate responses to a divine revelation in some contexts, but fear of God in the more positive sense of reverence or respect is more often in view. Note the examination of such terms and concepts in my chapter two.

[34] F. F. Bruce (*Hebrews*, pp. 397–398) describes this strange teaching which laid such insistence on food as 'probably some form of syncretistic gnosis, perhaps with Essene or quasi-Essene affinities'. The excursus by H. W. Attridge (*Hebrews*, pp. 394–396) surveys and comments on a number of possible approaches to this verse.

[35] This interpretation, which goes back to patristic times, is represented more recently by E. L. Randall, 'The Altar of Hebr. 13,10', *Australasian Catholic Record* 46, 1969, pp. 197–208, and P. Andriessen, 'L'Eucharistie dans l'Épître aux Hébreux', *NRTh* 3, 1972, pp. 275–276. The word *thysiastērion* ('altar') occurs in 7:13, with reference to the altar of the Jewish tabernacle (*cf.* 1 Cor. 9:13; 10:18), but is not used with reference to the Christian assembly until the second century AD (*cf.* Ignatius, *Phld.* 4; *Magn.* 7.2).

[36] Some interpreters argue that the 'altar' of Heb. 13:10 is within the heavenly sanctuary (so, for example, R. Williamson, 'The Eucharist and the Epistle to the Hebrews', *NTS* 21, 1974–75, pp. 308–309). The almost immediate reference to Christ's death 'outside the city gate to make the people holy through his own blood' (v. 12), however, suggests that the cross may be more specifically the altar on view in v. 10.

[37] R. Williamson ('The Eucharist and the Epistle to the Hebrews', p. 309) rightly concludes that there is 'little or no evidence in Hebrews of involvement on the part of the author or of the community of Christians to which the epistle was addressed, in eucharistic faith and practice'. To argue, however, that the writer was actually opposing the celebration of the Lord's Supper by engaging in a polemic against 'every form of cultus that placed a material means of sacramental communion between God and the worshipper' (p. 310) is to move beyond the evidence. *Cf.* F. F. Bruce, *Hebrews*, pp. 401–402.

[38] H. Koester, ' "Outside the Camp": Hebrews 13.9–14', *HTR* 55, 1967, p. 301. Koester too readily dismisses the view that the writer is calling for a decisive break with Judaism. While it is possible to generalize the call to abandon the security of cultic religion, the overall argument of Hebrews demands that Jewish tradition is the primary reference here.

[39] H. W. Attridge, *Hebrews*, p. 399. While it is true that we are to draw near to

Christ in the heavenly sanctuary, Heb. 13:13 suggests that, in another sense, we approach Christ by following his call to take up the cross and meeting him in the world, 'outside the camp'.

40 The 'sacrifice of praise' in the Old Testament may be a bloody sacrifice, a sub-class of 'peace offerings' (*e.g.* LXX Lv. 7:12; Ps. 26 [ET 27]:6), or the offering of thanksgiving itself, without an animal (*e.g.* LXX Pss. 49 [50]:14, 23; 106 [107]:22). The metaphorical character of the 'sacrifice of praise' in Heb. 13:15 is made quite clear by the use of the explanatory 'that is' (*tout' estin*).

41 *Cf.* Mt. 10:32 par.; Jn. 9:22; 12:42. O. Michel (*TDNT* 5. 207–217) shows the wide range of meanings that can be conveyed by the terms *homologoun* and *homologia* in the New Testament, but (pp. 209–210) unnecessarily restricts Heb. 13:15 to prayer and praise, and (p. 215) limits the 'confession' of Heb. 3:1; 4:14; 10:23 to 'a firmly outlined, liturgically set tradition by which the community must abide'.

42 There is no basis for finding an allusion to 'eucharistic sacrifice' in 13:15. 'Our author is simply not thinking of the eucharist at all... It is later associations, not the words of the text itself, which have led commentators to see in this passage a reference to the eucharist', H. W. Montefiore, *A Commentary on the Epistle to the Hebrews*, BNTC (London: Black, 1964), p. 248. *Cf.* R. Williamson, 'The Eucharist and the Epistle to the Hebrews', pp. 309–310.

43 'The new covenant community has a cult that is quite outside the realm of the cultic' (H. W. Attridge, *Hebrews*, p. 401).

44 *to euareston* ('that which is pleasing', 13:21) links back to the use of the corresponding verb *euaresteitai* in 13:16 and the adverb *euarestōs* in 12:28. Note also the same verb in the foundational teaching of 11:5–6 and the use of the adjective in Rom. 12:1, 2; 14:18; 2 Cor. 5:9; Eph. 5:10; Phil. 4:18; Col. 3:20; Tit. 2:9.

45 *Cf.* W. Schrage, *TDNT* 7. 841–843. Although a number of commentators have argued for a special meaning to be given to the word *episynagōgē* in this context, the majority view it simply as 'the regular gathering together of Christian believers for worship and exhortation in a particular place', according to P. E. Hughes, *A Commentary on the Epistle to the Hebrews* (Grand Rapids: Eerdmans, 1977), p. 418, concluding a helpful excursus on the subject.

46 The inhabitants of the heavenly Jerusalem in 12:22–24 are 'thousands upon thousands of angels' engaged in a great festival or celebration, together with 'the church of the firstborn (*ekklēsia prōtotokōn*), whose names are written in heaven'. The word *ekklēsia*, which means 'congregation', 'gathering' or 'assembly', was sometimes used in the Greek version of the Old Testament to denote the Israelites, assembled to meet the Lord (*e.g.* Dt. 4:10; 9:10; 18:16; 31:30; Jdg. 20:2). In Heb. 12:23 the reference is to the ultimate, completed company of the people of God – the heavenly or eschatological 'church' of God.

47 The new temple in Hebrews embraces 'both heavenly and earthly realities' to the extent that it identifies Christ's death on the cross as the new way to God (R. J. McKelvey, *The New Temple*, pp. 149–154), but the imagery of the temple is not specifically applied to the local congregation.

48 Although some writers have argued that *didaskaloi* ('teachers') in 5:12 indicates that the recipients of Hebrews were a special group within the Christian community such as priests converted from Judaism, such theories have not

commended themselves widely to scholars. Teaching others could mean professing and propagating the faith to unbelievers, as well as exhorting fellow believers.

[49] In common Greek usage, the verb *parakalein* and the noun *paraklesis* were employed with a great range of meanings, including calling for help, exhortation, encouragement and comfort. *Cf.* O. Schmitz, *TDNT* 5. 773–799, and D. G. Peterson, 'The Ministry of Encouragement', in P. T. O'Brien and D. G. Peterson (eds.), *God who is Rich in Mercy* (Sydney: Lancer; Grand Rapids: Baker, 1986), pp. 235–253.

[50] The expression *kardia ponēra apistias* means literally 'a heart that is evil because it is unbelieving'. B. F. Westcott (*Hebrews*, p. 84) rightly notes that ' "unbelief" (*apistia*) finds its practical issue in "disobedience" (*apeitheia*)'. *Cf.* 3:18–19 and compare 4:6.

[51] F. F. Bruce, *Hebrews*, p. 67.

[52] 'If there should be a concern of the individual for the community ("exhort one another"), there should also be a concern of the community for the individual ("lest any one of you...")', in line with the teaching of Paul that "if one member suffers, all suffer together" (1 Cor. 12:26)' (P. E. Hughes, *Hebrews*, p. 148).

[53] The exhortation *katanoōmen* recalls 3:1, where the same verb is used in a challenge to 'consider Jesus'. Hebrews thus calls for a continuing reflection on Jesus and what he has accomplished, together with a continuing reflection on the needs of other believers as they seek to live out their faith in Jesus and his promises.

[54] The present participle *engkataleipontes* in this context 'conveys the notion not simply of leaving, as no longer taking part in the assembly, but of abandoning, leaving the assembly exposed to period in the conflict' (B. F. Westcott, *Hebrews*, p. 327). *Cf.* 2 Tim. 4:10, 16; 2 Cor. 4:9; Mt. 27:46.

[55] O. Glombitza, '*Erwägungen zum kunstvollen Ansatz der Paraenese im Brief an die Hebräer – X, 19–25*', *NovT* 9, 1967, p. 147.

[56] N. A. Dahl, 'A New and Living Way: the Approach to God According to Hebrews 10:19–25', *Interpretation* 5, 1951, p. 409.

[57] Note the argument for such a general confession of sin as part of the ordinary gathering of the church by J. Calvin, *Institutes of the Christian Religion* III. 4. 11. With such confession, 'a gate to prayer is opened both to individuals in prayer and to all in public'.

[58] Against those who argue that there are many allusions to the Lord's Supper woven into the fabric of the author's argument, note the sober and careful response of R. Williamson, 'The Eucharist and the Epistle to the Hebrews', pp. 300–312 (focusing on Heb. 10:19–20 on pp. 306–307). *Cf.* my assessment of 13:9–10 above.

[59] O. Michel *TDNT* 5. 215–216. O. Glombitza ('Hebräer – X, 19–25', p. 142) argues that the perfect participles in v. 22b belong with the hortatory subjunctive in v. 23, making it clear that the exhortation is to hold fast to the baptismal confession of 'the hope that God has for us'.

[60] V. H. Neufeld, *The Earliest Christian Confessions*, NT Tools and Studies 5 (Leiden: Brill, 1963), p. 137.

CHAPTER NINE

Worship in the Revelation to John

What is going on around them, in the social and
political life of their own cities, is part of a conflict of
cosmic proportions, the eschatological war of good
and evil, the conflict of sovereignty between God and
the devil, in which they are called to take sides, to
take a firm stand, and by faithful witness to the truth
to play their part in resisting the pagan state and
pagan society.[1]

Without doubt, the Revelation to John is critical for a study of
the theme of worship in the New Testament. Visions of the
heavenly realm consistently portray the offering of adoration and
praise to God and the Lamb and the language of worship per-
vades the whole document. Most significantly, the worship term
proskynein is used twenty-four times, in ways that indicate the
centrality of this theme to the author's message. In most passages this word describes some form of homage to the living and
true God by heavenly beings or by those redeemed from earth
(Rev. 4:10; 5:14; 7:11; 11:1, 16; 14:7; 15:4; 19:4, 10; 22:9). Such
homage is offered by gesture and by words of acclamation and
praise.

Despite this interest in the worship of the heavenly host,
however, John's Apocalypse also concentrates on the earthly
scene. Various forms of idolatry are portrayed (9:20; 13:4, 8, 12),

together with prophecies of the awful judgment coming upon those who bow to false gods and refuse to acknowledge the living and true God. Surprisingly enough, the terminology of worship is not directly used to describe the response of Christians on earth to God and the Lamb.

For all that, a theology of worship can be constructed from what this book says about the role of Christians in their everyday discipleship. John is very concerned to show that Christian commitment has political, social and economic consequences. Acceptable worship involves faithfully serving God in the face of every conflicting loyalty. Nothing is specifically said about the function and purpose of Christian gatherings but, again, theological conclusions can be drawn from a number of John's perspectives.

The seductive power of false religion

The Revelation to John has been characterized as 'an apocalyptic writing in narrative form with a prophetic, eschatological aim and a pastoral touch presented in the form of a letter'.[2] It confronts a very specific social and historical situation in the first century AD, providing encouragement and challenge to groups of Christians in Asia Minor. The essential problem, as highlighted first in the letters to the seven churches, is one of conflict with the dominating cultural and religious ideals of the Greco-Roman world. John warns about the danger of compromise with or assimilation to pagan society. The false teaching coming from within the churches appears to be a sign that such compromise had already taken place in some of the cities addressed.[3]

From 9:20–21 it is clear that a large proportion of humanity worships 'demons and idols of gold and silver and bronze and stone and wood, which cannot either see or hear or walk' (RSV). The cults of paganism are linked with murders, sorceries, immorality and thefts, as an expression of the rebellion of mankind against the rule of God the Creator. So powerful are the forces of natural religion that people will not abandon its values and practices even in the face of God's terrible judgments. The focus in the rest of Revelation, however, is specifically on the worship of 'the beast' and the frightful judgment coming upon those who bow to his authority (13:4, 8, 12, 15; 14:9, 11; 16:2; 19:20; 20:4). Most commentators agree that the primary reference here is to the aggressive programme of emperor-worship being forced upon the population of the Roman Empire in the latter part of the first century.

The challenge of emperor-worship

Beginning with Julius Caesar, the Roman emperors were accustomed to receiving divine honours in terms of sacrifices, offerings of incense, processions, priesthoods, hymns and acclamations. They were commonly regarded as being set apart from ordinary mortals and standing in a special relationship with the gods of the various communities they had conquered. In the Greco-Roman world, all the important functions and spheres of life were thought to be activated by the gods and the object of religion was to secure their goodwill by faithfully carrying out the prescribed ritual. Since the ruler of the Roman Empire was regarded as having been elected by the gods and as manifesting their power for the benefit of all, 'it was impossible to consider the gods without reference to the emperor, just as to be reminded of the emperor was to be reminded of the gods'.[4]

There is no evidence to suggest that the average Roman citizen thought that the emperor possessed supernatural powers or could hear and answer prayers. The emperor as a god was associated with all the traditional gods in their temples, but never replaced them. The imperial cult was a symbol of the unity of the empire: the loyalty of the citizens was fostered by ceremonies taken from religion and focused on the emperor.[5] Religious, political, social and economic realities were thus linked together. Participation in the imperial cult helped people to affirm the values of their society and 'to express their own interest in the preservation of the world in which they lived'.[6]

The strongest centre of the imperial cult since the time of Augustus was in Asia Minor, where the seven churches were located. Indeed, there were imperial temples in each of the cities addressed by John.[7] By the time of Domitian (AD 81-96), emperor-worship had become 'the one religion of universal obligation in Asia'.[8] It was the Emperor Domitian who insisted on the designation *dominus et deus* ('Lord and God'), and in his time failure to honour the emperor as a god became a political offence and punishable.

From John's point of view, to engage in the imperial cult is to worship the 'beast coming out of the sea' (13:1). Moreover, to worship this beast is to give allegiance to 'the dragon', 'that ancient serpent called the devil, or Satan, who leads the whole world astray' (12:9). This is so because the beast gets his authority from Satan (13:4). In reality, the dragon and the beast are 'a diabolic duo who function as counterfeit counterparts to God and the Lamb'.[9] John also sees a second beast coming up 'out of the earth', who exercises all the authority of the first beast on his behalf, and whose task is to make the earth and its inhabitants worship the first beast (13:11–12). Its use of great signs to deceive people suggests that this beast represents 'the role of false religion in effecting the capitulation of mankind to the worship of the secular power'.[10] Those who will not worship the image of the first beast are to be slain (13:15). Only those who worship the first beast receive the mark on the right hand or the forehead, enabling them to buy and sell in the commerce of the empire. Clearly, economic privation or death await those who refuse to participate in the emperor-cult.[11]

Two categories of worshippers

A major theme of this book is the distinction between true worship and idolatry. John divides humanity into two categories, the worshippers of the dragon and the beast and the worshippers of God and the Lamb. The contrast between the two groups of worshippers reaches its climax in two visions at the end of the book. The vision of the fall of Babylon (17:1 – 19:10) represents the judgment coming upon human society in rebellion against God – the 'prostitute' seducing people away from the worship of the creator by her corrupt practices. The vision of Jerusalem (21:9 – 22:9) then portrays the future of the faithful in terms of a city where God himself dwells (21:22) and where his servants worship him unceasingly (22:3). The message of these two climactic visions is emphasized by their parallel conclusions (19:9–10; 22:8–9), which enable John to end both with the injunction 'Worship God!' 'The angel's refusal of worship reinforces the point: Do not worship the beast, do not even worship God's servants the angels, worship God!'[12]

John's Apocalypse teaches that 'the conflict between God and Satan takes historical form in the conflict of human allegiances manifest in worship'.[13] Satan works through the ordinary structures of society, as well as through the deceits of false religion, to capture the allegiance of people and to turn them from the service of God. John directs his original readers to recognize the religious dimension to their involvement in the Greco-Roman world. While some New Testament writers stress the importance of honouring and obeying the governing authorities (*e.g.* Rom. 13:1-7; 1 Pet. 2:13-17), John sees the need to warn Christians about rendering to God 'the things that are God's' (*cf.* Mk. 12:17). To participate in the imperial cult was to endorse beliefs that were alien to the gospel and to yield themselves to the control of Satan. Their relationship with God demanded a deliberate stand against every pressure to conform. In the face of such conflicting world-views, they could not simply 'worship' God in private but had to consider the social consequences of their Christian commitment!

Although the situation addressed by the Apocalypse is quite specific, there have been a number of parallels in the experience of God's people ever since. As with Old Testament prophecy, it is possible to see different levels of fulfilment for John's predictions. Whenever the state opposes Christianity with its own ideology and power, 'the dragon' is most obviously at work in the political arena. Christians in every age and culture need to discern how this conflict between God and Satan is manifested in their own particular context. Acceptable worship involves acknowledging and accepting God's claim for exclusive devotion and loyalty by rejecting every alternative. In the market-place, in politics, in the field of education or the arts, the Christian is constantly challenged to make the decisive choice for God that Jesus himself made, when he was tested so forcefully in the wilderness (*cf.* Mt. 4:8-10).

The call to worship the true God

The frightening prophecy of persecution for Christians who refuse to worship the beast and to bear its mark (13:1–18), is followed by a vision of 'the Lamb, standing on Mount Zion, and with him 144,000 who had his name and his Father's name written on their foreheads' (14:1–5). Glimpses of the final blessedness of God's people are interspersed in this book among the visions of judgment to encourage the readers to patient endurance and faithfulness in the present. Those who are 'redeemed from the earth' (14:3) are engaged in the worship of heaven, as they sing a new song before the throne and before the four living creatures and the elders and 'follow the Lamb wherever he goes' (14:4). The implication is clear: only those who abstain from worshipping the beast on earth will share, by God's grace, in the worship of heaven. John then goes on to give the message of three angels, each of which relates to the conflict of worship highlighted in Revelation 13.

The eternal gospel

The first angel summons people from every nation and tribe and tongue to 'Fear God (*phobēthēte ton theon*) and give him glory, because the hour of his judgment has come', and to 'worship (*proskynēsate*) him who made the heavens, the earth, the sea and the springs of water' (14:6–7). This 'eternal gospel' summons the whole creation to acknowledge God as creator, lord of history and judge of all. It recalls the vision of Revelation 4 and the claim of the heavenly host that he alone is worthy to receive 'glory and honour and power' (4:11) from everything that he has made. Notwithstanding the message of God's redeeming grace in Christ, which is so prominent in this book, the doctrine of creation is given as the primary reason for honouring God as God or worshipping him. Associated with this doctrine is the claim that every human being is accountable to God (*cf.* Rom. 1:18–25; Acts 14:15–17; 17:22–31). In line with other New Testament passages, Revelation 14:6–7 suggests that evangelism may be viewed as a call to worship God appropriately.

The second angel reinforces the proclamation that 'the hour of

his judgment has come' by announcing the fall of 'Babylon the Great' (14:8). The third angel brings a proclamation recalling the decree that those who would not worship the beast and his image or receive his mark should be persecuted and killed (13:15, 17). Now it is revealed that those who do worship the beast and bear his mark suffer a much worse fate at the hands of God (14:9–11). When the terrible fury of God is poured out upon them, 'There is no rest day or night for those who worship the beast and his image, or for anyone who receives the mark of his name' (14:11). God's wrath against the worshippers of the beast is then portrayed (16:2) and the punishment of the beast and the false prophet who had persuaded people to worship the beast is recorded (19:20).

The worship of the beast, which is effectively the worship of Satan, involves literally paying homage to an image in Revelation 13, but more profoundly giving the kind of allegiance to the state that belongs to God. This means a life-orientation as well as involvement in the emperor-cult. What, then, is the nature of Christian worship in the earthly sphere, according to John the Seer?

The priestly service of God's people

The angelic summons to worship God alone (14:6–7; 19:10; 22:8–9), broadly calls for submission and undivided allegiance to the creator. Beyond that, however, *proskynein* is not specifically applied to what Christians do here and now, even though it is liberally used in the visions of heaven. On the other hand, in a programmatic statement summarizing much of the teaching of the rest of the Revelation, we find this ascription:

> To him who loves us and has freed us from our sins
> by his blood, and has made us to be a kingdom and
> priests (to serve) his God and Father – to him be
> glory and power for ever and ever! Amen (Rev.
> 1:5b–6).

The NEB and NIV have added 'to serve' in the English translation to enhance the notion that the priestly service of the people of God is the end-point of Christ's redeeming work.[14] What was promised to Israel at Sinai ('You shall be to me a kingdom of priests, a holy nation', Ex. 19:6, RSV) has been fulfilled for a great multitude of believers in the heavenly or eschatological assembly of the people of God ('from every nation, tribe, people and language', Rev. 7:9–15). By virtue of his sacrifice, Christ has purchased a people for God from amongst the nations and has made them to be 'a kingdom and priests to (serve) our God' (5:10; *cf.* 20:6).[15] As in the Old Testament, redemption is for the purpose of worship or service to God.

1 Peter is the only other New Testament document that points explicitly to the priestly role of Christ's people. Those who come to Jesus are being built into 'a spiritual house', to be 'a holy priesthood' (1 Pet. 2:5).[16] They function collectively as priests by 'offering spiritual sacrifices acceptable to God through Jesus Christ'. The broader context of this letter would suggest that such 'spiritual sacrifices' are the good deeds performed by Christians in everyday life, in grateful obedience to God for all his mercies in Christ (*cf.* Rom. 12:1).

Peter goes on to explain more precisely how the role and function of Israel under the old covenant is to be fulfilled by Jewish and Gentile believers in Christ. 'You are a chosen people,' he writes, 'a royal priesthood, a holy nation, a people belonging to God, that you may declare the praises of him who called you out of darkness into his wonderful light' (1 Pet. 2:9). The priesthood in view is not a ministry within the church by certain selected individuals for the benefit of others, following the pattern of the levitical priesthood within Israel. Just as Israel was chosen from among the nations by God, to bear witness to his character and will (*cf.* Ex. 19:6), the people of the new covenant are to serve the nations by maintaining their distinctiveness as 'a holy nation' (*cf.* 1 Pet. 1:15–16), reflecting the character of God in all their relationships (*cf.* 2:11–12).

Another dimension to the 'priestly' calling of Christ's people in 1 Peter 2:9 is the charge to 'sound the praises' (*tas aretas exangeilēte*) of God. This adaptation of Isaiah 43:21 uses the language of the Psalms (*e.g.* Pss. 9:14 [LXX, 9:15]; 71:15 [70:15]; 107:22 [106:22]), suggesting that testimony to God's praise-worthy deeds in the gathering of his people is in view. The broader context, however, also suggests that believers fulfil this priestly role by giving an account of the gospel to unbelievers, whenever the opportunity arises (*cf.* 1 Pet. 3:15).[17] In short, Christians are to convey the character and purposes of God to the world by word and deed.

The notion of priestly service in the Apocalypse is particularly linked with that of Christ's coming reign on earth (5:10; 20:6), when every temptation to compromise and sin is removed.[18] Visions of the heavenly realm suggest that, as in 1 Peter, the service of God involves glorifying God in word and deed, following the Lamb 'wherever he goes' (Rev. 14:4). God's people serve him or pay homage to him in anticipation now, as they wait for the perfection of 'a new heaven and a new earth' (21:1).

Although it is not called worship as such, there is a clear alternative for Christians to the worship of the beast. Following the portrayal of the judgment of God on all idolaters, John's call is for 'patient endurance on the part of the saints who obey God's commandments and remain faithful to Jesus' (14:12; *cf.* 13:10). In their context, such verses function to define Christian worship as *faith in God's promises worked out in the obedience of everyday life.* The writer's aim is not simply to warn Christians of the persecution they must endure or of the danger of giving in to Satan's demands and becoming apostate. He writes positively to encourage his readers to persevere in their obedience to the Creator, to continue in their reliance on Jesus and his saving work, and to hold fast to the testimony about the future sent to them by the risen Christ (*cf.* 22:16–20).

> The decisive battle in God's eschatological holy war against all evil, including the power of Rome, has already been won – by the faithful witness and sacrificial death of Jesus. Christians are called to participate in his war and his victory – but by the same means as he employed: bearing the witness of Jesus to the point of martyrdom.[19]

In the context of temptation and trial, God can be glorified and served by taking a firm stand against paganism in all its forms and by bearing faithful witness to the truth of the gospel.

The worship of Christians on earth is the exact opposite to the worship of the beast and involves giving proper allegiance to God and the Lamb in every circumstance of life. In 22:6–15, the worship of God is closely associated with keeping the words of John's prophetic book and living in a godly way, awaiting the consummation of history.

Worship in the heavenly realm

The point has already been made that the visions of heavenly worship are given to encourage Christians to remain faithful to Jesus and not to miss out on the joy of serving God and the Lamb in the new Jerusalem. In these visions, the heavenly court regularly pays homage to God by some literal act of obeisance or homage in his presence. This is suggested by the regular coupling of *proskynein* with the verb *piptein*, 'to fall down' (4:10; 5:14; 7:11; 11:16; 19:4) or by the expression 'worship before you' (*proskynēsousin enōpion sou*, 15:4), with respect to God. Nevertheless, the worship envisaged is not simply an act of physical obeisance but an acknowledgment of God's character and purposes, as revealed in his righteous acts.

Praise of God the creator

At strategic points in the Apocalypse, the heavenly host falls down and worships God and the Lamb, ascribing certain characteristics and mighty acts to them. Here it is significant to notice that verbs of saying and singing are regularly coupled with *proskynein*. So, for example, the four living creatures 'rest not day nor night' ascribing holiness to God as creator (4:8–10). When this happens the twenty-four elders fall before the throne of God and worship him by saying:

> You are worthy, our Lord and God,
>   to receive glory and honour and power,
> for you created all things,
>   and by your will they were created
>   and have their being.
>   (Rev. 4:11; *cf.* 7:11–12)[20]

270

This ascription is fundamental to the teaching of the book, since it establishes God's absolute sovereignty over his creation and the fact that all life exists to reflect his glory and honour and power. The honour that is paid to God in the heavenly realm contrasts dramatically with the situation on earth, where few hold fast to his words and serve him faithfully. The link between praise and homage in Revelation recalls the pattern observed in some Old Testament cultic contexts (*e.g.* 1 Ch. 29:20–21; 2 Ch. 7:3–4; 29:28–30; Ne. 8:6).

The idea that heaven is God's dwelling-place is well-known from the Old Testament (*e.g.* 1 Ki. 8:30; Ps. 103:19; Is. 66:1). Sometimes his dwelling is portrayed as a heavenly temple (*e.g.* Is. 6:1–8; Hab. 2:20), sometimes as a celestial throne-room or court-room (*e.g.* 1 Ki. 22:19–22; Dn. 7:9–10; Zc. 3:1–7), and sometimes as both together (*e.g.* Ps. 11:4). In the inter-testamental period, there was a growing interest in the heavenly temple, and some identification of it with prophetic teaching about the establishment of a new temple in the End-time. Jewish writers even spoke about the heavenly temple descending to earth to replace the temple at Jerusalem (*cf.* Rev. 21:2–4).[21] John's description of the heavenly realm and its relation to life on earth shows many obvious links with biblical and post-biblical teaching. His outline of the ceremonial of the heavenly throne-room, however, also shows a striking resemblance to the ceremonial of the first-century Roman imperial court.[22]

Hymns and acclamations were offered to Roman emperors and governors by people from various social stations and regions, expressing consent to their rule, praise for their achievements, and hope for the continuation of their reign. The hymns and acclamations in the setting of the heavenly throne-room point to God's greater and more powerful kingship. They acknowledge the magnificent benefits of his rule and look forward to its consummation in the overthrow of all his enemies. 'The result is that the sovereignty of God and the Lamb have been elevated so far above all pretensions and claims of earthly rulers that the latter, upon comparison, become only pale, even diabolical imitations of the transcendent majesty of the King of Kings and Lord of lords.'[23] The message for those on earth is that public acknowledgment of the kingship of God or testimony to Christ as Lord has far-reaching political and social implications (*cf.* Acts 17:6–9).

Praise of Christ the redeemer

In Revelation 5, the same heavenly host sings a 'new song' to Christ as the Lamb. They fall on their faces before him, as he is revealed to be the only one worthy to open the scroll and its seven seals, thus setting in motion the final events of human history. His worthiness has to do with his redemptive work, which is briefly recounted in a credal form addressed directly to the risen and ascended Lord:

> You are worthy to take the scroll
>   and to open its seals,
> because you were slain,
>   and with your blood you purchased
>   men for God
>   from every tribe and language and
>   people and nation.
> You have made them to be a kingdom
>   and priests to serve our God,
>   and they will reign on the earth.
>   (Rev. 5:9–10)

A further ascription of praise to the exalted Christ follows, echoing to some extent the language of 4:11 – 'Worthy is the Lamb, who was slain, to receive power and wealth and wisdom and strength and honour and glory and praise!' (5:12). Indeed, the parallels between 4:9–11 and 5:8–12 make it clear that Christ is being adored on absolutely equal terms with God the creator![24] Jesus Christ is not an alternative object of worship in this book but shares in the glory due to God. He belongs with God, while angels are regarded as fellow-servants with all who hold to the testimony of Jesus (19:10; 22:8–9). Prohibition of the worship of angels does not prohibit the worship of Jesus.[25]

Revelation 5 concludes with the response of everything created, uniting in praise to God and the Lamb as a single act of worship or homage: 'To him who sits on the throne and to the Lamb be praise and honour and glory and power, for ever and ever!' (5:13; *cf.* 7:9–10). Remembering that John presents a fundamental challenge to those who dwell on earth to worship God as creator and judge (14:6–7), it would appear from the sequence of visions in Revelation 4 – 5 that only those ransomed by the blood of the Lamb can participate in the worship that is due to God from his creation.

Praise for the outworking of God's purposes

When the Lamb opens the seals to inaugurate a series of judgments on the earth (6:1–17), those who are redeemed from the nations are pictured as standing before God and the Lamb, crying out with a loud voice, 'Salvation belongs to our God, who sits on the throne, and to the Lamb' (7:9–10), while the angels, the elders and the four living creatures fall down on their faces and worship God with another hymn of praise (7:11–12). This passage suggests that no great stress should be placed on differences of posture (as if the heavenly host honours God more effectively by prostration than standing!). The chapter concludes with an identification of the redeemed as those who have 'come out of the great tribulation; they have washed their robes and made them white in the blood of the Lamb' (7:14). The victory of Christ in his death and resurrection has become their victory, and now they are 'before the throne of God and serve (*latreuousin*) him day and night in his temple' (7:15).[26]

With the sounding of the seventh trumpet, loud voices in heaven proclaim that 'the kingdom of the world has become the kingdom of our Lord and of his Christ, and he will reign for ever and ever' (11:15). This provokes the twenty-four elders, who are seated on their thrones before God, to fall on their faces and pay homage to God with an outburst of thanksgiving:

> We give thanks to you, Lord God Almighty,
>   the One who is and who was,
> because you have taken your great power
>   and have begun to reign.
> The nations were angry;
>   and your wrath has come.

The time has come for judging the dead,
  and for rewarding your servants the
    prophets
and your saints and those who
    reverence your name,
  both small and great –
and for destroying those who destroy
    the earth.

(Rev. 11:17–18)

The heavenly court is grateful because God has exercised his powerful rule over rebellious men and women by inaugurating the final judgment. The response to the outpouring of God's wrath in 16:5–7 is similar in sentiment.

Praise for the fulfilment of Old Testament hopes and promises

There are many ways in which the praise of the heavenly host in the Apocalypse proclaims the fulfilment of Old Testament hopes and promises. So, for example, the expectation that the nations would be united in the praise of Israel's God is shown to have been fulfilled in the visions of the heavenly Jerusalem (*e.g.* 7:1–17; 22:1–5) and is proclaimed in the song of the redeemed:

Great and marvellous are your deeds,
  Lord God Almighty.
Just and true are your ways,
  King of the ages.
Who will not fear you, O Lord,
  and bring glory to your name?
For you alone are holy.
All nations will come
  and worship before you,
for your righteous acts have been revealed.

(Rev. 15:3–4)

Again, the destruction of 'Babylon the Great', as portrayed in Revelation 17 – 18, represents the judgment of all the forces opposed to the people of God throughout their history (*cf.* Is. 13 – 24). A roar of praise goes up from the great multitude in heaven, glorifying God for his judgments, which are 'true and just', and rejoicing that final salvation has come (19:1–3). The twenty-four elders and the four living creatures echo this praise with cries of 'Amen, Hallelujah!' (19:4). Then a voice from the throne calls for all God's servants to praise him and the multitude shouts its response:

> Hallelujah!
>   For our Lord God Almighty reigns.
> Let us rejoice and be glad
>   and give him glory!
> For the wedding of the Lamb has come,
>   and his bride has made herself
>   ready.
> Fine linen, bright and clean,
>   was given her to wear.
>
> (Rev. 19:6–8)

Israel's hope of feasting together in the presence of the Lord (*e.g.* Is. 25:6–8) is fulfilled in the new Jerusalem for those who are wedded to the Lamb. He is the one who cleanses and clothes his 'bride', making her fit to share in this glorious event. This picture of the messianic banquet is another way of describing the joy of the new creation, as detailed in Revelation 21 – 22.

It is clear then that rejoicing in God, giving him the glory and praising him are all different aspects of the homage or worship that is due to him. Adoration and praise occur in the book of the Revelation as the events of the End-time are unfolded or as they are anticipated. Adoration and praise also function to recall the saving work of God in Christ and to spell out all its benefits.

The link between heaven and earth

The doxologies, acclamations and hymns of praise in John's Apocalypse have found their way into many Christian songs and liturgies throughout the centuries. This has happened because of the form as well as the content of these segments. With the greatest of ease, they can be adapted for congregational use.

Observing this, some scholars have proposed that John must have employed sentences and phrases taken from pre-existing liturgical sources in the first century.[27] Others have argued that Revelation reflects a whole pattern of congregational worship in the churches addressed, largely influenced by contemporary Jewish practices in temple and synagogue, or by those services together with aspects of the Hellenistic ruler cults.[28] It cannot simply be assumed from later liturgical use of the hymnic material in this book, however, that Revelation reflects first-century Christian liturgical usage.[29] Although elements of Christian and Jewish services may have been interwoven in the portrayal of the heavenly worship, it is now impossible to separate the details and see the basic lines of the primitive Christian service.

Affirming the victory of God

The elements of heavenly worship have their own special function in the structure of this book: 'they interpret the apocalyptic events, the peculiar meaning of which would not be completely clear without such interpretation. For this reason, they are quite closely linked, as regards their contents at any rate, with the visions of the future.'[30] John has made eschatological drama unfold from a heavenly, cultic setting. The heavenly liturgy regularly proclaims End-time realities prior to their presentation in narrative form (*e.g.* 15:1–4), or responds to God's actions in history, when they are set forth in a vision (*e.g.* 19:1–8). Since John was writing a book of prophecy, 'he structured the hymnic material so that it would serve a prophetic function, as he knew it in the life of the community'.[31]

In particular it is important to notice that the hymnic material emphasizes the victory already accomplished by Jesus through his death and heavenly exaltation. What remains to be worked out in history is an unfolding of the ultimate implications of that victory. The scenes of heavenly worship express fundamental theological truths represented in other ways in other New Testament books. By this means, John leaves his readers in no doubt that the End has come in the historic events of Jesus of Nazareth,[32] and on the basis he urges them to live patient, faithful and godly lives.

It is possible that the visions of the eschatological drama came to John when he was meeting with other Christians 'on the Lord's day' (cf. 1:10, 'On the Lord's Day I was in the Spirit'). He certainly wrote them down so that they could be read aloud in that context (cf. 1:3; 22:18–19). If his aim was to encourage Christians to maintain their faith in Christ and resist every temptation to idolatry and apostasy, the hymnic material, with its focus on the sovereignty of God and the victory of the Lamb, must have provided the original recipients with every encouragement to do just that. By implication, a theology of the Christian gathering emerges here.

Sharing in the worship of heaven

'Behold, I am coming soon!' says the risen Christ. 'Blessed is he who keeps the words of the prophecy in this book' (22:7). Meeting together to hear 'the words of the prophecy of this book' (22:18) being read and discussed would have been a particularly encouraging activity for those originally addressed. A natural response to the hearing of this prophecy in the congregation would have been some acknowledgment of the truths it expresses with acclamations and songs. John does not say as much, but such affirmations of trust and hope in God are surely a way by which believers on earth may share corporately in the worship of heaven and anticipate the unhindered service of the coming reign of Christ.

Against those who have argued that John has made the worship of heaven in some way a reflection of what was going on in the churches of Asia in the first century, it is more reasonable to suggest that the reverse is true. John wrote to encourage his readers to reflect the pattern of the heavenly assembly in their life on earth. This could happen when they gathered together and in everyday life situations, when they were faced with any new sign of the dragon's power or with any manifestation of God's wrath. It would be simplistic to say that John wanted the churches to imitate the actions of the heavenly assembly or merely to sing the same songs. What was needed above all else was to reflect the same confidence in God. With the qualification that Christian worship means more than singing hymns in church on Sunday, it is correct to assert that 'in its innermost meaning primitive Christian Worship was intended to be parallel to the Worship of heaven'.[33]

Singing the praises of God and the Lamb is undoubtedly an important Christian activity. It is a way of affirming fundamental gospel truths together and of acknowledging God's powerful but gracious rule over nature and history. Together with teaching and various forms of exhortation, it can strengthen Christians to maintain their confidence in God and in the outworking of his purposes in a world devoted to idolatry and every kind of God-rejecting activity. Testifying to the goodness and power of God in the congregation of his people can be a means of encouraging such testimony before unbelievers in everyday life.

The hymnic material in the book of the Revelation, however, should alert us to the importance of singing God's praise in a way that is truly honouring to him and helpful to his people. Do our hymns and songs concentrate on praising God for his character and his mighty acts in history on our behalf? Do they focus sufficiently on the great truths of the gospel? There is always a temptation to focus too much on the expression of our own immediate needs. Is the language we use as powerful and as simple as in the material given to us by John? We need to avoid the extremes of being trite and trivial, and loading our hymns and choruses with so much imagery that only the well-instructed can appreciate them. Do our hymns and acclamations help us to rejoice in God's gracious and powerful rule, acknowledge its blessings and look forward to its consummation in the new creation? Do they challenge us to take a firm stand against every manifestation of Satan's power and to bear faithful witness to the truth of the gospel in our society? It is not good enough to sing certain items merely because they make the congregation feel good!

Conclusion

Like Hebrews, the Revelation to John focuses on the heavenly realm, where Jesus the crucified Messiah reigns in glory. The whole of life is to be lived in relation to the new Jerusalem and the victory of 'the Lamb who was slain'. From the point of view of those still on earth, the holy city must one day come down 'out of heaven from God' (21:2). But confidence in the finished work of Jesus and his promises about the future is the way to share even now in the worship of heaven. Those who remain faithful to Jesus will enjoy the fruit of his victory in the full reality of his unshakable kingdom. Even those who feel overwhelmed by the powers ranged against them and who are persecuted for their faith should be moved by John's visions of heaven to live a life of joyful service to God in the present.

Christ's redeeming work creates a community of believers from every tribe and language and people and nation. Together, they fulfil the destiny of Israel, 'to be a kingdom and priests to serve our God, and they will reign on the earth' (5:10). Old Testament promises about the nations being united in the service of Israel's God are fulfilled by those who belong to the Messiah. As they await the consummation of God's purposes, they can offer to God the exclusive worship that is due to him by taking a firm stand against paganism in all its forms and by bearing faithful witness to the truth of the gospel in their everyday lives. The full exercise of their royal priesthood belongs to the time of Christ's return and his ultimate triumph.

More than any other New Testament book, the Revelation to John stresses the importance of praise and acclamation as a means of honouring God and encouraging his people to trust him and obey him. A key aspect of the 'priestly service' of the new covenant community is the sounding of his praises. This can find one expression when his people gather together and another in the context of everyday life and relationships.

Notes

[1] R. J. Bauckham, 'The Book of Revelation as a Christian War Scroll', *Neotestamentica* 22, 1988, p. 31.

[2] J. A. du Rand, 'The imagery of the heavenly Jerusalem (Revelation 21:9 – 22:5)', *Neotestamentica* 22, 1988, p. 70, summarizing the conclusions of a number of contemporary commentators. However, I am not satisfied with the expression 'a pastoral touch'. It seems to me that Revelation has a distinctly pastoral aim from start to finish.

[3] C. J. Hemer, *The Letters to the Seven Churches of Asia in their Local Setting*, *JSNTS*

11 (Sheffield: *JSOT*, 1986), p. 10, suggests that the readers were faced with the challenge of identifying either with pagan society (the 'Nicolaitan' answer), or with Judaism, on whatever terms would gain them acceptance in the synagogue.

[4] P. J. J. Botha, 'God, emperor worship and society: Contemporary experiences and the book of Revelation', *Neotestamentica* 22, 1988, p. 97. Earlier in this article he rightly warns about oversimplifying the evidence regarding a uniform cult throughout the Empire in the first century AD.

[5] *Cf.* K. Hopkins, 'Divine Emperors or the Symbolic Unity of the Roman Empire', *Conquerors and Slaves* (Cambridge, London, New York and Melbourne: Cambridge University Press, 1978), pp. 199, n. 3.

[6] P. J. J. Botha, 'God, emperor worship and society', p. 97.

[7] *Cf.* S. R. F. Price, *Rituals of Power* (Cambridge, London, New York and Melbourne: Cambridge University Press, 1984), p. xxiii.

[8] R. H. Charles, *The Revelation of St John*, *ICC*, Vol. I (Edinburgh: T. & T. Clark, 1920), p. xcv. *Cf.* G. B. Caird, *The Apostolic Age* (London: Duckworth, 1955), pp. 156–180. The earliest authorities are practically unanimous in assigning the Apocalypse to the last years of Domitian and the internal evidence points strongly in this direction (*cf.* R. H. Charles, *Revelation* I, pp. xcii–xcvii).

[9] D. E. Aune, 'The Influence of Roman Imperial Court Ceremonial on the Apocalypse of John', *Biblical Research* 28, 1983, p. 5.

[10] R. H. Mounce, *The Book of Revelation*, *NICNT* (Grand Rapids: Eerdmans, 1977), p. 259. The beast out of the earth is a deceiver (*cf.* v. 14). Elsewhere he is uniformly called the false prophet (16:13; 19:20; 20:10). Mounce suggests that 'in John's day the reference would be either to the local priests of the imperial cult or to the provincial council responsible for enforcing emperor worship throughout Asia'.

[11] On the forms of the imperial cult see E. Ferguson, *Backgrounds of Early Christianity* (Grand Rapids: Eerdmans, 1987), pp. 164–165. R. H. Mounce (*Revelation*, p. 33) rightly asserts that 'while the picture of universal enforcement of the imperial cult given in Revelation 13 is a forecast rather than a descriptive account of the conditions under Domitian, all the elements were present in the final decade of the first century from which a reasonable projection could be made'.

[12] R. J. Bauckham, 'The Worship of Jesus in Apocalyptic Christianity', *NTS* 27, 1981, p. 329 (emphasis removed).

[13] *Ibid*, p. 329.

[14] The verb *latreuein* ('to serve') is not used in the Greek text here, though it functions as an apparent equivalent for *proskynein* in 7:15 and 22:3, where we are told that the destiny of God's people is to worship or serve him for ever in the bliss of the new creation. The NIV has added 'to serve' also in 5:10 to make clear the implication of being 'priests to our God'.

[15] It is entirely unwarranted to say that 'corporately believers are a kingdom, and individually they are priests to God' (R. H. Mounce, *Revelation*, pp. 148–149). The allusion to Ex. 19:6 suggests that Christians function corporately as a priestly kingdom, reigning and serving as 'a holy nation', devoted to God and the Lamb.

[16] Although some have argued that the 'spiritual house' in 1 Pet. 2:5 is household rather than temple imagery, the house is defined as being 'for holy priesthood' (*eis hierateuma hagion*) and 'it is difficult to imagine a house intended for priesthood as being anything other than a temple of some sort', J. R. Michaels, *1 Peter*, WBC 49 (Waco: Word, 1988), p. 100.

[17] J. R. Michaels (*1 Peter*, p. 110) makes too much of a distinction between congregational praise and 'mission preaching' in opposing the one-sided emphasis of J. H. Elliott, *The Elect and Holy: An Exegetical Examination of 1 Peter 2:4–10 and the Phrase basileion hierateuma*, NovTSup 12 (Leiden: Brill, 1966), pp. 41–42. The allusion to Is. 43:20–21 in 1 Pet. 2:9 suggests an analogy between the situation of the exiles in Babylon and Peter's readers. In different ways they are to bring testimony about the character and purposes of God before the nations.

[18] Even if the present tense *basileuousin* ('they reign') is read instead of the future *basileusousin* ('they shall reign') in 5:10, the reference is probably future, 'the verb serving as a futuristic present and imparting a tone of assurance' (R. H. Mounce, *Revelation*, p. 149, n. 27).

[19] R. J. Bauckham, 'The Book of Revelation as a Christian War Scroll', p. 31. Bauckham notes that 'it is misleading to describe this as "passive resistance"; for John it is as active as any physical warfare and his use of holy war imagery conveys this need for active engagement in the Lamb's war'.

[20] RSV and NEB take the liberty of translating *legontes* in 4:8, 10 by 'singing'. It may be legitimate to argue from the parallel in 5:9 that these ascriptions of praise in the heavenly assembly are sung but the text of 4:8, 10 does not actually say so (*cf.* NIV).

[21] *Cf.* R. J. McKelvey, *The New Temple*, pp. 25–41. The Dead Sea Scrolls reflect the idea that the faithful on earth can participate with the angels in the worship of the heavenly temple (*e.g.* I QS 11:7–8; I QH 3:21–22).

[22] D. E. Aune, 'Roman Imperial Court Ceremonial', pp. 5–26. So, for example, 'the heavenly scene of the twenty-four elders throwing down their crowns before the throne (4:10) has no parallel in Israelite-Jewish literature, and become(s) comprehensible only in the light of the ceremonial traditions of Hellenistic and Roman ruler worship' (p. 13).

[23] D. E. Aune, 'Roman Imperial Court Ceremonial', p. 22.

[24] 'This chapter is the most powerful statement of the divinity of Christ in the New Testament, and it receives its power from the praise of God the Creator which precedes it' (J. Sweet, *Revelation*, Pelican Commentaries (London: SCM, 1979), p. 127.

[25] R. J. Bauckham, 'The Worship of Jesus', p. 329. Against the view that John included 19:10 and 22:8–9 to counter a tendency to angel worship in the Asiatic churches to which he addressed his work, Bauckham rightly argues from the structure of the Apocalypse that the angel's rejection of worship functions to claim for the whole book the authority, not of an angel (the creaturely instrument of revelation), but of God himself (as the transcendent source of worship), to whom worship alone is due.

[26] As noted previously, the service in view here seems to incorporate the notion of paying homage to God (*proskynēsis*) by word and deed. Perhaps *latreuousin* conveys more the sense of being entirely at God's disposal as a priestly kingdom.

[27] *E.g.* J. J. O'Rourke, 'The Hymns of the Apocalypse', *CBQ* 30, 1968, pp. 399–409. He makes his judgments on criteria such as: parallelism similar to that found in Psalms, solemn tone of expression apt for use in worship, and grammatical peculiarities.

[28] *E.g.* O. Piper, 'The Apocalypse of John and the Liturgy of the Ancient Church', *Church History* 20, 1951, pp. 10–22; L. Mowry, 'Revelation 4 – 5 and Early Christian Liturgical Usage', *JBL* 71, 1952, pp. 75–84 and A. Cabaniss, 'A Note on the Liturgy of the Apocalypse', *Interpretation* 7, 1953, pp. 78–80. M. H. Shepherd, *The Paschal Liturgy and the Apocalypse*, Ecumenical Studies in Worship No. 6 (London: Lutterworth, 1960) went so far as to propose that the outline of the Revelation followed the order of the Paschal Liturgy that was in the process of development in the first century and found full expression in the *Apostolic Tradition* of Hippolytus.

[29] *Cf.* D. E. Aune, 'Roman Imperial Court Ceremonial', p. 7.

[30] G. Delling, *Worship in the New Testament* (ET, London: Darton, Longman & Todd, 1962), p. 47.

[31] L. Thompson, 'Cult and Eschatology in the Apocalypse of John', *Journal of Religion* 49, 1969, pp. 330–350, (348–349). I would modify his basic thesis to this extent: heavenly worship is often 'the literary form by means of which the seer realizes the kingship of God and his judgment prior to the realization of these realities in the dramatic narrative form' (p. 342). Sometimes, as noted, praise follows the description of God's activity.

[32] G. Goldsworthy, *The Gospel in Revelation* (Exeter: Paternoster; Flemington Market: Lancer, 1984), pp. 100–112, rightly argues that the hymns are part of 'a framework of explicitly gospel-oriented material which prevents (the Book of the Revelation) from being a piece of purely Judaistic apocalyptic as far as its perception of the end is concerned' (p. 102).

[33] G. Delling, *Worship in the New Testament*, p. 45.

CHAPTER TEN

Worship and the gospel – a summary

As you come to him, the living stone – rejected by mortals but chosen by God and precious to him – you also, like living stones, are being built into a spiritual house to be a holy priesthood, offering spiritual sacrifices acceptable to God through Jesus Christ... You are a chosen people, a royal priesthood, a holy nation, a people belonging to God, that you may declare the praises of him who called you out of darkness into his wonderful light (1 Pet. 2:4–5, 9, NIV modified).

Throughout the Bible, acceptable worship means approaching or engaging with God on the terms that he proposes and in the manner that he makes possible. It involves honouring, serving and respecting him, abandoning any loyalty or devotion that hinders an exclusive relationship with him. Although some of Scripture's terms for worship may refer to specific gestures of homage, rituals or priestly ministrations, worship is more fundamentally faith expressing itself in obedience and adoration. Consequently, in both Testaments it is often shown to be a personal and moral fellowship with God relevant to every sphere of life.

God is worthy of homage, praise and grateful service because he is creator, lord of history, and judge of all. But humanly devised religion receives God's condemnation in Scripture. It cannot bring people into a right relationship with God or enable them to please him. God must rescue them from the darkness of ignorance and the corruption of sin, bringing them to a true knowledge of himself, if they are to worship him acceptably. Thus, the Old Testament insists that Israel could only draw near to the LORD because of his gracious initiative and provision. He uniquely revealed his character and will to them, rescuing them from captivity in Egypt, and establishing them in the land . where they could serve him without hindrance. Revelation and redemption are the basis of acceptable worship in biblical thinking.

God's self-revelation to Israel was particularly associated with Mount Sinai, the tabernacle in the wilderness, and then the temple in Jerusalem. Here the word of the LORD was given and received, and his rule over his people and his presence amongst them were powerfully represented. The ritual established in connection with these sanctuaries was to be Israel's way of acknowledging his kingly presence and God's way of sustaining a rebellious and unfaithful people in a relationship with himself. His special provisions for Israel were designed to bring blessing to the rest of humanity (*cf.* Gn. 12:3; Ex. 19:5–6). So worship and God's covenant are closely linked in Scripture.

Israel's compromise with other religions and the corruption of her worship was a significant factor in the divine judgment that eventually came upon the temple and the nation. Nevertheless, the prophets predicted that the temple would be restored and that Israel's worship would be renewed 'in the last days'. This was another way of saying that the covenant would be renewed (*cf.* Jer. 31:31–34). The relationship of the people with God would be transformed so that his intention of blessing the whole world through them might be fulfilled. The word of the LORD would go out from Jerusalem and the nations would be drawn to worship God in the fellowship of his people, in his holy 'house'. Acceptable worship is thus an important aspect of biblical eschatology.

When the apostle Peter asserts that Jesus Christ is 'the living stone – rejected by mortals but chosen by God and precious to him', he indicates the fulfilment of these Old Testament hopes in

the person and work of the Messiah. God is building a new 'spiritual house' with Jesus as the 'cornerstone' or 'keystone' (*cf.* Eph. 2:20). This temple of 'living stones' is really the community of those who have come to Christ. They are 'chosen' and 'precious' because of their link with him. God dwells in their midst through his Spirit (*cf.* Eph. 2:21–22) and he has chosen to manifest his glory to the world through them. As a 'holy priesthood' they are called to live out the role given to Israel at Mount Sinai and to be 'a holy nation'. But they do this by 'offering spiritual sacrifices acceptable to God through Jesus Christ'. Jesus replaces the levitical priesthood and the sacrificial system designed to maintain the holiness of God's people and facilitate their service to God.

The starting-point for Christian reflection on this matter appears to have been the conviction that God fully and finally manifested himself in the person of his Son. Jesus Christ is at the centre of New Testament thinking about worship. He is the ultimate meeting point between heaven and earth and the decisive means of reconciliation between God and humanity. He is the centre of salvation and blessing for all nations. While some passages suggest that Jesus is exclusively the new temple, others show how temple ideals are also fulfilled in the church. Thus, it is in Jesus and the community that he gathers to himself that we see the full reality towards which the temple pointed.

At one level, the New Testament shows how the earliest disciples were drawn into a worshipping relationship with the risen Christ. At another level, we are shown how Jesus made possible a new relationship with the Father by means of his death, resurrection, ascension, and subsequent outpouring of the Holy Spirit. Through the ministry of the Son and the Spirit, the Father obtains true worshippers. Thus, the doctrine of the Trinity lies at the heart of a truly Christian theology of worship. Each person in the Godhead plays a significant role in establishing the worship appropriate to the new covenant era.

Central to New Testament teaching is the insistence that Christ's death is the ultimate sacrifice, provided by God to cleanse his people from the defilement of sin and consecrate them to himself in a relationship of heart-obedience. The victim and the priest of the new covenant are one, because Jesus offered perfect worship to the Father by a lifetime of obedience, culminating in his death. A special inspiration for Christian thinking about the sacrificial significance of Jesus' death appears to have been his own reinterpretation of the Passover for his disciples at the Last Supper. By means of his sacrifice and heavenly exaltation he has opened the way for Jews and Gentiles to approach the Father together. They can draw near with the certainty that their sins are forgiven and that they have been accepted into the life and fellowship of his coming kingdom. They can serve him with gratitude and whole-hearted devotion because of their trust in what God has done for them through Christ. Fundamentally, then, worship in the New Testament means believing the gospel and responding with one's whole life and being to the person and work of God's Son, in the power of the Holy Spirit.

Evangelism is the means by which people are initially drawn to present themselves to God as 'a living sacrifice'. The New Testament also shows that, if Christians are to be motivated and equipped to serve God in their everyday lives, they need to be exposed to an ongoing, gospel-based ministry of teaching and exhortation. Throughout Scripture, the word of God is fundamental to a genuine engagement with him. While it is true that worship terminology can be applied to every sphere of life, missionary preaching, the establishment of churches in the truth of the gospel, and support for such ministry are viewed as specific and particular expressions of Christian worship in the New Testament. At the same time, they are clearly a form of service or ministry to the churches.

Jesus removes the need for a cultic approach to God in the traditional sense. Yet the New Testament demonstrates that our understanding of his work can be greatly enriched by viewing it in terms of transformed worship categories. His sacrifice on the cross, his entrance into the heavenly sanctuary, and his intercession for us, provide the only basis for relating to God under the new covenant. The whole of life is to be lived in relation to the cross and to the sanctuary where Christ is enthroned as our crucified saviour and high priest. Indeed, it is ultimately our destiny to share with him in the fellowship of that heavenly or eschatological reality and to 'serve him day and night in his

temple' (*cf.* Rev. 7:15). Meanwhile, we worship God as we acknowledge these truths and respond to his mercies with grateful obedience. What, then, is the character and function of the gathering of his people on earth?

The uniqueness and total adequacy of Christ's work is obscured by any doctrine of human priesthood, charged with some form of sacrificial ministry in the Christian congregation. There are no sacred buildings where God is especially present in the gospel era. There is no divinely ordained ritual of approach to God for believers under the new covenant. Nevertheless, several texts suggest that God presences himself in a distinctive way in the Christian meeting through his word and the operation of his Spirit.

The purpose of Christian gatherings is the edification or building up of the body of Christ. We minister to one another as we teach and exhort one another on the basis of his word, using the gifts that the Spirit has given us, in the way that Scripture directs. Edification is to be our concern even when we sing or pray to God in the congregation. All this is not a purely human activity, however, for God is at work in the midst of his people as they minister in this way. Edification is first and foremost the responsibility of Christ as the 'head', but he achieves his purpose as the various members of the body are motivated and equipped by him to play their part. We meet together to draw on the resources of Christ and to take our part in the edification of his church.

From one point of view, the gathering of the church is meant to be an anticipation of the heavenly or eschatological assembly of God's people. It is to be characterized by worship or divine service in the form of prayer and praise directed to God and in the form of ministry to one another. Worship and edification are different dimensions of the same activities. Put another way, participation in the edification of the church is an important aspect of that total obedience of faith which is the worship of the new covenant. From another point of view, we gather together to encourage one another to live out in everyday life the obedience that glorifies God and furthers his saving purposes in the world.

The gospel is the key to New Testament teaching about worship. The gospel declares to us the ultimate revelation of God in the person of Jesus Christ and the ultimate redemption in his sacrificial death. He fulfils and replaces the whole method of approach to God associated with the Sinai covenant. The teaching and practice of the Old Testament is not discarded but is transformed in the New Testament. It becomes the means for understanding the work of the Messiah and how we can relate to God under the new covenant. Through the gospel message of God's mercy in Christ, and through his Spirit, men and women from all nations are united in his praise and service.

Epilogue

Anyone could tell from the way the members of this congregation related to one another that their Sunday gathering was an expression of genuine Christian community. It was clearly a high point in their week, but not the only time when most of them met together or engaged in ministry together. Their conversation, their prayers and their contributions during the service reflected an obvious concern for one another in a whole range of situations. This was no spiritual ghetto, since it was clear that members desired to welcome strangers and to minister to the needs of those outside their fellowship. Many seemed to be actively involved in evangelism, pastoral care, or social action groups in the wider community.

The service began with a time of informal singing, as the congregation remained seated and latecomers continued to arrive. Song leaders and instrumentalists had carefully planned this segment so that people were reminded of the significance of their gathering together, distractions were removed, and minds were focused on God's character and promises. Every contribution to the service seemed to be motivated by a desire to encourage the congregation in their relationship with God and with one another. This was no entertainment extravaganza, but it was certainly an involving experience that was far from dull. The time of informal singing led quite naturally to the reading of a few verses from Scripture and a challenge to draw near to God with repentance and faith.

Perhaps the most surprising aspect of this service was the fact that it happily combined a set 'liturgical form' with informal and spontaneous elements. The prayer of confession, which all said together, and the assurance of God's forgiveness which followed, were the beginning of the formal liturgy. Song leaders and instrumentalists then led another segment of praise and thanksgiving, responding to the reminder of gospel promises which had just been given. When two members of the congregation read the set lessons from the Bible, one from the Old Testament and one from the New, it was obvious that they had prepared well and anticipated that God would encounter his people through this ministry.

The sermon which followed was based on one of the readings for the day, though it incorporated insights from the other reading as well. Sometimes sermons were topical or thematic and sometimes they involved the explanation and application of key verses from Scripture. Mostly they were systematic expositions of biblical passages, working through a series of chapters for six to eight weeks, and then moving to another part of Scripture for variety of content and style. When a sermon series proceeded systematically through a segment of the Bible, home groups were encouraged to discuss several set questions each week, based on the exposition given that Sunday. Such questions were prepared in advance by the preachers, to enable members of the congregation to work hard at discovering the implications of the text. With such an integrated programme of adult education in the parish, people were more motivated to listen to the Sunday sermon and were actively involved with one another in implementing its teaching. Many prepared for the next Sunday by studying the relevant Bible passage in advance.

On this occasion the sermon was a careful explanation of a brief passage, well applied to the situation of the listeners and delivered in a compelling fashion. Since the subject was coping with suffering, at an appropriate point in the sermon the preacher asked a lady to share briefly how God had helped her in her recent distress. This unusual contribution really helped to bring the message home. It was one of several creative techniques used from time to time to involve people in the public teaching ministry, giving a voice to their hopes and fears, their victories and defeats. You could tell from the way the preacher handled the Scriptures, exalting the Lord Jesus Christ and challenging the congregation to relate every aspect of their lives to God and his promises, that this was viewed as an opportunity for the congregation to engage with God, in the Holy Spirit, through his words. The prayer before and after the sermon certainly conveyed something of that expectation.

The hymn after the sermon was carefully chosen to draw out some of the consequences of the sermon and enable the congregation to make a further response to what they had just heard. Then followed a time of announcements and informal ministry. A married couple asked for prayer about important family matters. A girl shared how God had answered a recent prayer and challenged the congregation to be bold themselves in intercession. Another person gave news of some missionaries who had gone out from the church and offered prayer for them. A man and a woman made specific responses to the sermon, giving ideas about the practical application of the biblical text. When this activity was first introduced into the Sunday services, people were slow to contribute, but the right sort of leadership encouraged even some of the most timid to share after a while. It was really an extension of the sort of ministry that members of the congregation were already exercising in home groups throughout the week.

The service leader then began a time of corporate prayer, in which he nominated areas of concern and called upon people to pray spontaneously about these concerns, closing each segment with a set prayer. On other Sundays a few people would be asked to prepare the prayer segment in advance and to lead it from the front. Sometimes the whole congregation broke into small groups, sharing in prayer with those seated near them. The matters that were contributed during the announcements and time of informal ministry were incorporated into the intercessions. The focus was not merely on the needs of the local church, however, but on the world and its problems.

On this particular Sunday, a hymn formed a bridge to the celebration of the Lord's Supper. A time of preparation was followed by a prayer of thanksgiving for Christ's saving work and a recollection of his words at the Last Supper. To express their commitment to one another as the body of Christ, members of this fairly large congregation passed the bread and the wine to each other, using appropriate words. On other occasions, they were encouraged to come forward in groups, stand in a circle and share the bread and wine with one another. When segments of the church were away together for weekends of teaching and fellowship, they celebrated the Lord's Supper quite informally, in the context of an ordinary meal.

The meeting finished on a note of thanksgiving and rededication to God. This was expressed in prayer and singing. In fact, much of the service seemed to be concerned with what would come after – in the time of informal conversation after church, in home groups during the week, and in the opportunities for ministry that many shared in the neighbourhood, in the workplace and beyond. Although the focus of the gathering was on heavenly or spiritual realities, the relevance of these truths to the world in which they lived was the preoccupation of those who participated.

Such an outward-looking emphasis, in the teaching, the prayers and other contributions, served to enhance and not to diminish the importance of the Sunday gathering. The congregation enjoyed meeting together to renew their relationship with God and with one another. But it was not the sum total of their involvement with each other or the ultimate expression of their commitment to Christ! It was a time to draw collectively on all the resources available to them in Christ, through the local congregation. It was a time to serve the Lord by participating in the building up of his body, and to be encouraged together to honour him in everyday life.

This brief portrait of an imaginary church shows what it might be like to put into practice the principles enunciated in this book, without necessarily discarding everything traditional. It draws together insights from several churches that I have visited or joined. Of course, the application of biblical principles to the life of the local church will vary according to the demands of the particular situation. Doubtless, every experiment will have its critics and some ideas will work better in one context than others. But a congregation desiring to please God will continually assess its activities and be willing to reform itself in the light of Scripture. Members will seek to discover how every aspect of congregational ministry may be a means of offering to God acceptable worship.

It may be very difficult in some churches to reassess the role and function of the congregational meeting in God's purposes and to take stock of what we are doing, Sunday by Sunday. Ecclesiastical traditions have a strangely powerful grip on many of us and some are fearful of the slightest change. Even the terminology we use to describe our activities can be a way of holding us back from reform. Indeed, spiritual inertia can justify itself in an amazing variety of ways! However, those who know and love the Scriptures will be concerned to teach them faithfully and to encourage God's people to work hard at applying them in the contemporary situation. In churches where significant changes are taking place, sermon series are given on the relevant themes, parish conferences are devoted to exploring the implications of biblical teaching, and small committees are appointed to promote and monitor new initiatives in various areas of congregational life.

Christians of every tradition need to be regularly exposed to the breadth and depth of the Bible's teaching on worship and to understand how it relates to evangelism, edification, faith and obedience. Above all, they must come to grips with the New Testament perspective that acceptable worship is an engagement with God, through Jesus Christ, in the Holy Spirit – a Christ-centred, gospel-serving, life-orientation.

INDEX OF SCRIPTURE REFERENCES

301

INDEX OF SUBJECTS

INDEX OF MODERN AUTHORS